D1459535

Talking
with
Serial Killers

STALKERS

Born in 1948 in Winchester, Hampshire, Christopher Berry-Dee is descended from Dr John Dee, Court Astrologer to Queen Elizabeth I, and is the founder and former Director of the Criminology Research Institute (CRI), and former publisher and Editor-in-Chief of *The Criminologist*, a highly respected journal on matters concerning all aspects of criminology from law enforcement to forensic psychology.

Christopher has interviewed and interrogated over thirty of the world's most notorious killers – serial, mass and one-off – including Peter Sutcliffe, Ted Bundy, Aileen Wuornos, Dennis Nilsen and Joanna Dennehy. He was co-producer/ interviewer for the acclaimed twelve-part TV documentary series *The Serial Killers*, and has appeared on television as a consultant on serial homicide, and, in the series *Born to Kill?*, on the cases of Fred and Rose West, the 'Moors Murderers' and Dr Harold Shipman. He has also assisted in criminal investigations as far afield as Russia and the United States.

Notable book successes include: *Monster* (the basis for the movie of the same title, about Aileen Wuornos); *Dad Help Me Please*, about the tragic Derek Bentley, hanged for a murder he did not commit (subsequently subject of the film *Let Him Have It*) – and *Talking with Serial Killers*, Christopher's international bestseller, now, with its sequel, *Talking with Serial Killers: World's Most Evil*, required reading at the FBI Behavioral Science Unit Academy at Quantico, Virginia. His *Talking with Psychopaths and Savages: A Journey Into the Evil Mind*, was the UK's bestselling true-crime title of 2017; its successor volume, *Talking with Psychopaths and Savages: Beyond Evil*, was published in the autumn of 2019, while a new edition of his *Talking with Serial Killers: Dead Men Talking* appeared in 2020.

https://www.christopherberrydee.com/

Talking
with
Serial Killers

STALKERS

The world's most sinister sexual
psychopaths – in their own words

Christopher Berry-Dee

JOHN BLAKE

First published in the UK by John Blake Publishing
an imprint of Bonnier Books UK
80-81 Wimpole Street, London, W1G 9RE

Owned by Bonnier Books
Sveavägen 56, Stockholm, Sweden

www.facebook.com/johnblakebooks
twitter.com/jblakebooks

First published in paperback in 2020

Paperback ISBN: 978-1-78946-267-8
Ebook ISBN: 978-1-78946-268-5
Audiobook ISBN: 978-1-78946-310-1

British Library Cataloguing-in-Publication Data:

A catalogue record for this book is available from the British Library.

Design by www.envydesign.co.uk

Printed and bound in Great Britain by Clays Ltd, Elcograf S.p.A

1 3 5 7 9 10 8 6 4 2

Text copyright © Christopher Berry-Dee 2020

John Blake Publishing is an imprint of Bonnier Books UK
www.bonnierbooks.co.uk

For
Frazer Ashford

Contents

PREFACE
Health Warning

In our modern times we have become all too immunised to the horrors, pain and suffering caused by the likes of some of the human predators featured in this book – many of whose awful crimes have become the subject material for bums-on-seats movies, with us, sitting in our comfortable armchairs, or in a cinema with a mouthful of popcorn, being 'entertained' with a glorified account of the crimes – most often far removed from reality and the twisted sexual psychopathology of the killers themselves, and without even considering the untold human suffering caused in extremis.

Let us *never* forget that these evil men and women are bottom-feeders; the scum of humanity who seek out, stalk, and torture in ways that are incomprehensible to you and me, who callously rape and kill our siblings, our parents, our loved ones and the most vulnerable in our societies, and don't give a damn.

I do not suggest for a millisecond that I have got everything right and proper in this book, for there will be many 'professionals' who disagree with me, who'll question every dot and comma, even flyspeck state of mind throughout, but, one might consider that if it were *your* terrified young son or daughter, much-loved boyfriend or girlfriend, or beloved spouse who had been stalked, lured to some dark place, stripped naked, hung from a beam and then skinned alive, would you truly give a damn about the killer's state of mind?

Now, as I reflect on the how's and why's, I have struggled hard to rip away the gloss that is often painted over the criminals' narratives, and get inside their heads – to try to understand, in some small way, what makes them tick.

Acknowledgements

To start the ball rolling, why do I dedicate this book to Frazer Ashford? Well, it celebrates seventeen years of being published by John Blake Publishing, and it all started decades ago when I met Frazer.

> This has to be the most awful typescript I have ever laid my eyes upon but your research into the PC Gutteridge murder is flawless. Would you consider allowing me to co-write this book, with you as the lead author?
>
> ROBIN ODELL, AUTHOR AND TRUE-CRIME
> HISTORIAN, TO THE AUTHOR

Way back in the early nineties, one the world's finest true-crime historians and crime writers, Robin Odell, spotted my first clumsy attempt at writing and showed it to Eric Dobby at W. H. Allen & Co. Together we published *The*

Long Drop, thereafter, *Dad, Help Me Please*, *Ladykiller*, and, later, *A Question of Evidence*.

Virgin Books published *Monsters of Death Row*, and during this time I met Frazer Ashford, who was MD and producer at CrystalVision TV, based in Croydon. Here we did a short piece based on my book, *Dad, Help Me Please* (the Craig and Bentley case), which went on to become the 1991 British drama film, *Let Him Have It*, directed by Peter Medak, starring Christopher Eccleston, Paul Reynolds, Tom Courtenay and Tom Bell.

Several years later, Frazer and I hooked up again and, as a result, we made the twelve-part television documentary series *The Serial Killers* – the first-ever TV series that allowed serial killers to tell their story in their own words. Of course, we included many next-of-kin, judges, cops and attorneys so that they could say their bit . . . then along came publisher John Blake.

Talking with Serial Killers, published in 2003, became the first-ever true-crime book in its genre to include the killers' own words and many of their letters as well. This was a risky and controversial move by John Blake, yet even today the book remains an international bestseller.

Seventeen years on, I am still with more-or-less the same publisher and there is a symbiotic literary thread running through from the start. Robin Odell sometimes wrote with the doyen of true-crime writing J. J. Gaute, and also with Colin Wilson – famous names, indeed, with decades of criminological research and expertise between them, of which, to a large extent, I have been the beneficiary because it was Robin who 'showed me

ACKNOWLEDGEMENTS

the ropes'. Then it was Frazer Ashford who first saw the potential of my interviewing these highly dangerous criminals, some of them psychopaths, face-to-face, and capturing it all on film. So it was these first on-screen TV-making experiences that helped me during the television documentaries I appear on, and in my lectures and talks, today.

Thank you again, Frazer. Bless you.

For many years now, Toby Buchan has been, and he still is my editor-in-chief, so I owe him a great debt of gratitude. Indeed, if I may say so, the idea for this book was his, with it coming across a table in Jamie Oliver's Italian restaurant in Tooley Street, South Bank, London, to be precise, when my publishers treated me to a celebratory lunch on 5 July 2018, when I was in town signing my books in Waterstones and Foyles. Thank you again, my dear friend, and thank you, too, Kelly Ellis, then the head of John Blake Publishing, for your much-needed support.

I also extend the same heartfelt sentiments to all the publishing team and to my US publishers, Ulysses Press, in California, for I have always regarded successful book publishing as a team effort; one that extends all the way from the process of research, writing through to marketing, cover design, goodness knows how many edits, along to sales in the bookstores and online. For my part, I merely consider myself as the guy who pushes a pen around – because no matter how great an idea is, if we writers had no loyal and dedicated publisher we would be wasting our time.

Next up are my family and close friends: Claire, the

mother of my wonderful son Jack, her parents Trevor and Carol, sister Lizzie and Clan Stothard, my loving partner Maui; pals Boris Coster, Tony Brown, Ann Sidney (former Miss World), Rev. Chris Richardson, Claire Louise, Clive Sturdy, Dan Zupansky, Denis Claivaz, Gary and Anita Roberts, the amazing Hollie, Jan Fuller, Jay, Jenni, Jenny (WRN) Wiseman, Jon Sotnick; long-time buddies Karl Spencer-Smith, Robert Pothecary, Roger Holman, Linda and Sherri from the 'Offie', Martin Mahoney, Paul Bell, Jay Thorley, Steve McCullough, Liam Greaney, Wayne Jowers, Willy B. Wilhemsen, Tony Brown, Yang Lu, and last but not least, the incorrigible Pete 'Bitcoin Pete' Aldred, who is one of the nicest guys one could ever meet.

I could, of course, go on ad infinitum with thanks, for there are scores of newspaper journalists, columnists, TV producers and their crews from as far afield as 'down under' with Executive Producer Ray Pedretti of 'Blizzard Road Productions' (*35 Serial Killers*). With Monster Films: Davis Howard and Rik Hall (CBS Reality *Voice of a Serial Killer* and *Murder by the Sea*); then StoryHouse Productions in Germany (*Killing for Kicks – Serial Killer Joanna Dennehy*), also springing to mind – but to include everyone who has supported me over the years would exhaust the 75,000-word count allocated me in the book you are about to read. So, if your name doesn't appear in these pages, you will know who you are anyway – so thank you all once again.

CHRISTOPHER BERRY–DEE

Introduction

STALK: 1: to follow or approach (game, prey, etc.)
stealthily and quietly. 2: to pursue persistently and,
sometimes, attack (a person with whom one is
obsessed, often a celebrity) ... 3: to search (a piece
of land) for prey.
COLLINS ENGLISH DICTIONARY

In itself, serial homicide is a grim, if fascinating, subject;
one where, in the main, we appear to focus our attention
on the homicides themselves and the techniques used
by law enforcement to bring the offenders to justice.
Thus, the most gruesome of cases inevitably result in the
making of movies designed to put bums on seats – for
blood-and-gore sells well these days. Criminal literature
seems lacking in studies of what motivates serial killers
and other types of criminals to stalk and hunt down their
prey, what is going through their minds and the oft-times

uncontrollable emotions that accompany the pre-kill process, and this is what I hope to address in this book. Principally, therefore, this book concerns itself with the manner in which serial killers and sex offenders hunt prey, and it goes without saying that stalking comes in many different forms.

Over the past few decades there has emerged a proliferation of these predatory individuals who infest the internet; deviants who rob, steal, assault, con, rape – and kill. Men and women alike, they will use any subtle method to entice an intended victim into their web, and we will meet many of these evil personalities throughout this book.

I have drawn upon historic and contemporary cases alike. However, in one specific chapter – that of the historic rape murder of a south London woman called Muriel Maitland – a delicate issue arose: the man in question was still at large within our society until he died of natural causes a few years ago. I met him, had tea with him several times at his squalid home in Portsmouth, and I found him the most manipulative and dangerous person I have ever encountered outside of prison walls, and I have interviewed face-to-face over thirty sado-sexual serial killers in my time, so this is saying something because Gordon Jowers was evil.

What we do know about this appalling murder is worthy of the entire chapter dedicated to the memory of Muriel Maitland, for if ever there was a case of homicidal stalking this is a prime example. Indeed, I have decided to include it because it is of a type that most women will identify with as being their worst nightmare. But there is another sadness here and it is this. As this cold case was belatedly focusing in on the offender, it came to pass that police had lost all of the forensic evidence, which included any traces on the victim's underwear (that could, much later, have yielded material for DNA testing), and a cigarette butt that her killer had discarded at the crime scene – all of which could well have linked him firmly to the murder. There was no sign of any of the case papers, either. However, more by luck than design I located copies of these very valuable documents in a dusty cellar at the South London Coroner's Court, just days before they were due to be incinerated, to be, quite obviously, lost for ever. God moves in mysterious ways!

Of course, stalking a victim to kill sits at the extreme end of the human behavioural spectrum – saintly do-gooding at the other – but it would be remiss of me not to include within these pages perhaps what might erroneously be judged a much lesser degree of criminal activity – that of the scammers who trawl the internet using various 'honey trap' guises to lure potential victims into their web; gullible if not foolish souls who are often fleeced for every penny they have, in the worst cases ending up dead.

My book *Murder.com*, was written with the cooperation of many law-enforcement agencies, with the FBI and St Petersburg Russian State Police heading the list. Of late I have worked with more-or-less the same agencies focusing on Facebook Messenger and Hangouts, also Craigslist, to reverse the honey-trap methods used by scammers, and turn the tables on them. One might judge this as illegal entrapment of sorts, but this legal issue is easily circumvented when 'focused intelligence' combined with documentary material such as, emails, text messages, photographs, Western Union receipts, as well as gift cards and fake IDs, prove beyond doubt that this is worthy of police attention. It should not be forgotten that in many cases like this men and women have been lured to their deaths, so it is a very serious matter indeed. So I have included details of several of the cases I have worked on, and, if anything, this most valuable information should provide as a stark warning that financial stalkers and blackmailers infest the internet, so punters seeking love online beware – you could also end up dead – if you are lucky in a pine box – or never to be seen alive, or dead, again!

There, that's the end of my Introduction. A very short one it is too, yet the book itself will be a scary read. I can assure you of this because the most terrifying thing for anyone is to feel that someone is watching you, sometimes with your awful, sudden blood-drenched murder in mind.

CHRISTOPHER BERRY–DEE
SOUTHSEA, UK
EL NIDO, PALAWAN, PHILIPPINES

1

Lenny the Lizard

PREDATOR: 1: any carnivorous animal.
2: a predatory person or thing.
COLLINS ENGLISH DICIONARY

The word 'predator' derives from the Latin *praedator*, meaning 'plunderer', from *praedare* ('to loot', 'to pillage'); to which is related *praeda*, meaning 'booty', 'spoils' – and 'prey' (which derives from the same root). A grim definition indeed, yet an apt one with which to label the twisted humans who stalk, hunt down, entrap, then rape and/or slaughter our men, women, children, the infirm and even babies – for sexual satisfaction, for money and for fun.

I have been interviewing and corresponding with homicidal psychopaths for almost a quarter of a century, and have had some thirty-six books published on the subject of serial killers; I also give talks on serial murder, after which I am frequently asked the question 'What makes these monsters tick?'

In *Talking with Psychopaths and Savages: A Journey into the Evil Mind* and its sequel *Talking with Psychopaths and Savages: Beyond Evil*, I have I hope managed in some part to answer this question. As my readers will have quickly realised, the answer is multi-faceted and far from simple. A basic dictionary definition of 'psychopath' goes along the lines of 'a person who has a chronic mental disorder characterised by bouts of irrational, abnormal and/or violent behaviour'. As I explained in my earlier books, there are chemical imbalances or deficiencies within the brain, which often remove or reduce the ability to make moral judgements, to hold back urges (sexual ones commonly) or to empathise with the pain or suffering of others. But it is a lot more complicated than that. Not all such individuals become killers, nevertheless some of the most horrific murders are perpetrated by psychopaths. But – as my loyal readers know is my wont – I digress: it is specifically stalkers I am dealing with in this book.

In 2018, as I mentioned in an earlier book, I visited the fabulous Manila Ocean Park in the Philippines. There, in the 'World of Creepy Crawlies', I gazed through the glass of tank after tank. In each I could see nothing but green leaves and brown twigs. It took some time – as most things do at my age – for what I *didn't* see to penetrate my mind, the thought itself happy to wander around for a month before a flicker of light lit up the neurons in my brain and the penny dropped.

In each of those tanks was a hidden predator primed to strike. In this case, a lizard – perfectly camouflaged, undetected by its prey – and, of course, 99.99 percent of the time, its victim is dead as soon as spotted.

They were dead as soon as I saw them.
DESCRIBING HOW HE ZEROED IN ON HIS MANY
VICTIMS, THE SERIAL KILLER, MICHAEL BRUCE ROSS ON
DEATH ROW AT OSBORN CORRECTIONAL INSTITUTION,
SOMERS, CONNECTICUT, INTERVIEWED BY THE AUTHOR
26 SEPTEMBER 1994

Michael Ross's method of catching his prey, then torturing and killing to satisfy his uncontrollable perverse sexual hunger wasn't so much using the technique of lying in wait, he was rather more of an opportunist coming upon his victims by happenstance. This is not to say that he was *not* thinking about committing rape and murder when going about his day-to-day business as an insurance salesman, for those acts were constantly somewhere in his mind. Actually, he was *unconsciously* hunting for prey, and then, when a young woman provided him with 'opportunity' and it was the right place for him and the wrong time for her, these evil thoughts would jump into his consciousness and he would strike. We will meet other killers like Michael later in this book.

Other serial murderers and rapists stalk their victims, often for hours, days, even months before springing carefully laid traps. And, as shocking as this may seem, it is true that these highly dangerous people get as many thrills out of this predatory stalking phase as the actual killing time itself, for it gives them a sense of power over their forthcoming prey. Just like the big game hunter, or a military sniper, even an assassin, there is a great degree of adrenalin-fuelled planning and excitement in the hunt, too. Moreover, stalking then killing to eat or for the purpose of eliminating rivals is writ large throughout our DNA, dating back millennia to the time when our ancestors lived in caves; this, however, stems from a basic instinct – that of survival.

Of course, Lenny the Lizard doesn't think in a predatory sexual way, bless him, neither does he actively stalk – he just merges into the background to wait patiently for dinner to appear on the horizon. The tiger, on the other hand, stalks its prey through the jungle, and African wild dogs will stalk theirs in a pack, hidden by tall savanna grasses. In all such cases, however, this is to feed themselves and their young, an important distinction.

Man, it is often said, is the only animal who hunts and kills for fun, but while this may not be completely true, it is true that animals kill mostly for understandable and acceptable reasons – they kill for food, they kill to protect their young, or in self-defence. Perhaps, occasionally, they appear to kill for enjoyment – as when they get carried away by the excitement of it (the fox in the henhouse, for example) and cannot stop themselves. This could especially be the case among pack animals where excitement mounts to frenzy. Or they could equally be behaving in this way for more obscure, and instinctive, reasons, maybe to do with pack survival and rivalry.

But this book is about human predators, mostly psychosexual, and I'd love to hear from anyone who can tell me the name of a single creature – other than us – that kills for sexual kicks. My ears are wide open. And it is humans, too, not other animals, that get a kick out of torturing their victim. Cruelty is our prerogative. What about the domestic cat playing with a mouse? you ask. The behaviour is instinctive: a cat's killing method is to break the neck of its prey – a quick and efficient system – but with a small wriggling mouse it is hard to get a firm grip without being bitten. One explanation put forward to explain the 'playing' is that tossing the mouse about will break its neck; another is that it enables the cat to catch the mouse by the nape to kill it with a single bite.

Whatever an animal's reason for killing, it is likely that most of the time some instinct, however obscure or distasteful to us humans, is at play. Nothing can compare with the lone and warped human serial rapist/murderer, who *should* have a moral compass but hasn't; one who kills not for territorial rights, for food or a family dispute, but one who lies in wait, or stalks his prey, unconsciously or consciously, with the premeditated intention to commit the most atrocious acts of barbaric cruelty on the helpless and vulnerable.

And this is where we look at crypsis (the avoidance of observation), first turning to Lenny the Lizard and his kind: the predators of the animal kingdom are aided in their stalking by their camouflage (and indeed many of their prey are similarly kept hidden by theirs). Lizards, leaf-green or bark-brown or rock-grey, blend in with their surroundings, hidden from both prey and predator; tigers stalk their prey unseen through long grasses, an owl is lost in the mottled grey and brown of a tree trunk . . .

So, when reading this book, think of camouflage in all of its different guises – please keep in the back of your mind the hunter, the sniper, the assassin and the different masks they wear to stalk, entrap and kill their prey. Humans have mostly had to resort to creating their own camouflage – thus we have the well-known soldier's camouflage battledress which is printed in disrupted patches of various colours to resemble its intended background – jungle, desert, snowy, rocky terrain, etc. – and similarly painted artillery and aircraft. The most elaborate form of camouflage clothing is the 'ghillie suit', which might include netting and strips of burlap or jute, and leaves and twigs plucked from local plants, the more the better, or lumps of mud, all added to the camouflaged garment.

Lenny the Lizard's camouflage is his outer 'skin', the ghillie suit perhaps. Another form of crypsis may be found in the waters of southern Australia's coast, where the predatory leafy seadragon avoids recognition by other predators by using alga-like colouration and protuberances to appear as no more than a bit of floating seaweed. This allows otherwise visible organisms to remain unnoticed by predators or prey. In much the same way, our serial killers and others use a form of crypsis too.

My point here is that all the serial killers and other offenders included in this book used a ghillie suit of sorts. A uniform, for example, could be a way of hiding the wolfish self in sheep's clothing to gain the trust of a potential victim. David Alan Gore (1953–2012) was a Floridian sado-sex serial killer who launched his vile career of rape-degradation-murder from behind the uniform of auxiliary deputy sheriff; he was executed after twenty-eight years on death row. In London. John Christie (1899–1953) similarly used his role as a special constable in the War Reserve Police, even long after he'd left the force, to give himself a façade of respectability and gain the confidence of young women.

At the other end of the offender spectrum we find the internet scammers who use camouflage, guile and cunning as well. Allegedly young and beautiful, innocent busty blondes posing as love-lost, life torn apart by some cheating partner, they sit in social media sites and on internet chat forums, waiting for some guy to happen upon them. Oh, and do they plan their predations with military precision? Yes, they do, for there are many well documented cases where a man who should have known better falls in love with some Russian 'dolly bird', flies out to meet her with his wallet stuffed full of dollars, gets off the plane at Moscow's Sheremetyevo Airport, and is never seen alive again. So, think again about the deadly spider sitting in the middle of its web and you'll find another meaning to the World Wide Web.

As we move through this book we will find that many of these offenders use various different types of bait to lure their victims to their doom, just like the fly fisherman who will use hand-tied flies that resemble natural invertebrates, baitfish or other types of lures to provoke the fish to bite at the fly.

Let's just pause and think for a moment about our fly fisherman, or even a beach caster. In every respect they are hunters. To enhance chances of success, the more experienced of them know where the fish swim, maybe singly in a deep, shaded pool or in shoals just offshore. These fishermen know which bait or lure to use, then they cast out their lines. Many of the serial killers I have interviewed do this too. The British serial killer, Peter Sutcliffe (June 1946–) murdered mostly prostitutes, as did the US 'Monster of the Rivers' Arthur John Shawcross (1945–2008). They, and so many more like them, specifically target these 'working girls' because they know exactly where they gather (swim) in numbers; being in dark, seedy red-light districts and with the offer of money for short-time sex, they make for easy catching and killing. The term 'red-light district' of course indicating a lure to entice clients, too. Indeed, a common phrase used by these street girls is 'fishing'. The girls go onto the streets, into bars or clubs, wearing sexy clothes, being their own bait, to fish for customers, but, often in doing so put their own lives in great peril into the bargain. Nevertheless, the derogative term 'hooker' means exactly that. They cast their own sex bait and hook their clients much in the same way as scammers do on the internet.

The grotesque-looking anglerfish (*Melanocetus johnsonii*), which gets its name from the long, modified dorsal spine tipped with a luminescent organ known as a photophore, uses its light as a lure to attract its prey – and, yes, there are a few of these in the Manila Ocean Park too.

One of the UK's medieval serial killers who used light as a lure was the so-called Mad Monk of Gidleigh.

We are now back to the thirteenth century, when a small, private chapel was built just outside Gidleigh in Devon which became known as the Chapel of La Wallen, dedicated to the Blessed Virgin Mary. It was deconsecrated in 1332 and subsequently used, if at all, as a cow byre.

It was here, that, according to the local bishop's register, the monk Robert de Middlecote 'did maltreat' Agnes, a local miller's daughter, and murdered her unborn child; history does not relate whether the child was a result of the so-called maltreatment, or whether he was helping her out with an amateur abortion, and neither does it tell us what became of the unfortunate Agnes. He was indicted for trial but somehow managed to escape. At about the same time, a monk or cleric by the same name settled in the remote Lidwell Chapel, also dedicated to St Mary, in Haldon Forest. By all accounts he was a devout and compassionate man – by day. At night he placed welcoming candles in the windows to entice weary travellers on their long nocturnal walk home to pop in for a bite to eat and a short nap from which they never awoke. Legend has it that they were robbed of what little they possessed, killed and their bodies thrown down the well, which is still in situ today. He was eventually overpowered by one of his victims-to-be, went for trial and was sent to the gallows in 1329. (Strangely, there exists a nineteenth-century account of a monk called Simon who settled there in the mid-1500s and committed exactly the same murders – a case of copy-cat crime or of confused records?) Now a Grade II-listed building, the ruined chapel may be found at grid reference SX 92411 76098, and I can testify that it is a damned difficult ruin to visit at the best of times – that is of course if one wishes to leave a perfectly safe road to stumble, even plunge, down a treacherous, rock-strewn, moss-carpeted track into a boggy field. This place is scary so my advice is don't go down there in the dead of night – especially under a full moon.

Now you may think that I am going right off the wall here, but stay with me please, and think 'smugglers' and 'wreckers' who used to tie lanterns to their horses' tails, or held lamps aloft on a long pole to lure ships onto the rocks where they would founder and be plundered. The Mad Monk was a human predator, as were the smugglers and wreckers, who like the aforementioned anglerfish used a light to lure his prey.

But, for many serial killers, specifically the breed who use guile and cunning, 'light' might be viewed in a slightly different way – as 'hope'; and they use hope and the promise of good things to come, as a beacon to attract a specific type of prey, who then shows an interest and walks freely into the trap.

Yes, the offer of hope is a big thing amongst internet scammers too. Some crusty old guy is nose-deep in some online chat room when he comes across 'Miss Bosom Heavy' from Detroit. He is one of those guys with 3,500 'friends', all of them beautiful gals but as fake as a fashion watch with a bamboo spring. Hope springs eternal now when he sends her a message and *wow!* she responds. Within minutes they are in love, engagement is on the cards. Next minute they are on Hangouts. Oops, so enraptured is he now that together they can overcome the fact that she has no ID, bank account, that any Western Union money can be sent to a 'friend' in Nigeria or in Belarus, or that she only wants gift cards that cannot be traced, for it is the *hope* that counts – the hope that our man has that this blonde bombshell will be happy to shift him around in his wheelchair and she wants a child with him too. So our hypothetical – but all too typical – hero flies out to meet her. Then, when he gets off the plane at the airport, apparently still unsuspicious, he is met by some big fella who assures him he'll take him to where she is waiting. He is robbed, his bank account emptied and, if he is lucky, he'll escape with a severe beating; at worst he will never be seen alive again. This scenario – and variations of it – is all too commonplace.

Of course, it's not only men who fall for this kind of trap. Springing to mind is 'Bodies in Barrels' sado-sexual US serial killer, John Edward Robinson (1943–). His camouflage – his ghillie suit – was that of a bespectacled, respectable, community-minded Christian – a successful businessman, married with children and involved in charitable works. Underneath this shiny façade was a true monster if ever there was one: he was a conman, embezzler, forger, kidnapper – and an internet stalker. While researching one of my books, I got to know him well. Known to have committed at least eight homicides, Robinson, who prefers to be called 'JR', is now residing on death row in Kansas's El Dorado Correctional Facility. It is believed that he is the first serial killer in history to use the World Wide Web to capture his victims, his post-1993 ones, enticing them into his own carefully spun web, having made contact with them through online chat rooms and shone for them a ray of hope for a better future. And, his modus operandi was so simple.

Under the name 'Slavemaster', Robinson roamed various social networking sites fishing for women who enjoyed playing the submissive partner role during sex. Posing as a very rich man, he offered women – apart from kinky S&M sex – the chance to work full time for him, to act as carer for his now long-dead mother, and to sail on his non-existent yacht. And these young women took the bait and were easily lured into visiting JR, not imagining for one minute that they would soon be swindled, have their lives bludgeoned out of them, and end up dead and rotting in their own stinking bodily fluids in steel barrels. Of him, I will speak again later.

Well it's time to say goodbye to Lenny the Lizard. Right now he is probably tucked up nice and warm amongst some leaves and waiting for a tiny unsuspecting bug to chance to come his way. In the scheme of things the bug won't have a clue that two beady eyes are watching him, for he is merely crawling along a twig himself looking for a snack. Serial killers work in pretty much the same way. When the time is right they pounce and by the time you realise what's happening to you it will be far too late.

Welcome to the dark world of homicidal stalking. Sweet dreams!

2

Premeditation:
Murder in Mind

'Premeditation' is the act of considering, deliberating or planning something in advance – which by its very definition indicates an intention to commit the act under consideration, and it is important to consider premeditation as a factor in the crimes committed by the offenders you will find in the pages of this book.

Nearly all criminal stalkers plan their moves, often in great detail. And this is of course not restricted to serial killers as we usually define them. On Tuesday, 2 October 2018, Jamal Khashoggi (1958–2018), a Saudi dissident, journalist for the *Washington Post* and former General Manager and Editor-in-Chief of the Al-Arab News Channel, was murdered in the Saudi consulate in Istanbul by a group of Saudi Arabians. It is clear that a great deal of forward planning went into this killing: the crime was premeditated, so it effectively follows that Mr Khashoggi was under covert surveillance for a considerable time – his every move was observed, he was stalked, and then lured into a trap from which there could be no escape. These killers were organised criminals – acting under orders or not!

Therefore, the term 'stalking' implies premeditation, whether for a big-game hunter or someone like the American man hunter, Richard Beasley, whom we will meet later. And with the advent of the internet, rapists and killers increasingly stalk their intended victims from afar, even thousands of miles distant. While the game hunter will use guile and his knowledge of the lay of the land in a very physical sort of way, predators who use the internet as their hunting ground. They know where to find potential prey – and they have numerous target options open to them – and look on dating sites, in chat rooms and blogs, until they've pinpointed a possible victim. Then they stalk their chosen quarry, planning their next steps with meticulous care and premeditation.

Throughout this book you will find examples of how and where these types of organised offenders spent lengthy periods in premeditation: selecting victims, watching, and covertly stalking their intended prey until their carefully laid traps snap shut. Elsewhere, one will find human predators who spot, watch, catch, rape, kill – literally in an unbroken sequence, as if it is all carried out on the 'spur of the moment' from start to finish. However, whereas it was once thought that premeditated behaviour could be defined as a period lasting hours, days, weeks, months or even years, during which time an offender planned and executed his acts, now we can safely say that even if someone does act on the spur of the moment, if the intention *is* to cause harm then premeditation exists. And this is why the subject of premeditation linked to stalking is particularly interesting when considering the psychopathology of rapists and killers.

The Connecticut serial killer Michael Bruce Ross (1959–2005), whom I mentioned earlier, acted more-or-less on the spur of the moment. If he saw a potential female victim at the right time and place for him (the wrong time and place for her) then he zeroed in almost instantly. Ross, who committed sickening crimes, was addicted to hardcore pornography; sex was always consciously, or subconsciously, in his mind. In fact, even while on death row (he has since been executed) he masturbated to his sexual fantasies up to forty times a day to the degree he caused sores on his penis. When he was out and about working as an insurance salesman his overwhelming sexual needs were ever present. He was, in effect, hunting, consciously or unconsciously primed to commit murder.

So, imagine if you are a woman or young girl walking home alone from the store or school and someone like the well-groomed young, bespectacled, bookish-looking Michael Ross drives past you. His car brake lights go on . . . he stops . . . waits . . . and when you pass him he pleasantly asks you directions; then he seizes hold of you, covers your mouth with a hand and takes you away to be raped and murdered. Indeed, Ross didn't just snatch and grab like this at night, he did so in broad daylight, on well-travelled busy roads, too.

So, here's a piece of advice. If a man slows down his car

and starts asking you for directions, stand well back and treat him with suspicion. We have sat nav these days, do we not?

Here I turn to Freud's theory of the human personality, which he divided into three parts – the id, which contains our primitive drives and operates largely according to the 'pleasure principle', whereby its two main goals are the seeking of pleasure and the avoidance of pain; the superego, the lofty, ethical part, which acts as moral conscience; and the ego, the realistic component, which negotiates between the impulses of the id and the ideals and prohibitions of the superego. The id has no perception of reality, its actions stemming from two major instincts:

Eros: the life instinct that motivates people to focus on self-preservation and pleasure-seeking (e.g., sexual urges).

Thanatos: the death instinct that motivates people towards destruction, including that of other people and also of themselves.

The late Dr Don Bannister, a British psychologist who was not entirely in agreement with Freud, summarised, with gentle mockery, such psychoanalytic theories as suggesting that man:

> . . . is essentially a battlefield, he is a dark cellar in which a maiden aunt [the superego] and a sex-crazed monkey [the id] are locked in mortal combat, the affair being refereed by a rather nervous bank clerk [the ego].

Notwithstanding Don Bannister's views, his lively inter-pretation of Freud's three components of personality is echoed by Michael Ross's description of the struggle he experienced from day to day, month in month out:

I felt like a spider trying to climb up a glass window. I wanted rid of the terrible thoughts inside my head but as soon as I got near to the top I fell down again. And it was like having an obnoxious neighbour who kept coming round uninvited and getting on my nerves. When I was under medication this neighbour lived down the hallway and left me alone. As soon as the medication was stopped he came back again.

For Michael Ross, his car played the part of trap, and elsewhere in this book are examples of other vehicle users, taxi drivers amongst them, who have the same sexual mindset as had Ross. Just like Michael, they often spend hours in their vehicles fantasising about sex. Men such as Antoni Imiela (1954–2018) were, and are, addicted to internet porn, spending hours in sex chat rooms or on dating sites. Like Ross, they didn't consciously go about their daily employment with the premeditated intention of committing rape or murder, but their subconscious minds were always consumed with sexual fantasies. So, when a young woman, possibly intoxicated, hailed their cab, their thoughts awoke up from the subconscious in a Dr Jekyll/Mr Hyde sort of way. She was vulnerable and he could do as he pleased with her. As Ross once told me: 'I saw them. I wanted them. I used them, I raped them and I killed them. Then I dumped their bodies like so much trash. What fuckin' more do you want to know?'

On the other hand, about the same number of taxi drivers around the world are murdered by their passengers, which kind of makes it quits, I suppose, but for different reasons. Those who murder taxi drivers do so for money, while taxi drivers who kill women do so with sex to the forefront of their minds.

With these opportunist killers, it seems to me that while subconscious premeditation is always present, off-the-cuff opportunities arise when their sexual fantasies are irreversibly triggered. Even in perfectly normal people like you and me, emotions are often sparked reflexively and without concern or an understanding of the consequences. The hypothalamus seeks pleasure and satisfaction, and whether the stimulus is thirst or sexual hunger, the basic message is 'I WANT IT NOW!' Fortunately, you and I have the ability to control ourselves. With sexual psychopaths, however, there is no consideration of the long-term consequences of their acts because they have no sense of morals, danger, values, logic or right and wrong. Where there *should* be a conscience there is a black hole, and each and every offender in this book had no moral compass at all.

We will also meet serial rapists and killers – all of them psychopaths through and through, who, having selected their victim either by chance or design, methodically and consciously plan and execute their offences over a longer period of time.

The serial killer George Joseph Smith (1872–1915), active during the early twentieth century and perpetrator of the 'Brides in the Bath' murders is a prime example, as was the 'Acid Bath Murderer' John George Haig (1909–1949), both of whom killed for financial gain, as did the serial killer John Martin Scripps, the 'Tourist from Hell', whom I interviewed a few days before he was hanged, aged thirty-seven, at Changi Prison, Singapore, on 19 April 1996. They were organised killers, their crimes planned and prepared for beforehand.

Then there are the serial killers who combine a mix of organised – or premeditated – and disorganised offending. US serial killer, Harvey 'The Hammer' Louis Carignan (1927–), motivated by lust as much as by hate, sometimes used 'Wanted' ads to lure female victims into his clutches, while most other times he simply snatched them off the streets.

Another US killing machine, Paul John Knowles (1946–1974), was even more random, killing men, women and children in an orgy of slaughter, just as did tag team Henry Lee Lucas (1936–2001) and Ottis Elwood Toole (1947–1996). Carl Panzram 1892–1930) and German-born Werner Boost, now aged ninety-two, are another two men whose bitter hatred of mankind led them to kill again and again.

The bottom line is that these killers, and countless others, were, and are, predators, even the most disorganised. Of the more organised, premeditation was certainly behind their actions – and very often this involved stalking their victims.

Before I go any further, I should remind you that stalkers come in all sorts – jealous lovers or would-be lovers, strangers besotted with certain celebrities, exes who can't let go … all of these might stalk the object of their obsession. Some might stalk in person, hanging around the person's home and watching them, perhaps following them, others stalk them online. These situations usually cause great distress, and can result in assault or even murder – but I am talking about a different kind of stalker. I am talking about that most sinister of serial killers, the one who stalks his victims.

3

The Watchers

There was this guy standing on the stairs. Lots of
girls saw him. He didn't dance or drink or mix with
us. For a long time he just stood there and watched
us. It was kind of creepy. He gave us all the creeps.
FORMER CHI OMEGA SORORITY STUDENT,
TO THE AUTHOR DURING THE MAKING OF THE
TWELVE-PART TV DOCUMENTARY SERIES *THE SERIAL
KILLERS*, FLORIDA STATE UNIVERSITY CAMPUS,
TALLAHASSEE, 1995

Within an hour of this unnerving experience, another
Chi Omega student, Margaret Elizabeth Bowman, aged
twenty-one, was bludgeoned and strangled as she slept
in her dorm bed. Moments later, Lisa Levy, aged twenty,
was also beaten, strangled to death then posthumously
sexually assaulted. Shortly after, Cheryl Thomas, aged

twenty-one, was bludgeoned as she slept in her condo just eight blocks away. Somehow, she survived.

The date was Sunday, 15 January 1978. The silent watcher was kidnapper, rapist and sado-sexual lust serial killer, Theodore 'Ted' Robert Bundy (1946–1989), known to all true-crime buffs as being perhaps the most heinous serial murderer in US criminal history.

While researching and making the TV documentary, my producer Frazer Ashford, our film crew and I had been in Florida's state capital, Tallahassee, and we'd done all the usual things that crime-film crews do: eat lots of junk food; argue; bicker; pester witnesses and cops for interviews; have a ride-along in a police cruiser, blue strobes flashing . . . We talked to police chiefs; the Florida Department of Law Enforcement (FDLE); crime technicians; lawyers; visited crime scenes; we drank weak beer and ate even more crap food – oh, for a true-Brit Sunday roast with all the trimmings!

I even got to handle Ted's dental moulds, I kid you not. These were the casts taken from his mouth after his arrest under the pretext that he might need dental treatment. This exercise would soon demonstrate that he had, indeed, bitten into Lisa Levy's buttocks just before she died, for the impressions matched perfectly. The definition of such work is included within the science known as 'forensic odontology'. It is truly a subject to get your teeth into and chew over at your leisure.

Levity aside, I have two particularly vivid memories of that visit to Tallahassee; the first being the words, quoted above, of one of Margaret Bowman and Lisa Levy's sorority sisters; the other that I was presented with a clear plastic (or similar transparent composite material) 'Florida Law Enforcement OLYMPICS' mug inscribed with 'Building a Stronger Bond Between Law Enforcement Officers' on the reverse side.

Have you ever had an unhealthy sense of unease accompanied by a slight twinge of rising hair on the nape of your neck, perhaps even a shiver down your spine, a sensation that you are being watched? This could have happened at any time, in any place and at any time of the day or night, so please give this question some thought.

If you *have* had this experience, then you most probably shrugged it off to forget about it within the minute – that is, until at some other time, in some other place, you get that same sensation again. Coincidence? Maybe or maybe not. But consider the words of the student quoted earlier; it is horribly clear that the most awful death could have been merely a dorm away for her; the stalking Ted Bundy had been watching her too – watching, waiting; overwhelmed by an controllable urge to bludgeon, rape, abuse, maul and kill.

I now think about Shirley Ann Banks.

One of four siblings Shirley was born in Edinburgh on 4 August 1958. She had recently married and was living in Bristol. On Thursday, 8 October 1987, this slim, attractive, hardworking young woman left work at the end of the day with plans to go shopping for a new dress. Having studied every one of the hundreds of police documents on this shocking case, and having interviewed and corresponded with her killer at length, I know that at 7 p.m. that evening Shirley went into the Debenhams department store in Broadmead, Bristol, and started browsing – eventually opting for a full-length navy-and-white print spun-viscose dress. The price was a reasonable £24.99, so she bought it.

Shirley's badly decomposing body was later found in a Quantock Hills stream locally known as 'Dead Woman's Ditch' by a couple, Basil Hooper and his wife Jill, out walking on Saturday, 2 April 1988.

But let us return to Debenhams and the Top Shop (now Topshop) part of the store where John David Guise Cannan, thirty-three years old, tall, smartly suited and well-groomed, had zeroed in. He was covertly watching Shirley, who without a care in the world, wandered from rail to rail, picking up dresses, holding them up against herself in front of a full-length mirror to see whether they suited her.

All women do this, correct? Some guys do, too, bless them.

Perhaps Shirley spotted the charming-looking John Cannan. Who knows?

The innocent prey being watched by a killer – Shirley was more or less dead the moment Cannan spotted her.

Maybe for a fleeting second it might have crossed her mind to wonder what a lone man was doing in a woman's clothing area. Of course we will never have the answer to that thought, if it existed at all. What we do know, however, is that Cannan followed Shirley out of the store to where she had parked her Austin Mini car. It was here that he pounced. He pushed the terrified woman into her own vehicle, cuffed her and drove her back to his Foye House apartment just across Isambard Brunel's Clifton Suspension Bridge where he held her for a couple of days or so and raped her. He then dragged her to nearby woods and bludgeoned her to death. Cannan is also prime suspect in the murder of Suzy Lamplugh, for, although her body has never been found, and he strongly denies having ever met her, there are solid grounds for suspecting him, as I demonstrate in my book *Prime Suspect*.

Although Cannan has voiced numerous theories as to who *might* have murdered Shirley Banks, he has always maintained his total innocence, when in fact he is as guilty as sin. In truth, we may never know exactly when he first spotted Shirley but all the indications are that he first noticed her someplace inside the Debenhams store where he was either subconsciously or consciously on the hunt for prey. I suspect it was the former. Whatever the case, he then zeroed in on the pretty blonde. For a while he would have furtively watched her, just observing to check if she was alone.

Now, we have in Cannan an 'organised offender', because when he was satisfied that she was by herself, and only then he moved in closer, and wearing a gracious smile he might have even told her that he was also looking for a dress that might suit his (non-existent) girlfriend. So, can you see them both now. . .can you now see this man's devious mind working?

Taking this stalking technique a little further, we

all watch natural history programmes where a single predator stalks a group of animals, always waiting for one to stray too far from the herd, where it is, almost risk free, pulled down. Risk-averse Cannan was doing precisely the same thing. He was weighing up the odds of Success *v.* Failure. He was in a location where it could be said women swim in shoals, and his camouflage – his ghillie suit, or guise, for he is aptly named – being smart business attire, spotlessly clean shoes, and the persona of a well-spoken, well-groomed, slick and charming to a fault, young man.

Although serial killer Ted Bundy was by and large a 'snatch and grab' serial killer; meaning that more often than not he, like Michael Ross, just happened by chance upon his victims, as, incidentally, did Cannan in the two rapes of which he has been convicted, the stalking by Bundy on the FSU campus has all the hallmarks of a psychopathological modus operandi. We will see more examples of this type of MO throughout this book, some being conscious and premeditated, with others being subconscious in origin. However, it is the watching element that this chapter is concerned with. So the question of where the wellspring of stalking is in a serial murderer's psyche is a subject worth examining. To try to answer this question one has to go back through an offender's back history, his criminal narrative, and look at earlier crimes, because sure as eggs are eggs, most of these offenders have had brushes with the law before. In police parlance, they have 'form' – for my American readers, a 'rap sheet'.

Homicidal psychopaths do not just pop into existence out of nowhere, although this will always seem to be the case to their victims who never knew what was coming until it hit them.

Serial sex murderers 'evolve', and perhaps the best way I can simplify this is by saying that many of them start their 'careers' as peeping Toms or voyeurs (from the French *voir*, meaning 'to see' or 'to view'), or as people with a particularly unhealthy addiction to pornography – these days, internet-generated hard porn. Once a voyeur focuses on a specific individual or specific individuals, and watches or follows them exclusively and repeatedly, he or she is a stalker.

Of particular interest to us, is that in the fourth edition of their *Diagnostic and Statistical Manual of Mental Disorders* (DSM-IV, published 1994), the American Psychiatric Association has classified certain voyeuristic 'fantasies, urges and behaviour patterns as a paraphilia if the person has acted upon these urges, or the sexual urges or fantasies cause marked distress or interpersonal difficulty'.

A 'paraphilia' is a condition characterised by abnormal sexual desires, typically involving extreme or dangerous activities. We might also call this 'sexual perversion' or 'sexual deviation' and it may also be labelled as 'sexual fetishism'.

DSM-IV goes on to define voyeurism as 'the act of looking at unsuspecting individuals, usually strangers, who are naked, in the process of disrobing, or engaging in sexual activity'.

Furthermore, DSM-IV states that: 'In order to be *diagnosed* [my italics] with voyeuristic disorder the symptoms must persist for over six months and the person in question must be over the age of eighteen.' However, to be '*diagnosed* with voyeuristic tendencies' does not imply that this disorder didn't exist much earlier. Many very young children who metamorphose into sexual psychopaths in adulthood were subjected to some sort of unhealthy sexual imprinting, which affected them to the extent that some of these unhealthy experiences became precursors to or triggers for more adult forms of voyeurism in their teens.

Of course, it goes without saying that only a minute fraction of people who are into voyeurism turn into homicidal maniacs; nevertheless, when linked to an emerging psychopathy, or the more PC sociopathy – an antisocial personality disorder – sooner or later voyeurism can become addictive, with the individual needing more enhanced sexual stimuli over and over again.

In the case of Michael Ross, he undoubtedly formed an addiction to voyeurism in his very early teens and was fixated on pornographic reading material. He, like Ted Bundy, then moved on to become a Peeping Tom. So uncontrollable were his sexual urges that Michael Ross used to masturbate constantly while reading porn magazines, then still he demanded sex from his girlfriend at least three times each day.

I fantasise over the crimes every day and every night. I would masturbate to the point of, um, actually having raw spots on myself from the masturbation. I would bleed. It's weird. I get a lot of pleasure from it. It is really a pleasurable experience. But, when it's all over, it's a very short-term thing. I guess it's like getting high. You know I've never used drugs, but you can get high, then you come down and crash. That's almost how it is. It's just not an easy thing to live with.

MICHAEL ROSS TO THE AUTHOR AT INTERVIEW

Ted Bundy was similar. He too had become fixated on pornography as a teenager then went on to become a voyeur. Just hours before his execution, on 9 February 1978, he admitted on camera to a Dr Dobson that hard porn had more-or-less started him off in becoming a serial killer. That that might be any form of honest mitigation for committing sado-sexual serial homicide, I think not!

Just as voyeurs get a sexual kick out of reading pornographic material, or viewing similar material on the internet, it has to be agreed that both forms of exposure allow 'watching', and through the fantasies generated by this paraphiliac form of addictive watching comes the Peeping Tom stage, broadly defined by DSM-IV as 'the act of secretly looking at unsuspecting individuals, usually strangers, who are naked, in the process of disrobing – or engaging in sexual activity' – in effect a form of stalking.

However, I think we can go further than this when we look at 'victimology' later in this book – defining 'victimology' as being a serial killer's preferred type of victim: young, old, tall, short, petite, obese, male, female, blonde, brunette, types of clothing, red high heels or sandals, etc. Way back in an offender's history there has to have been a 'sexual trigger' of sorts – what turns him or her on or off – something that is associated with sexual pleasure, excitement, fulfilment, empowerment, fear, pain or other sensation.

Voyeurs have their own preferences too, and this, to a lesser degree, may well entail ogling, discreetly following a pretty young girl down the street to her home in the hope of being able to see her strip naked – as did Michael Ross, Ted Bundy, and hundreds more of their type who obtain a sexual kick, and the sense of power, that comes with 'I'm watching you'– thus, somewhat perversely, 'I am in control'. And, indeed, in so many ways these offenders *are* in control, for under the right circumstances they will have the power over life and death.

Not a comforting thought.

To these truly vile individuals there is to be found 'exhilaration' in the act of secretly following, watching . . . stalking. Indeed, it is a fact that when being interviewed by homicide police many serial sex murderers freely admit that they had got as much 'fun' out of this stalking phase as the actual killing itself. These monsters merely see the dead body in front of them as the 'end result'. The stalking is over with. The victim has been trapped, used, abused, with the body being dumped like so much garbage; therefore, it is now time for the offender to cool down, to hope and pray that they had not been seen, chill out and wait until the next time round, when, they vow to themselves, they'll have more fun. It all comes back to the Id and Eros (pleasure-seeking/sexual urges), and Thanatos (the death instinct that motivates people to use aggressive urges to destroy.)

Michael Ross looks so normal he could be the guy next door. If I was walking down a dark alley at night, heard footsteps behind me, and turned around, well, I would have been relieved to see Michael Ross. That's how normal the guy looks.

KAREN B. CLARKE, AN EXPERIENCED NEW YORK
JOURNALIST, WHO VISITED ROSS IN PRISON

Following the peeping Tom stage, the 'emerging serial sex offender' may move on to commit a sexual assault. This may amount to some type of fondling, or perhaps an act of indecent exposure – both of which will give the offender sexual satisfaction, at least initially. Unless apprehended, a rape almost inevitably follows.

I use the criminal narrative of Michael Ross quite often. Indeed, I lecture on this man frequently because his is as good an example of this 'graduation process' from hard-porn voyeurism to becoming a sado-sexual psychopath as any I can find. There are many other examples I could cite, but, for the purposes of this book, there is no better.

While he was studying for a degree in agriculture at the prestigious Cornell University, Ithaca, New York, Michael went from Peeping Tom to committing what he called 'minor sexual assaults'. He started following vulnerable young co-eds around the campus at night. Then, when he could contain himself no longer, he sexually assaulted a young woman, and then another, then another, with thoughts of taking them back to a secret dungeon, tying them up and using them as sex slaves. He had metamorphosed into a serial rapist, with cooling-off periods in between the 'events'.

Inevitably, it went further, and tragically for Dzung Ngoc Tu, Ross would make her his first dead victim. He followed her through the campus grounds, sprang out from bushes, raped her and strangled her. Thinking that she was now dead, he callously tossed her body over a bridge into the swirling waters of Beebe Lake. She wasn't actually dead at the time, as was discovered at autopsy when it was determined that she had drowned.

I spent four years corresponding with Mike Ross. I interviewed him twice on death row at Somers Prison, Connecticut.

He was likeable, the beast sleeping within concealed. Outwardly, there was absolutely no hint whatsoever that he was a monster: one of the most twisted serial killers in the state's history. His demeanour was pleasant, self-effacing. He was highly intelligent. Articulate. Non-threatening. With his boyish smile, he was the all-American boy. This was Michael's ghillie suit. He could so easily be the guy living next door to you . . . but . . . he would have raped and killed any parent's daughter and he would not have given a damn.

Although he was convicted of having killed five times, prior to me interviewing him he had never admitted murdering Dzung Ngoc Tu. During my last filmed interview with Michael, I managed to get him to admit the murder – and also that of a schoolgirl called Paula Perrera, eventually making a total of eight kills. For this I received letters of commendation from the New York

State Police and Crystal Run PD. It brought long-awaited closure to the grieving next of kin. He once said to me, 'I didn't actually kill Dzung. It was proven that she had drowned.' Then he smiled. How cold-blooded is that?

My book, *Talking with Serial Killers*, includes a chapter devoted to Ross's life and crimes. But what I will say is that much has been written about Michael, much of which is true, much of which is not. I have been with him and I have the T-shirt to prove it − I found being in the presence of true evil a very interesting exercise indeed.

In November 2018 there was a national media frenzy regarding the aforementioned John Cannan, who, as many will know, is the prime suspect in the disappearance, now presumed murder, on Monday, 28 July 1986 of twenty-five-year-old south London estate agent, Suzy Lamplugh. Indeed, such was this media interest I was called back to the UK from Manila to be interviewed by numerous newspapers and appear on TV to give my thoughts as to why the police had suddenly decided to dig up Cannan's mother's former garden looking for a body *thirty-two years* after Suzy went missing.

Those of you who have read my book *Prime Suspect* will know the story of Cannan's life and his awful crimes. It is a fact that as the result of letters Cannan wrote to me, the Metropolitan Police were able to locate a red Ford Sierra motorcar that Cannan was using on 28 July 1986 − the precise day Suzy vanished. It was found in a scrapyard. Forensic examination of the interior yielded both Cannan's and Suzy's DNA. Yet, despite this, the Crown Prosecution Service (CPS), whom the lead investigators snapped at during an unprecedented TV broadcast conference, labelling them the 'Can't Prosecute Service', defended their position. DCI Jim Dickie and DCI Ault, from the elite SOII squad based at Buckingham Palace Road police station, criticised the decision not to charge Cannan on the grounds of insufficient evidence. It is now unlikely that Cannan will ever stand trial for the murder of Suzy Lamplugh.

The very belated digging up of Mrs Cannan's Sutton Coldfield garden was not only a complete waste of valuable and finite police resources, not to mention taxpayers' money, as the police should have known that Cannan could not have interred Suzy there following an earlier police investigation in 1986. Perhaps they would have been better occupied in looking again into the Sandra Court homicide for which Cannan is also suspected. With regard to Suzy Lamplugh's case, Cannan – who had been transferred from HM Prison Bristol, where he had served five out of eight years for a horrific rape, to a pre-release hostel near Wormwood Scrubs Prison – had now been released.

It is known that Cannan, wearing a smart business suit and a 'kipper-style' tie, frequented wine bars in Fulham, which is where he might have met Suzy. Upon returning to her office she made a note in her diary: '12.45 Mr Kipper – 37 Shorrolds Road o/s' ('o/s' indicating that she had arranged to meet the prospective client – Mr Kipper – outside the property, which was not far from her office in Fulham Road) for the following afternoon – on the day she went missing.

Several witnesses later told police that they saw Suzy and a man of a similar description to Cannan outside the property. Shortly thereafter, at about 2.45 p.m., a friend of Suzy's, Barbara Whitfield, spotted her driving her white Fiesta car along Stevenage Road, near the river, and about a mile from Suzy's office. There was a man, again with a similar description to Cannan, in the front passenger seat. Suzy, she said, looked terrified. Her car was later found abandoned near the Thames. Local people recalled seeing a red Ford Sierra parked close by. Suzy was never seen alive again.

In fact, when one thoroughly studies Cannan's back history – his narrative – aligning all of this with his modus operandi, his rapes, robberies and the way he has manipulated the police over several decades till the present day, it is no surprise that Cannan remains the prime suspect for the murder of Suzy Lamplugh and has been investigated for the murder of Sandra Court.

Of course, not all serial killers wear outer disguises like smart business attire as ghillie suits. Sexual predators such as deviant clergy wear the cloth of their so-called Christian faith to disguise their evil intentions. Others wear the guise of the learned schoolteacher, thus gaining the trust of impressionable pupils. Medical people, like the UK serial killer Dr Harold Shipman, wore a musty tweed jacket and cavalry-twill trousers. Killer nurses, like Beverly Allitt, wore the crispy white apron of a nurse to camouflage their premeditated homicidal intentions.

An accomplice can occasionally play the part of a killer's camouflage. Serial sex murderers, such as Ian Brady and

Fred West, might never have killed had they not had a female partner alongside them when they first approached their selected prey. An ingrained but mistaken belief that a female posed no, or at least much less, threat would put the intended victim at ease, and make the killers' chances to carry out their evil intent easier – and perhaps more enjoyable. Where two perpetrators are involved, there has to be an element of planning – and very possibly of stalking.

4

Modi Operandi and Criminal Signatures

Crime scenes can reveal a lot about the crimes' perpetrators, the modus operandi displaying traits and preferences which can indicate whether the perpetrator is an 'organised' or 'disorganised' offender (of which more below). With serial killers there tends to be a signature, too – a kind of personal stamp – not always unintentional, as while some are the result of a psychological deviance, others are just for effect. These – the modus operandi, the signature (should one be present) and other factors, all help investigators build up a profile of the offender, which, it is to be hoped – will sooner or later lead them to the offender.

THE MODUS OPERANDI

In my books I have spoken many times of offenders' modus operandi. Literally, it means way or method of doing something, of operating, and in the case of serial killers and other criminals, it is their method of perpetrating their crimes. There is usually some sort of pattern or common thread to be discerned in an offender's modus operandi (MO), which, like the signature (should there be one), helps to create a serial offender's profile. The MO can be something as simple as a killer's favoured killing instrument – a knife, a gun, strangulation, poison or something else; or it might be how bodies are treated after death, and how they are hidden, or left in plain view . . . Criminologist Dr Scott Bonn, in an article published in *Psychology Today* of 29 June 2015, gives as an example Jack the Ripper's MO, which 'was that he attacked prostitutes at night on the street armed with a knife'.

In the same article, Dr Bonn observes that 'Significantly, the MO is a "learned behaviour" that is subject to change, for a serial killer will alter and refine his MO to accommodate new circumstances or to incorporate new skills and information. For example, instead of using rope to tie up a victim, the offender may learn that it is easier and more effective to bring handcuffs with him.'

THE CRIMINAL SIGNATURE

Whereas virtually all crimes have an MO, not every crime has to have a signature. And, unlike the MO, the signature, as Dr Bonn writes, 'serves the "emotional" or "psychological" needs of the offender. The signature comes from within the psyche of the offender and probably reflects a deep fantasy need that the killer has about his victims.' He goes on to observe that 'the essential core of the signature, when present, is that it is always the same because it emerges out of an offender's fantasies' – and these fantasies had often existed well before any crime was committed.

There are numerous examples of criminal signatures, all too many adding a grotesque twist to a foul act. Certain offenders might pose corpses in a provocative sexual position, as did the US serial killer tag team, the 'Hillside Stranglers' Kenneth Bianchi and Angelo Buono; others carve something, some symbol, say, like a pentagram, or a letter, onto a body; others might insert items into the body, as did US homosexual serial murderer, Randy Kraft who, on one occasion, stuck a chrome car-door handle into a victim's body; or they take 'souvenirs', a lock of hair perhaps, or an item of jewellery, as did Long Island serial killer, Joel Rifkin.

I say 'souvenirs' when I really mean 'trophies', in much the same way as a big-game hunter will take the horns of a shot animal to exhibit on the wall of his den. Some fishermen do the same thing in having their prize catch cleaned, stuffed and framed for all to see, and for them to remember what a fight the fish put up before it was taken into the net.

Many serial killers do precisely the same thing in as much as they take away a lock of hair, a ring, a necklace, the victim's underwear, just so that they can relive over and over again the terrible crimes they have committed. Some offenders take photographs or video recordings of their victims' suffering. And, in other cases, the killer will 'gift' an item of a victim's jewellery to a wife or a partner so that he can enjoy a continuing perverse thrill out of seeing a dead woman's necklace around a living person's neck.

I have before me the crime-scene photographs of all the victims of the so-called Hillside Stranglers, in situ. These photos are not for public viewing because, to be honest with you, it is stomach-curdling to see the way Bianchi and Buono treated the innocent young women and two young schoolgirls who were all raped, tortured and strangled. Their broken bodies were dumped like trash, by the roadsides around Los Angeles, naked, legs wide open with their eyes closed in a travesty of peace. This was their killers' signature – their way of saying, '*Fuck you*! Catch us if you can!'

Signature analysis has not been subjected to many systematic studies, and so a myth has arisen that signatures always present in the same way. In fact, however, as with the MO, different victims and different situations might present opportunities to tinker and improve, or might necessitate some new ritual.

Ted Bundy's signature is said to have been the bites he inflicted on his victims (ultimately, this could be what sealed his fate: investigators were able to compare photographs of the bite marks with an impression of his teeth – a case, perhaps, of the biter bit); some would tie ligatures with an unusual knot; a serial killer in India left beer cans next to victims, while in Greece, a killer stabbed each of four elderly prostitutes exactly four times in the neck; a serial murderer in Germany usually inflicted left-slanted parallel stab wounds, which helped to link his victims.

Between 1990 and 1991, three prostitutes were murdered in Texas. At autopsy, it became clear that their eyes had been skilfully removed. A tip from another prostitute led police to fifty-seven-year-old Charles Frederick Albright, aka the 'Dallas Ripper'. A hair and fibre analysis of debris from his home, a blanket, and the victim's, provided circumstantial physical evidence that implicated him. He had a fixation for eyes, seemingly from his background in taxidermy, and a long history of deception and fraud. Albright was convicted of the murders, and now, as inmate No. 00606168 he is currently at the West Texas Regional Medical Facility Unit, at Lubbock, where he occupies himself by drawing pictures of women's eyes.

In 1960s Poland the shadowy killer Lucian Staniak – whose very existence has been called into question – would leave a signature comparable to that of London's Jack the Ripper, as, like the Ripper, he purportedly disembowelled his female prey – although, unlike Jack's, none of his victims were prostitutes. Again like the Ripper supposedly did, he sent letters to the press. These, written in red, earned him the nickname Red Spider, thanks to his spidery scrawl.

The Red Spider is alleged to have confessed to twenty killings – four times as many victims as the Ripper but over three years compared to Jack's ten weeks. Finally and critically, the Red Spider was identified, arrested and incarcerated, partly thanks to an analysis of the red 'ink', which showed it was artist's paint. Two of the victims (sisters) had been members of the same art club as Staniak – which led police to Lucien Staniak, twenty-six, a government translator and an artist who'd once depicted a mutilated woman.

Serial killer, Roger Reece Kibbe, aka the 'I-5 Strangler', was a henpecked husband with a longer-than-average criminal record for non-violent crimes. Since boyhood he had had a fetish for cutting female clothing in unusual ways. Twice a week, he'd stolen such items from clothes lines, and after clipping them he'd often bury them. The same odd cutting patterns were found on the clothing of a number of Kibbe's seven murder victims: his signature. Reportedly, he'd used his mother's scissors. His MO was consciously stalking the freeways south of Sacramento late at night looking for women driving along the highway. If they seemed lost or were having car trouble, he would generously offer them assistance; alternatively he would pretend to be disabled and ask for their help. He would then abduct them, drive them to remote locations and strangle them with their own clothing. Two pieces of chance evidence – a length of cord of a sort he was known to use, with traces of red paint also found in Kibbe's vehicle, and also cat hairs that matched those of his cats – linked Kibbe to one of the killings. In 1991, he was tried and convicted of one count of first-degree murder and sentenced to prison for twenty-five years. Kibbe is now inmate No. E98227 at the Mule Creek State Prison (MCSP), Ione, California. Years after his incarceration, at a parole hearing, he confessed to a further six murders in order to avoid the death penalty. It is therefore doubtful that he will ever be released.

Then, of course, there's BTK's notorious signature,

the three letters stylised so that when placed together they formed a shape resembling a female torso. Dennis L. Rader, who announced himself as BTK, wanted his crimes linked and was frustrated when they weren't. Having created his signature, he'd often anonymously tip off the police himself, or send items to ensure that his BTK ('bind, torture, kill') persona got credit. He crafted his signature for effect, as well as to set him apart as an elite killer. Inmate no.83707 Rader is serving a natural life sentence at the El Dorado Correctional Facility in Butler County, Kansas.

ORGANISED, DISORGANISED AND MIXED OFFENDERS

Now to return to my earlier mention in this chapter of organised and disorganised killers. The categorisation of serial offenders into three types: 'organised', 'disorganised', and 'mixed' (i.e., those who exhibit both characteristics) is to be found in the FBI's *Crime Classification Manual*. Classifying an unknown killer as one of these types forms part of creating a criminal's profile, potentially leading investigators to identify the offender.

Once again, I turn to Dr Bonn who, writing in *Psychology Today* (17 June 2018) explains that:

Profilers use a list of factors such as whether the victim's body was positioned or posed by the killer, whether sexual acts were performed before or after death and whether cannibalism or mutilation was practised on the body. These factors are used to predict whether an unknown offender is an organised or disorganised killer. The organised/disorganised classification of offenders is the centrepiece of the FBI profiling approach.

Throughout this book, I talk about organised and disorganised killers – so I plead guilty to repeating myself here. But where serial killers are concerned, it makes an important contribution to offender profiling, and is a much-discussed aspect of serial murder.

At the beginning of this chapter, I mentioned crime scenes – with organised killers there are usually three: where the killer advances upon the victim, where he or she kills the victim, and where the victim's body is disposed of. Little evidence is found at any of the scenes, for the offender is careful to clear away anything that could lead police to them. The organised killer is intelligent, efficient, controlled and educated; they take an interest in news reports of their crimes; they are probably employed and might well lead an apparently blameless domestic life with a partner who is completely unaware of their crimes. They are frequently capable of turning on the charm to get what they want. Organised offenders plan their actions methodically, and they are generally meticulous in covering up evidence of their crime, and try to remain one step ahead of those investigating their crimes. According to the FBI's classification scheme, they are antisocial and often psychopathic. But they are not insane, and they do know right from wrong; they are incapable of showing any remorse. Ted Bundy is a typical example of an organised killer, as is Dennis Rader.

As a rule, serial killers tend to be more organised than disorganised – unsurprisingly, as they are more likely to evade arrest and reoffend for long enough to become serial killers.

Disorganised serial killers are considered generally less intelligent than organised ones, and they are often found to have a history of mental illness. There is nothing to suggest that they planned their murders, and neither are there signs of much effort having been put into clearing up afterwards, with little or no attempt made to hide the body or wipe away fingerprints and other incriminating bits of evidence. Often the murder weapon is left at the scene, suggesting it was picked at random.

Disorganised killers are possibly young, and are likely to be unemployed, and to be loners with few friends. The crime scene often shows signs of the attack having been frenzied, and there may be signs of sexual violence and/or necrophilia. Dr Bonn suggests that such killers are 'likely to come from an unstable or dysfunctional family, perhaps having been abused physically or sexually by relatives. They are often sexually inhibited, sexually uninformed and may have sexual aversions or other pathologies.'

Serial murders can – and frequently do – display signs of being both types. Scott Bonn, published in *Psychology Today* (June 2018), observed:

It is also important to note that a serial murder case can also be a mix of organised and disorganised. This occasionally occurs, for example, when there are multiple offenders of different personality types involved in the killings. It can also occur when a lone offender is undergoing a psychological trans-formation throughout his killing career.

STAGING AND POSING

Sometimes there are signs of the crime scene having been altered – usually in order to mislead crime investigators, but sometimes as part of the criminal's signature.

In this context, the reader might be interested in the case of Darlie Lynn Routier, who stabbed to death her two sons: Devon, aged six, and Damon, aged five, at the family home on 6 June 1996. Routier is currently on death row at Mountain View Unit, Gatesville, convicted of the murder of Damon. Her case might be seen as a prime example of an alteration of the crime scene – in this instance an attempt to stage the crime scene to make it look as though an intruder had broken into the house and attacked both her and her two boys as they slept downstairs in the living room. There is still much controversy surrounding this dreadful murder but red flags quickly indicated that Routier was a practised liar.

On the other hand, if the crime scene alterations only serve the fantasy needs of the offender, then they are considered part of the signature and they are referred to as 'posing'. Sometimes a victim's body is posed to send a message to the police or public. For example, Jack the Ripper sometimes posed his victims' nude bodies with their legs spread apart to shock onlookers and the police in Victorian England. The 'Hillside Stranglers' mentioned above did likewise.

So, as we work our way through the cases in this book, readers might wish to come to their own conclusions as to whether a killer is 'organised', 'disorganised' or 'a bit of both', and to differentiate between MO and signature.

5

A Master Class in Stalking

I want to master life and death . . . What's one less
person on the face of the earth, anyway?

TED BUNDY

On Sunday, 14 July 1974, two young women disappeared
from the Lake Sammamish State Park, a freshwater lake
approximately ten miles east of Seattle, King County,
Washington, United States. While a film crew and I
were making a TV documentary about Bundy, years
later we visited the lake and one can imagine it back in
the seventies: a hot day; the perfect picnic spot, the park
crowded with hundreds of young people taking in the
sun.

In the midst of the crowds on that sunny day was
a watcher. He was covertly selecting his prey. He was
weighing up his chances of a successful kill, indeed, such

was the skill of this hunter he would kill two birds with more-or-less one stone, for he took two girls in broad daylight from that lakeside throng the same day; this was his technique.

At around noon, a wavy-haired handsome young man with his arm in a sling approached a girl named Doris Grayling. He asked her if she would help him lift his boat onto his car, a brown Volkswagen 'beetle'. She accompanied him to the car but then he told her the boat (which did not exist) was further up the hill by a line of trees. Unwilling to go further with the stranger, she excused herself and walked off; Bundy was thwarted. Doris had smelt a rat, probably asking herself why the stranger had not asked one of the hundreds of fit young men around to assist him, and with his arm in a sling what would he be doing with a boat? Her caution, her gut feeling, saved her life.

Within the hour, Bundy approached a pretty twenty-three-year-old named Janice Ott who was sunbathing alone by the lake. In other words she had strayed a little too far from the herd. When he asked her to help him with his boat, she invited him to sit down and talk. People sitting only a few yards away heard him introduce himself as 'Ted', and noted that he had an accent that might have been Canadian or even British. They talked for ten minutes about sailing and, in response to Janice saying, 'sailing must be fun, I've never learned how', Bundy offered to teach her. They set off together. She never returned to her place by the lake.

Only a couple of hours later, eighteen-year-old Denise

Naslund left a group of friends and went to the ladies, or the 'washroom' as our US friends call it. When she failed to return after four hours her friends reported her disappearance to a park ranger.

In September 1974, the remains of Janice Ott, Denise Naslund, and a third unidentified body (just a thigh bone), were found two miles east of Lake Sammamish Park in dense woodland. Ted Bundy later confessed to seven other attacks – with a single survivor – earlier that year, but at this stage he had merely started his killing spree. He would not finally face justice until 1979. He finally confessed to thirty murders in all; the actual total of his victims remains unknown.

As I have mentioned earlier, it would be redundant of me to detail Bundy's crimes again in this book for there are fuller accounts published elsewhere. However, what we are concerned about here is his MO: his stalking and hunting techniques, all of which he developed and polished to perfection as time passed by. He was able to adapt to suit his surroundings just like a chameleon.

> He should have recognised that what fascinated him was the hunt ... searching out his victims.
>
> BUNDY, IN THE SECOND PERSON
> REFLECTING ON HIMSELF

A noteworthy aspect of this human predator is that he had a preferred victim type (his victimology). The reader might wish to look at photos of many of Bundy's victims – easily found on the internet – and compare their faces and hairstyles. I suggest that they look so similar they could have been sisters – indeed a number of them were sorority sisters.

An example of Ted's cunning as a hunter is well documented in the homicide case of eighteen-year-old Georgann Hawkins whom he abducted on Tuesday, 11 June 1974. Several students recalled a stranger on crutches carrying a briefcase and dropping his textbooks in a dark alleyway adjacent to the Beta House Hall of Residence, University of Washington, where Georgann had suddenly vanished into thin air. Shortly before his execution, Bundy admitted this murder saying that the crutches (a bit like the sling he used when entrapping Janice Ott and Denise Naslund) was the none-threatening bait he'd used to lure these unsuspecting victims into his trap, adding: 'A pretty naïve young co-ed would have never refused to help a fellow student on crutches struggling to pick up his books or help him move his boat. Basically they were stupid.'

So, we can see that Bundy was choosy when selecting his victims. Wearing the ghillie suit of a university student, and using the sling and the crutches as a type of 'duck or goose call', to allay any suspicions, he knew where he could hunt and find exactly what he was seeking. Indeed, he did this time and again. He knew what worked and what did not work, and used the same technique with twenty-two-year-old Brenda Ball who was snatched on Saturday, 1 June 1974. Friends of Brenda later told law enforcement that they had last seen her talking to a handsome young man with his arm in a sling outside a bar near SeaTac airport. With Ted, this luring technique was used over and over, employing chameleon-like, subtle changes, on the same theme.

Under false pretences, as 'Officer Roseland', Bundy used a police badge to order women into his car, abduct then kill them. At his trial in Florida commencing 25 June 1979, he adopted the pseudo attorney persona of a first-rate lawyer, which, in truth, even impressed the sitting judge, Edward D. Cowart. This is how convincing this extremely narcissistic sado-sexual psychopath could be. However, during my time researching the life and crimes of Ted Bundy, the question has always come to mind: 'Where did his plunge into Stephen King-horror-like depravity all start?'

Much mockery has been poured over Bundy's death-row 'confessions': that the use of pornography was a prelude to him committing his dreadful crimes. Many sex offenders also confess to the use of porn, yet the link between porn and sex crime is very hard to pin down because many such criminals, and their lawyers, often use this addiction to porn as some form of mitigation – as an excuse for offending. However, this does not wash with me at all, simply because there are millions of people across the world who are addicted to pornography and they don't all turn into sado-sexual serial killers, do they? And there is no empirical evidence to even suggest it. But, there may be some, for where Bundy's alleged addiction to porn does have a ring of the truth rests with the 'graduation period' I referred to in the previous chapter. In Bundy's case we cannot dismiss him out of hand when in jail he explained that the pornography he used had a 'major influence upon him' and incited him to commit sexual violence. Again, I say this cannot be considered as mitigation for his crimes, but it is a factor to ponder as some form of early addiction to porn and the over-whelming need for sex have played a part in a sado-sexual killer's development as may be seen in Michael Ross and many of the other serial killers I have worked with over the past decades. Nevertheless we have to distinguish between proof and evidence. The 'proof' linking pornography and sex crime is similar to proof linking cholesterol to heart disease: there is no fixed linkage. But despite that, there is reasonable evidence to assume that there is a connection between the two, and that one leads to the other . . . often with fatal consequences.

'Hardcore porn' encompasses almost every form of pornography. This includes anything from the relatively tame magazines found in sex shops up to magazines and videos with bestiality, paedophilia, and extremely violent sadomasochistic material. This last category includes what are called 'snuff' films, in which the sadism is genuine and not acted: women are mutilated for real, terrible wounds are inflicted, and, in the most prized snuff films, actual murder is committed and filmed on camera. Thus, it could be said that any murderer who videos the rape, torture and killing of his victims is making his own snuff movie – one that he will keep as a trophy to watch over and over again.

Illegal in the UK, most printed hardcore pornography is available on the continent and across America. It is on this hardcore pornography that the complex debate about the influences leading to sex crime centres.

Nancy Steele, a prison social worker in the US, who deals directly with convicted rapists, has said – and this might like stating the obvious – 'Certain types of [sex criminals] live in a fantasy world, isolated from real human relationships', for it is a recognised feature of sex offenders that their emotional lives are most often empty, and they have difficulty forming loving relationships, or any relationship they do have is superficial. However, many authorities suggest that these people are mistaking the sex they see in pornography for love – which I do not believe is completely the case.

There was no definite tie-up between the de-censoring of hardcore porn and the growing occurrence of sex crime, but now with the internet there is a definite increase in sex-related crimes and sex-related homicide. In fact there is a veritable rip tide of general stalking flooding the internet today and there is no stopping it.

The flip side of this argument is that in some countries, following the liberalisation of censorship laws there has been a fall in these types of offences. It is popularly thought that this decrease is due to freely available pornography reducing the urge to commit sex crimes by providing a harmless 'release' for sexual excitement. However, where this may have applied many decades ago, most sociologists and prison psychologists refute this popular theory, and view pornography as a highly toxic incitement to sexual violence.

From my many decades of working with, interviewing

and corresponding with over thirty serial killers and one-off murderers, I say that far from being satisfied with photos on a page or a TV or PC screen, potential rapists, and sex killers, with their distorted image of women gleaned from hardcore pornography, want to try it out for themselves, and what is certain is that pornography is used by 80–90 per cent of sex offenders – including the likes of Ian Brady, Ted Bundy and Michael Ross, and many more – as an incitement to crime.

With this being said, I am confident in saying that in the majority of cases of stalking – after all, a form of voyeurism – with homicidal intent, much of this springs from exposure to hardcore porn, fantasising about sex with women who become mere objects of desire, through to voyeurism, stalking, sexual assault, rape, serial rape, sexual homicide to serial sexual murder. It is a graduation process from pornography through to murder. For these people now in the grip of this form of addiction, there can be no turning back.

6

Thierry Paulin and Kenneth Erskine: Stalking and Killing the Elderly

Perhaps another master-class example of conscious stalking with homicidal intent can be found in Thierry Paulin, dubbed by the media 'the Grim Reaper of Paris', aka 'le Monstre de Montmartre', who, for the three years from 1984 to 1987, roamed the avenues and tenements of Paris. His death toll is uncertain but it is believed to have been between eighteen and twenty-one. Indeed, this is quite an unusual case because on the surface the deaths had no sexual motive, yet robbery *was* involved. All of his victims were often frail and without the means to defend themselves particularly vulnerable as they lived alone, had few friends, relatives or visitors, and, for those without a telephone, little contact with the outside world.

This type of prey was Paulin's victimology and he knew they would make for easy pickings once he'd zeroed in on them. So, what and where was his stalking and hunting ground?

This has always been a tough area. People kill for fifty francs.

PIERRE BLOCH: DEPUTY MAYOR, XVIIITH
ARRONDISSEMENT, PARIS

At the time of the killings, the XVIIIth arrondissement had one of the most elderly populations in Paris, with a total of about 43,250 people aged over sixty representing almost a quarter of the 189,340 inhabitants. This arrondissement (borough) lies north of the Seine and stretches from the Boulevard de Clichy up to the périphérique motorway that encircles the city. Even today it is one of the most socially diverse districts of 'Gay Paree', encompassing the beautiful villas of the Avenue Junot in Montmartre, but, back in the eighties, also the dilapidated tenement buildings of the Goutte-d'Or, and the pornographic cinemas of the Boulevard de Clichy. At the time, drug dealers, prostitutes and petty crooks lived here, but also immigrant families, artists, actors and singers, side-by-side with the retired on modest incomes.

For the purpose of this book I will be brief in summarizing Paulin's victims, as follows.

Friday, 5 October 1984. Non-fatal attack on Germaine Petitot, ninety-one, in her small apartment on the Rue Lepic. She was bound, gagged and beaten by two men, then relieved of all her savings.

Friday, 5 October 1984. Police found the body of Anna Barbier-Ponthus, eighty-three. She lived in a modest apartment in the Rue Saulnier. It transpires that towards the end of the morning she returned home after doing her shopping. No sooner had she put the key in the front door than she was attacked, beaten and suffocated with a pillow. Her body was discovered gagged and bound with a curtain pull string. The contents of her purse – between 200 and 300 francs (less than £50) – had been stolen.

Tuesday, 9 October 1984. The body of eighty-nine-year-old Suzanne Foucault was discovered – she'd been dead for about two days. The apartment had been set on fire. The old lady had been suffocated with a plastic bag. Her watch, worth 300 francs, and 500 francs in cash were missing.

Monday, 5 November 1984. Seventy-one-year-old retired teacher Iona Seigaresco was found dead in her apartment in the Boulevard de Clichy. She had been beaten to death after being bound and gagged with an electric flex. In this case the violence of the murder was horrific. Her nose and jaw were fractured and a scarf had been used to half-strangle her. The autopsy revealed that all the ribs on her right side were shattered. Her killer got away with 10,000 francs in treasury bonds.

Wednesday, 7 November 1984. Alice Benaïm, eighty-four, was found dead by her son André, little more than two hours after she had died, when he had called in to have lunch with her at her apartment on Rue Marc-Séguin, as he did every day. Alice had been hit in the face and viciously tortured, probably to make her reveal where she had hidden her savings. She had been forced to swallow caustic soda and, while her mouth and throat burned with the acid, she had been bound with an electric flex, hands secured behind her back. She had been gagged with a dishcloth and thrown on her bed. Cause of death was strangulation. Around 400 to 500 francs was missing – a shockingly meagre return for such homicidal violence.

Thursday, 8 November 1984. The body of eighty-year-old Marie Choy was found – she had been dead for about three days. She lived just twenty metres from Alice Benaim. Marie had been tortured, bound with wire and gagged with a dishcloth. At autopsy it was revealed that, amongst other trauma, her skull had been fractured. Her killer stole between 200 and 300 francs.

Friday, 9 November 1984. Discovery of the body of Maria Mico-Diaz who, aged seventy-five, met a death similar to those of Maria Choy and Alice Benaim; this time, however, her body had been slashed with a knife.

Monday, 12, November 1984: Jeanne Laurent, who was eighty-two, was found bound with flex and murdered in her top-floor apartment, which had been vandalised. Nothing, apart from a very small amount of cash was stolen.

Four hours later, a second body was found, less than a kilometre away: Paule Victor, aged seventy-seven, had been killed in her home, a plastic bag pulled over her head, and a pillow placed on it. It was determined at autopsy that she had been killed about a week before.

I ask all pensioners to be on their guard, without becoming paranoid [about an attack].

J. Franceschi, Secretary of State
for the Elderly

There is some debate as to when 'offender profiling' came about and who actually invented the technique. Many claim that it came from the FBI, while others say in the UK. Maybe it was an Anglo-US effort, but I do know that Professor David Canter first developed it in the UK and applied Offender Profiling very successfully in the 1985–6hunt for sex killer John Duffy, aka 'the Railway Killer', during 'Operation Hart'. Nevertheless, during the search for a man who was now bringing terror to the elderly in Paris, it has to be said that French law enforcement were using offender-profiling techniques, throwing every resource and all the manpower they had at their disposal in trying to track down the now dubbed 'Grim Reaper of Paris'.

As the murders escalated, abject fear began creeping all over the city, settling in particular on the XVIIIth arrondissement and, as is so often the case, the media started lambasting the police, accusing them of incompetence in having failed to track down the killer. Indeed, the press even started furnishing their readers with the gory details of the killings, all of which spread more alarm amongst the citizens, seriously hampering the cops with their investigation and, in doing so, scared off Thierry Paulin and his lover Jean-Thierry Mathurin, who was also his accomplice, who moved to Toulouse. Paulin didn't return to Paris until December 1985 – when the killings began again.

So, let's now look at Thierry Paulin a little closer, but skipping past his early life. He was now twenty-two, not only a gay in Gay Paree, a homosexual transvestite addicted to hard pornography, as poor as a homeless church mouse, but also a drifting drug addict, an alcoholic, who, with his lover Jean-Thierry Mathurin, was living a life of nightclubs, champagne and cocaine that neither could afford. The seedy glamour and the glittery transsexual nightclubs of Toulouse appealed to them and as Paulin's father lived there, they went to stay with him for some months.

Paulin and his lover lived in a world where lead balls bounce, pink elephants fly and fairies reign supreme, dreaming of one day having their own nightclub and getting rich. Paulin's father in the meantime did not want to put up with Mathurin any longer and many a row ensued until the two young men split up and Mathurin returned to Paris. Thierry Paulin meanwhile, obsessed with the idea of doing his own musical act, worked hard at creating his 'image', and made sure that he was seen in all the right places, offering champagne and cocaine with money he had gained from thieving and killing, to all those around him, hoping that this would win him friends and useful contacts.

As unprofessional as this observation may seem, what an egotistical, insufferable little prick Paulin was. Oh, why do such people try to build such great mansions on shifting sands? However, if one can give any credit to this serial killer of the elderly (and I am *not*), it has to be said that despite his degenerate, flawed psychopathology, he persisted in his pie-in-the-sky schemes, moving on to launch a business called La Transforme Star – an agency for transvestite performers. It failed. Now deciding that Toulouse was no longer the place to be, he returned to Paris, still clinging to his unrealistic thoughts of riches and glory.

> I thought he [Paulin] was a born schemer, maybe even a [drug] dealer. He always had too much money.
> EMPLOYEE OF LE PALACE, ONE OF PARIS'S HOT
> NIGHTSPOTS FAVOURED BY TRANSSEXUALS.

Then, to the utter shock and dismay of Paris police and the city itself, suddenly the murders of elderly people started all over again:

Saturday, 20 December 1985. In the XIV arrondissement, Estelle Donjoux (ninety-one) was strangled in her home.

Sunday, 4 January 1986. Andrée Ladam, aged seventy-seven, suffered the same fate.

Thursday, 8 January 1986. Yvonne Couronne, aged eighty-three, was murdered in her home on Rue Sarrette.

With the killings of Estelle, Andrée and Yvonne all perpetrated in the XIVth arrondissement within a radius of 400 metres from the Saint-Pierre-de-Montrouge church of d'Alésia, it was clear to the police that the scenario was the same, with the victim being spotted, stalked to her block of flats, followed to the landing where she lived, and then pushed into the interior of the apartment as soon as she opened the door. Then she was attacked, suffocated or strangled.

Monday, 12 January 1986. On this day Marjem Jurblum, aged eighty-one, from the Rue Pelé in the XIth arrondissement, and Françoise Vendôme, eighty-three, who lived in the Rue de Charenton, XIIth arrondissement, were discovered dead in their apartments. Both widows had been strangled and robbed of what little money the killer could find. Françoise was independent and worked part time at the Louvre art museum. Her hobby was painting.

Thursday, 15 January 1986. Yvonne Schaiblé, seventy-seven, was discovered dead in her apartment, this time in the Vth arrondissement.

Saturday, 31 January 1986. Virginie Labrette, who was seventy-six, was murdered in her apartment in the XIIth arrondissement.

Tuesday, 14 June 1986: brought the discovery, this time back in the XIV arrondissement, of the body of a seventy-eight-year-old American widow, Ludmilla Liberman.

Then came another short lull in the killings. Paulin was arrested and jailed for eighteen months for beating up a cocaine dealer in Alfortville because the wrap did not contain the amount of coke he had paid for. He was released from prison in September 1987.

I was always surprised at his calm, yet one evening I learned that he was violent; he had recently beaten a nightclub boss with a baseball bat.

C<small>O-ORGANISER OF THE TRANSVESTITE PARTY</small> U<small>N</small>
L<small>OOK D'</small>E<small>NFER</small> ('L<small>OOKING</small> C<small>OOL</small>')

Soon the murders resumed.

25 November 1987. Seventy-nine-year-old Rachel Cohen was killed in her home in the Rue du Château d'Eau in the Xth arrondissement. That same day, barely a kilometre away in the Rue d'Alsace, Madame Finaltéri, aged eighty-seven, was left for dead by her attacker who had tried to suffocate her with a mattress. She survived and this spirited old lady was able to give graphic details of her ordeal and furnish police with an excellent description of her would-be murderer. A photofit was drawn up and circulated to every police officer in Paris.

27 November 1987: Geneviève Germont, aged seventy-three, became Paulin's final victim. She was robbed, suffocated then strangled to death at her home at 22 Rue Cail.

After signing his bail conditions on Tuesday, 1 December 1987, as Paulin wandered a short distance from the Porte Saint-Denis police station in the Xth arrondissement, Superintendent Jacob was chatting to a few shopkeepers in the street. He had a copy of the photofit folded in his pocket. As he gossiped, his glance fell upon a young man: mixed race, of athletic build, walking towards him. The law officer stopped him to ask for his ID papers. Paulin was arrested, soon to confess to twenty murders.

Alas, my allocated word count for this book does not permit a much deeper account and examination of Thierry Paulin's life from cradle to grave – no doubt for the reader who is keen to dig deeper there is much information to be found elsewhere. However, it has been stated time and again that killing for financial gain was never a motive in this killer's mind. I say that it was, because we all do things for a reason – good or otherwise – and serial killers are no exception. And, as any lawyer, or judge, will confirm: the commonest motives are:

1 to avenge some real or fancied wrong
2 to get rid of a rival or obnoxious connection
3 to escape from the pressure of pecuniary or
   other obligation
4 to obtain plunder
5 to gratify some other selfish malignant passion

These may be summed up concisely as Hatred, Money and Sex.

In Thierry Paulin we find an ill-born homicidal trans-vestite psychopath, a cocaine addict, an alcoholic, a dreamer and schemer who, when the mood took him, was quite able and fit enough to resort to committing acts of extreme violence upon anyone who crossed him. This is a given fact, but it is the stalking, his hunting down of his victims, that concerns us in this book, and in Paulin's case, I would say that motives 1, 3, 4 and 5 apply.

It has to have been this way with Paulin, for why beat and torture some old lady within an inch of her life until she finally tells him where her money – usually a pitiful amount of cash – is hidden away in her home?

Paulin was a degenerate loser living a fantasy-driven existence. He needed money to support his seedy lifestyle and his wild dreams of making a fortune. He needed quick money and plundered the lives of the elderly with as much compassion as one swats flies.

What we do *not* see is Paulin stalking and hunting down men. No way would he take on a man. We do know is that he was a predator who preyed on the most weak and vulnerable of society. Such easy pickings for him, indeed

– but what of his 'camouflage', his 'ghillie suit' – what made him undetectable for so long?

The answer to this question can be found in that in the flamboyant if seedy company that he kept he would never have stood out: he was one of them, and did not fit in with the petty but violent criminals common to the deprived areas of the city that he prowled in.

Paulin's hunting ground, his killing ground, was the then rundown Paris arrondissements – ideal territory to locate elderly ladies, follow them to their homes, maybe even offer to help them with their shopping bags as they climbed steep, rickety stairs to their rooms.

At the time of his arrest, Paulin was HIV-positive. He confessed to the murders and implicated Jean-Thierry Mathurin, who was convicted of the first nine murders and given a life sentence, eventually being released in 2009. Paulin, however, was never convicted as while awaiting trial in jail he succumbed to AIDS. He died on Sunday, 16 April 1989.

There can be no doubt that Thierry Paulin was an inner-city killer who murdered for financial gain, but what of other inner-city sadists who also exploit the cover of city life to stalk and prey on their helpless victims?

Up next is Kenneth Erskine, nicknamed 'the Stockwell Strangler'. The only person to survive a murderous attack by Erskine repeatedly referred to his whispering voice and frightening grin. At least seven other elderly people were not so lucky – like scenes out of nightmare horror movie they were found dead in their beds after he had visited them in the dead of night.

Erskine was an 'equal opportunity offender', for he targeted both men and women. We may never know how many defenceless elderly people he murdered. After he was sent to prison for the remainder of his natural life for seven known killings, detectives closed their files on four other deaths – simply because there was not enough evidence to support a conviction.

Although very little is known about Erskine's early life, we do know that he held a deep-seated grudge and hated both his English mother, Margaret, and his Antiguan father, Charles; that he was born in Hammersmith and brought up in a council flat in Putney, south London; that he was the eldest of four siblings and, as a youngster, was an avid Bible reader who allegedly believed in love and peace. But Erskine soon became difficult to manage, notably after his parents' divorce, so he received quite a bit of his education at a series of schools for maladjusted children where he was prone to bursts of violence against his teachers and fellow pupils alike.

To his tutors, young Erskine lived in a fantasy world where he took on the role of Lawrence of Arabia, attacking and tying up smaller, weaker children. He even tried to drown several of them on trips to the local swimming pool, holding their heads under water until staff intervened. By his early teens he was already exhibiting homicidal tendencies, and on one occasion, he attacked a teacher with scissors. Shortly thereafter he took a psychiatric nurse hostage when she tried to examine him, holding a pair of scissors to her throat. Moreover, whenever female staff tried to show him affection, he would do his best to shock them by rubbing himself against them, or exposing his genitals. Violent behaviour resulted in Erskine being ousted from the family home, and he spent seven years drifting through the twilight world of London's homeless and rootless, living mainly in squats in Brixton and Stockwell, indulging in petty crime. A recidivist burglar, he served time in Feltham Young Offenders Institution, reverting to his life of petty burglary, which went on for several years before he began targeting the elderly in their homes and killing them.

I was absolutely terrified but there was nothing I could do. He was sitting on my chest with his fingers clutching at my neck. I thought I was a goner.

FREDERICK PRENTICE, TO POLICE AFTER
BEING ATTACKED AND LEFT FOR DEAD BY THE
'STOCKWELL STRANGLER'

At this point, it might be worth thinking of how it must feel utterly terrifying, most especially for a frail, elderly person, to be woken in the dead of night and see a shadowy figure standing silently, glistening blade in hand, at the end of one's bed. Well, it was at 3 a.m., Friday, 27 June 1986, when seventy-three-year-old retired civil engineer Frederick Prentice was lying in his bed in an old people's home in Cedars Road, south London, when he heard footsteps in the passage outside. He sat up, then saw a shadow through the glass door, which the figure opened, and a stranger entered his room.

Only through autopsy can a dead person speak, but Fred Prentice does give us an insight into how Erskine treated his murder victims before they died. It makes for shocking reading.

Fred remembered screaming as loud as he could but no one could hear him. He was disabled and barely able to struggle. His attacker, reeking of filthy clothes and drink, was young and strong. As far as Mr Prentice could recall, the attacker's motive was not one of theft. 'I kept pleading with him to let me go and take whatever he wanted . . .' the old man told detectives . . . 'but he took no notice. It was a nightmare. He told me that he had only come to kill me.'

Three times Erskine tried to throttle the life out of Fred Prentice, who nevertheless managed to press the alarm button by his bed – on the final occasion the attacker 'chucked my head against the wall and ran off,' Fred said. There was one other detail he recalled: 'I shall always have his face in my memory. He's ruined my life.' But Fred's life had already been wrecked. Three years earlier, just after his wife had died, three men had burst into his home in nearby Brixton, tied him up, and ransacked the place. Fred, however, considered himself lucky in a sense, for he was the only person attacked by Kenneth Erskine who lived to tell the tale.

Wednesday, 9 April 1986. Nancy Eileen Emms, a seventy-eight-year-old spinster was found strangled and sexually assaulted in her bed in West Hill, Wandsworth.

Monday, 9 June 1986. Janet Cockett, a widow of sixty-seven, was strangled in her bed in her first-floor flat on the Overton Road council estate in Stockwell. Mrs Cockett, who had led an active life as chairwoman of her local tenants' association, had two broken ribs, the result of Erskine kneeling on her chest. Her nightdress had been ripped off and left neatly folded. Erskine's palm print was later found on the bathroom window and his thumbprint on a plant pot. A lock of her hair was later found in his bedroom; he had taken it as a 'trophy' of his kill.

Tuesday, 10 June 1986. Two men, Polish pensioners, war veteran Valentine Gleim, aged eighty-four, and Zbigniew Stabrawa, ninety-four, were murdered at an old people's home, Hastings House, in Stockwell Park Crescent. Both had been strangled and sexually assaulted.

Tuesday, 8 July 1986. William Carmen, eighty-two years old, was killed in his bed at his flat in Sybil Thorndike House, Clephane Road, on the Marquess estate in Islington. Like the previous victims Bill had been strangled and sexually assaulted. His daughter found his body. Her photographs in his flat had been turned to face the wall.

Sunday, 20 July 1986. William Downes, seventy-four, was sexually assaulted and strangled to death in his flat in Holles House, on the Overton Road estate, where Janet Cockett's home was. Erskine's palm print was found on the garden gate, and on a wall in the bedsit.

Wednesday, 23 July 1986. Partly blind and deaf, and only able to get around using a walking frame, eighty-year-old Florence Tisdall was found strangled and sexually assaulted in bed at her flat in fashionable Ranelagh Gardens Mansions, Hurlingham, near Putney Bridge in south-west London, by the caretaker. The day she was killed, Mrs Tisdall had enjoyed watching the wedding of Prince Andrew and Sarah Ferguson on television. God bless her, she had even had her hair done for the occasion. She was frail, and any shouts for help she may have uttered would have been drowned out by the noise from a celebration disco in the Eight Bells public house opposite. Florence loved cats; she had three of them and regularly brought in strays that could come and go as they pleased. Tragically, the police concluded, her cats might have led indirectly to her death, as she used to leave a window open to allow them in and out. Forensic examination of her home proved that Erskine entered her flat via that window, then exited through the front door.

Before we move onto his stalking modus operandi, there were certain aspects of Kenneth Erskine's murders that puzzled police, and still mystify aficionados of true crime: the first being lack of the motive of killing for financial gain, for it appears, that unlike Thierry Paulin, a desperate need for ready money was not on Erskine's mind.

Looking back to motives again we find:

1 to avenge some real or fancied wrong
2 to get rid of a rival or obnoxious connection
3 to escape from the pressure of pecuniary or other obligation
4 to obtain plunder
5 to gratify some other selfish malignant passion

Once again, all summed up concisely as Hatred, Money and Sex. In the Stockwell Strangler's case I believe, when we look much deeper into his twisted psychopathology, that 1, 2, 4 and 5 are present.

Having studied most of Erskine's psychiatric reports, I am convinced that from his earliest years as the weakest of four brothers, the odds were stacked up against him. His parents more or less left him to his own devices and his childhood was spent drifting in and out of special schools Many of the killers I have interviewed recall spending much time in their bedrooms, often looking out of their windows for hours on end, or playing quietly, some inventing a make-believe friend – an alter ego whom they talk to about their worries and fears. This was the case with Kenneth Bianchi, one of the Hillside Stranglers. Under those conditions, youngsters can fester; start to conjure up schemes on how to exact revenge.

I think that it would not be far off the mark to consider a steam boiler full of water being constantly heated by fire, not emotion, with the safety valve jammed shut. Eventually, the pressure becomes too much and there is a catastrophic explosion. And, of course, the chances of such an explosion are increased through issues such as poor water treatment causing scaling and over-heating of the plates – in other words lack of care and maintenance.

In many respects, I see a parallel here with the developing human mind. Having abusive parents or caregivers, being subjected to a dysfunctional upbringing are all to be found in so many serial killers' narratives. The child cannot rebel against its parents, so the mind may fester and seek revenge, which it cannot act out in the form of physical or psychological release. This is why so many killers have a history of torturing animals and birds, simply because these creatures are now a repository for all of the mental pressures building up within. It might take many years before a person blows his or her top, but when it does blow, just like the steam boiler, the results can be catastrophic.

During Erskine's schoolyears, he rebelled against teachers who, like his parents, tried to enforce a strict regime, and he bullied his more vulnerable peers. To him, now free of his parents, he found himself able to assert himself aggressively.

The second motive – that of getting rid of a rival or obnoxious connection resonates with me too. Leading psychologist Dr Anthony Storr adds weight to my theory that Erskine had developed a homicidal hatred for old people, that he wanted to avenge himself on 'old people who are perfectly innocent, *probably for some incident/s in his past* [my italics]'. There is no doubt in my mind that there are those who truly want to wipe their parents off the face of the earth but simply cannot do it. So they wreak vengeance on others who to them appear to be cast in the same mould as their parents.

The motive of obtaining plunder is an interesting one because we usually associate 'obtaining plunder' with the act of stealing goods from (a place or person), typically using force and in a time of war or civil disorder. But when we drill down into that verb we find discreetly tucked away 'rape'. In fact, when the reader examines any sexual homicide case, what does one find: the plundering and or stealing of an innocent human life, that is what it is and always will be, which leaves us with gratifying some other selfish malignant passion, and this where things get even nastier.

It is possible that Kenneth Erskine was bisexual. At one time he stated that he could 'fuck man and beast'. He was a petty thief and burglar – even his Rastafarian fellows called him an 'ankle swinger' (short jeans) – who appeared before magistrates at least eight times and served four short jail terms before he was finally arrested for murder by police on Monday, 28 July 1986, at a social security office (DHS). Police were then able to match his palm print to one left at one of the murder scenes, after which he was identified in a police line-up by seventy-four-year-old Fred Prentice who identified Erskine as the man who had tried to strangle him in his bed just a month earlier.

To say that Kenneth Erskine was 'unhinged' might seem

to be an understatement, but later psychiatric reports said Erskine was severely schizophrenic at the time of the south London killers. In 1982, when he was serving time in borstal for burglary, he shocked staff by painting pictures of elderly people in bed with gags in their mouths, burned to death, or with daggers in them. Other drawings showed headless figures with blood spurting from their necks. This was a chilling foretaste of what was to come. Indeed, the prison doctors were so alarmed by his behaviour they literally begged the authorities not to release him. However, it seems that nothing much has changed, even to this day. We are still releasing homicidal maniacs back into society to kill and kill again.

He is dangerous and desperate. Erskine is a diabolical monster.

CHIEF SUPERINTENDENT KEN THOMPSON

As part of Erskine's mitigation at trial, it was put forth by his defence team that he had a mental age of just eleven, and thus he was somewhat not responsible for his actions as being merely a child. A senior professor of psychology at King's College, London, and expert on forensic psychiatry, interviewed Erskine and noted that he 'lives in a world of his own. At times he cannot distinguish between reality and fantasy' adding, '… he behaved strangely during consultations. He would giggle, smile and stare out of the window when important matters were discussed.'

The jury were not swayed by potential mitigating reasons for the man's behaviour. They found Erskine guilty on all counts; while probably bearing in mind that his mental age of eleven didn't prevent the accused from systematically selecting and stalking and raping and killing the most precious in our society – the elderly, often infirm, weak and vulnerable. The jurors also probably considered the fact that Erskine had managed to cover his tracks to the degree that it would take all the expertise of law enforcement to finally track him down. On appeal, however, his convictions were reduced from murder to manslaughter on the grounds of diminished responsibility. At the appeal hearing in 2009 the Lord Chief Justice, Lord Judge, concluded, that 'It is overwhelmingly clear that, at the time when the appellant appeared at trial, there was unequivocal contemporaneous evidence that his mental responsibility for his actions at the time of the killing was substantially impaired.' It was accepted that his mental condition was chronic and incurable, requiring life-long treatment – and a minimum of forty years in Broadmoor Hospital was recommended.

Following Erskine's conviction, the police closed their files on four more murders thought to have been perpetrated by the 'Stockwell Strangler'. There was not enough evidence to convict Erskine.

Tuesday, 4 February 1986. John Jordan, fifty-seven years old, found strangled and sexually assaulted beside his bed in his flat at 4 Josephine Avenue, Brixton. He could have been the first of Erskine's victims – however, given the frailty and ill-health of many of the elderly who died around that time, there could have been deaths that were ascribed to natural causes, which were not – as so nearly happened in the case of Miss Emms. As a senior detective is quoted as saying, 'There is simply no way of knowing just how many defenceless old folk he has killed, it could be dozens.'

Tuesday, 6 May 1986. Charles Quarrell, seventy-three, was found suffocated on his bed at his home in King James Street, Southwark.

Wednesday, 28 May 1986. Wilfred Parkes, 70, found choked to death in the bedroom of his flat in Albemarle House, Stockwell Estate.

Saturday, 12 July 1986. Trevor Thomas, aged seventy-five, was found dead in his bath at his home in Barton Court, Jeffreys Road, Clapham. He had been strangled and sexually assaulted.

The main problem faced by the 350 police officers, including a team of 150 detectives plus senior officers from the C1 Murder Squad, all led by Detective Chief Superintendent Ken Thompson from Scotland Yard's elite Serious Crimes Squad, was that they had no clear description of the killer.

This offender entered the homes of old people silently, did his dreadful deeds, and just as quietly left again. And, although it was midsummer, he operated only in the early hours of the morning, when it was completely dark. In addition, when the photofit based on Frederick Prentice's description was released to the press, there were scores of phone calls to the police but not one single person came forward to say that they had known Erskine. Thus, he was never 'in the frame', for here was a murderous phantom, an out-of-control sexual predator who knew his prey, and his hunting grounds, like the back of his hand.

Back then, the area in and around Stockwell was a small corner of poorer London consisting of a mixture of windy council estates; rows and rows of small terraced houses; badly-lit alleyways, side streets littered with broken-down cars and trash, nestling between the more cosmopolitan Brixton, and the more gentrified, upmarket expanses of Clapham, all enabling him to move around unnoticed during the black hours of night.

Did Kenneth Erskine actually stalk his victims in the hunter's sense? I think not because unlike Thierry Paulin who *did* stalk, follow and kill, Erskine, in a most predatory, basic animal sense, knew precisely where to locate weak prey, how to enter their space when they were most vulnerable, asleep, and do as he wished with them without fear of being caught. He hit his helpless victims when they thought that they were completely safe – in their beds at home where in fact they were not safe and had no chance of defending themselves at all.

..

7

Who Stalked and Murdered Muriel Maitland?

You can drink the coffee. I could easily beat you to
death right now but the coffee is not poisoned.

GORDON F. G. H. JOWERS, AT HIS PORTSMOUTH
HOME, TO THE AUTHOR, SEPTEMBER 2012

*NB: This chapter is based on official documents presumed lost
yet discovered by myself, exclusive interviews with the late Mr
Gordon Jowers, his brother Ronald Jowers, and police. The quotes
are taken verbatim from historic witness statements. Mr Wayne
Jowers (son of Gordon Jowers) has given his full permission to be
quoted where applicable.*

We all love a good TV whodunit, and this real-life cold-case
homicide is as fascinating as it is gruesome. In investigating
it, I held lengthy interviews with the prime suspect, who
blamed his identical twin brother for murder most foul.
This chapter draws upon historic police documents and

plans previously believed to have been destroyed. And the plot thickens when we learn that there were *two* Muriel Maitlands and the two identical Jowers brothers (recently deceased) knew or knew of both women.

This chapter attempts to deal in detail with the subject of stalking with the intention to rape and kill. However, such was the flood of information regarding the private lives of the Jowers twins that eventually came to my attention, that it has been extremely difficult for me to sort the wheat from the chaff; and not to become sidetracked and led up blind alleyways to lose sight of who did what, and why.

For fear of repeating myself, there are tens of thousands of us who are glued to the television when the *CSI* documentary series is screened, but with this account of murder most foul, I can only present what *is* known and invite my readers to come to *their own* conclusions as if they were members of a jury.

One might say that what I will present is circumstantial evidence and only that, but this circumstantial evidence has been strong enough for the Metropolitan Police to reopen this cold-case homicide even when they have far more contemporary cases pressing in on their finite resources. To give MetPol all due credit, they have assigned a forensic case officer to search for the case exhibits in the hope of extracting DNA – all somewhat hampered by the fact that the Forensic Science Laboratory, Lambeth, London – which once held these exhibits – closed down in 2013. The reasons why can be found in a BBC online news article of the time, 'Higher cost of Forensic

Science Service closure' by Paul Rincon (https://www.bbc.co.uk/news/science-environment-21251162).

With that being said, all of this extremely important information and material passed into the private forensic sector and we know what happened then: in Muriel Maitland's case her killer's true identity may never be verified as valuable DNA evidence that could have proved guilt without any doubt cannot be traced.

What will become obvious to the reader is that whoever killed Muriel was a very strong and powerful man and most certainly a sexual sadist who must have committed violence in some form or another against women in his past, a man possessed with an explosive temper. The rape/murder of Muriel was overkill because it went far beyond just a killing. That it was committed in a rage, with an utter contempt for his victim and hatred for her will jump from the pages of this chapter. Yet when this monster calmed down after his kill he calmly lit a cigarette, tried to bury evidence of his crime and without a care in the world just wandered off. This man treated and dumped widower Muriel, a young mother of two little girls, like trash, so please let us not forget her.

Muriel Gwendoline 'Gwen' Maitland was born 6 September 1921, at Wareham in Dorset, to Mrs Kate Hobbs, *nee* Waghorn and her husband whose name escapes me. The couple had sixteen children. Muriel was the fourth child. For our purpose we shall refer to her as 'Gwen', and she will like this very much indeed.

The family moved to Hounslow around 1927, and here

the green-eyed lass attended Hounslow Heath School, leaving at the age of fifteen. She was a quiet youngster and had only one young man in her life, his name being George William Maitland. They married in December 1942, and had two children: Sandra and Linda (both now deceased). They lived in a neat semi-detached house at 72 Eton Road, Cranford, having done so since 1947/8.

George Maitland passed away following a heart attack on 26 August 1956. According to Gwen's brother-in-law, Edward John Rossiter, George Maitland had been insured, so after his death Gwen was left financially fairly well provided for. The house they lived in was all but paid for, with about £200.00 left on the mortgage, and she had received something in the region of £800 in cash – added to which were the couple's savings of about £80. But, not long after her husband's death, because she wanted to be able to get a few extra things for the house and her little girls, Gwen took up part-time work from 9 a.m. to 4 p.m. at the Nestléchocolate factory, off North Hyde Road, in Hayes.

Every Saturday, Gwen and her two daughters visited her mother at 89 Barrack Road, Hounslow: in doing so they walked directly past the front window of the home of Mrs Jowers, where both Gordon and Ronald periodically lived.

Muriel has spoken to me about having scares in the wood. Twice since Christmas she has said she had a scare going through the woods, that a man on a bicycle had watched her. One of these occasions was just before Easter when she said, 'I've had another scare in the woods.' She was a very reserved girl. She was devoted to her daughters and she did not give me any details of the man or his actions. I think that she knew the man and did not want any trouble.

KATE HOBBS, THE VICTIM'S MOTHER, TO WPC JEAN MUNROE, 'T' DIVISION, 25 MAY 1957

Gwen's last-known movements were given to police by her daughter Sandra, thirteen at the time, who recalled that on Tuesday, 30 April 1957, she did not feel well and stayed home from school. Both girls had toast and a cup of tea for breakfast. At about 8.30 a.m., ten-year-old Linda went off to her classes. Their mother left home for work at about 8.50 a.m.

She never returned.

Sandra told the police that, ' . . . Mummy wore a red coat [of much significance later], a pair of brown court shoes . . .' She said that on this particular morning she was wearing either a red button-through dress or a grey dress that 'flaps over'. That sometimes Mummy wore a woollen scarf over her head with 'maroon in it'. Gwen always wore her wedding ring. She rode an old-fashioned black and white French bicycle. The three-speed gears didn't work and the glass on the front lamp had a little piece of glass broken out of the top. It had a half-chain guard, an old black leatherette saddlebag, and she always carried a small green plastic bag with beige handles with her lunch in it. The handlebars were painted a silver colour, 'chipped off a bit'. The pedals had rubbers and several were missing.

So now we find Gwen Maitland riding to work. She

rode north along Rendall Avenue, over Cranford Lane, around a stile into Cranford Park and cycled north along a wooded footpath close to the slow-moving River Crane.

The park consists of 144 acres of woods, meadow, wetlands, the medieval St Dunstan's church and graveyard. For those with an interest in the macabre, it also hosts two resident ghosts – a man who peers through the coach-house windows and, yes, you've guessed right, a Grey Lady who is said to haunt the park.

Along the west side of the park that morning, at a small bridge crossing the river into deep woodland and at a point not 800 yards from the Nestlé chocolate factory, Gwen encountered a man who suddenly dragged her into what is known locally as Bluebell Woods. Here, he raped her, vaginally and anally, then tried to strangle her to death after repeatedly punching her in the face: blows so heavy they broke her nose and smashed her front teeth. After smoking a cigarette – the butt of which he casually flicked onto the ground – he forced her head into soggy mud under an uprooted elm tree hoping that she was dead. She wasn't, for she drowned after sucking water, dirt and dead leaves into her lungs.

In the immediate aftermath, her killer buried some of Gwen's personal possessions close by and tossed her bicycle into the Grand Union Canal about 300 yards from the crime scene. The cycle was discovered a year later when a fisherman snagged his line.

When their mother failed to return home from work that late afternoon, Muriel's worried daughters went to their Uncle Edward Rossiter's home at 247 Waye Avenue, where they arrived at 5.30 p.m. At 6.15 p.m. Rossiter, an aircraft shop foreman by trade, went to 72 Eaton Road and searched through each room. There was no sign of Gwen so he called the police.

At about 4.20 p.m., Friday, 3 May 1957, PC 202 'T' Division, Paul Capon, along with WPC 474 'T' Division, Marsh, stationed at Norwood Green Police Station, were members of a party searching the woods in Cranford Park. Capon saw a partly uprooted elm tree about 50 yards in from the River Crane, and peered into the cavity. Beneath the roots he saw a mound of earth. He poked into it with a stick and felt something solid. He got down on his knees and raked the dirt away and, about one inch (2.5 cm) from the surface, he exposed the left hand of a woman. The two constables blew their whistles to summon aid and senior officers soon arrived on the scene.

One of the first to arrive was Detective Chief Inspector Peter Sinclair, stationed at Ealing Police Station. He ordered that the immediate area be cordoned off and searched for clues. Then, at about 7 p.m., a civilian volunteer searcher called Michael Durn found a hole in the ground 137 feet (approximately 42 metres) from the body. In the hole he saw a small purse and a pair of lady's brown court shoes. Also there was a bucket-type lady's bag and a black saddlebag. All were bagged up and taken to Ealing Police Station. Gwen was taken to Hampton Mortuary.

At 11 p.m. on 4 May, Edward Rossiter was called in to identify his sister-in-law. Here is his statement witnessed by Detective Sergeant P. Langley, 'T' Division:

I attended Hampton Mortuary where I was shown the body of a woman whom I identified as my sister-in-law, Mrs Muriel Gwendoline Maitland, who was reported as missing from her home at No.72, Eaton Road, Hayes. Apart from the fact that I knew Mrs Maitland had a wart on the right side of her nose, I was quite certain of the identification. I should mention that Mrs Maitland only had dentures in the upper part of her mouth.

Since describing my sister-in-law's cycle to you I have heard that the white grips were removed and replaced by black plastic ones which broke away leaving the cardboard base.

Every crime scene tells a story, and, in this case Muriel Maitland will be telling us how she died, so of specific interest to the reader will be the following document (amongst many more) that I recovered from the West London Coroner's Office just a day before these papers were to be incinerated. It is quoted verbatim and I have highlighted several items in italics because they will have much significance later.

This is the first time this document has been published; and it was drawn up by Lewis Charles Nickolls, MSc, FRIC, Director Metropolitan Police Laboratory.

The Metropolitan Police Laboratory
New Scotland Yard
LONDON, SW1
21st May 1957

Preliminary report on the examination of the following materials received in connection with the death of Mrs. Maitland:

Removed from the scene where body found:
One khaki [army-type] button
Two samples of earth taken from above the public region
Sample of ova removed from nasal orifice

Removed from hole in ground:
Left and right shoe
Purse containing one latchkey
One plastic and cloth shopping bag
One leatherette cycle bag

Removed from body in Mortuary:
One roll-on
One pair panties
One petticoat
One vest
One brassiere
One frock
One cardigan

Body samples:
Two vaginal swabs
One vaginal smear
One sample of blood
Upper and lower dentures

Sample of pubic hair
Sample of head hair
Stomach and contents
Right- and left-hand fingernail clippings
Two jars containing mud
One jar containing water
One cigarette end (from soil of body)

I have examined all of these samples and the following facts have been elicited.

The two samples of earth taken from the pubic region were similar to the earth on the clothing and revealed nothing of note. No spermatozoa could be detected in them.

The same of ova removed from the nasal orifice consisted of eggs from one of the dipterous insects of the blowfly type. These eggs had been recently laid, their normal period of incubation being in the region of twelve hours.

The left and right show constituted a pair of brown court type shoes. Apart from the dampness in the region where they were muddy, which was chiefly confined to the right shoe, the shoes were in a dry condition and had not suffered immersion in water. There was nothing else to note.

The purse was made of red plastic, suitably embossed to imitate leather, with a metal catch. An inner pocket of the purse contained a Yale type latch key attached to a metal ring. There was also a compartment in this purse for notes which was empty. The purse was wet and in a muddy condition.

The plastic and cloth shopping bag, green in colour with yellow binding around the top and yellow handles was in a muddy condition and empty. The yellow binding material is of plastic material.

The black leatherette cycle bag was in poor condition and mud stained.

There are attachments at the back of the cycle bag, which consist of three pieces of wire. One side appears intact, the wire being yellow and black in colour. On the other side, the only piece of wire remaining is yellow in colour and it would appear that this has been broken away, the remaining wire being left with the cycle. The bag is empty.

Clothing removed from the body in mortuary: All this clothing shows evidence of immersion in water.

One black cardigan: 8 buttons down the front, all buttons are present, heavily mud stained. Mud stains do not appear to be localised in any one place, except that in the right shoulder region at the back and the right waist region.

One cotton frock: blue with a black pattern, very muddy condition, consistent with immersion in

water. Handkerchief found in left-hand pocket.
Frock opens all the way down the front and would
normally have been fastened by two buttons at the
waist. Both these buttons are missing and the right-
hand buttonhole is torn. The seam of this frock is
split at the waist on the right side, no hole centre
back. No seminal staining could be traced on this
garment.

One slip: black lace, very muddy condition
consistent with immersion in water. A number of
holes in the region of the right shoulder blade,
garment torn in region of back by the right
shoulder strap. No seminal stains detected.

One brassiere: The left top shoulder strap broken,
in dirty condition, consistent with immersion.
Inside of cups show no obvious blood staining to
correspond with breast injury.

One elastic roll-on: Uniformly muddy, consistent
with immersion. No seminal staining detected.

One vest: Original colour white, but complete
garment discoloured due to the presence of mud
from immersion. Right shoulder strap torn away at
back. No spermatozoa detected.

One pair of panties: Aertex type. Originally white
in colour, uniformly muddy due to immersion. In
the centre of the back of the panties there is a hole
4 ½" from the waistband. The hole is horizontal

in direction, 7 ¾" long. The ends of this hole are turned back. No spermatozoa detected.

Samples removed from the body of deceased:

The materials removed from the vagina show the presence of human spermatozoa: *These are not numerous but are in good condition consistent with intercourse at or about the time of death.*

The anal swab is positive for human spermatozoa: *In view of this finding and that fact that there was no injury to the anus or sphincter muscle, Dr Teare [pathologist] removed this part and further swabs were taken under laboratory conditions.* These consisted of a high anal swab, which was again positive for human spermatozoa and a swab of the area taken between the anus and vagina. This last swab gave no satisfactory result. The further swabs were taken because of the possibility of spermatozoa draining from the vagina into the vicinity of the anus, but the high anal swab, being positive, precludes this possibility, *and it would appear that intercourse via the anus was performed* [my italics].

The sample of blood was human blood of 'Group A': It contained no alcohol.

The upper denture: had the right side of the plate broken away and teeth missing from the front.

The stomach: contained two ounces of viscous

greyish/black fluid. No food particles could be recognised. Microscopic examination of the contents showed it to consist of water containing a high proportion of mud. This mud contains vegetable debris, quartz grains and diatoms similar to the samples of mud.

<u>The clippings of the right- and left-hand fingernails:</u> revealed nothing of note.

<u>The earth removed from the scene:</u> revealed nothing of note.

<u>The right and left lungs</u> were examined microscopically: and quartz grains and diatoms were found in large amount in the bronchioles and also disseminated throughout the lung tissue.

The findings in the stomach and lungs would indicate that the body had been immersed in water while still living.

(Signed) L.C. Nickolls
MSc, FRIC
Director
(Lewis Charles Nickolls)

Medical examiners are the only doctors whose patients are dead and therefore silent. They cannot explain why they died, so we have to find out in other ways. We are detectives of death – we visit the crime scene; we examine the medical evidence and the laboratory findings and put them together with the circumstances and the patient's medical history. Through the autopsy, we make the body speak to us. Deciphering the message is an art as well as a science.

MICHAEL BADEN MD, *UNNATURAL DEATH: CONFESSIONS OF A MEDICAL EXAMINER*, FIRST PUBLISHED BY SPHERE BOOKS IN THE USA IN 1989, AND IN THE UK IN 1991

Lewis Charles Nickolls, and the famous senior British pathologist Dr Robert Donald Teare, FRCP, FRCPath (1911–1979), did just that when asking Gwen how she died as she lay, an ice-cold, mutilated corpse on the mortuary slab.

She told them that a man had suddenly appeared from nowhere as she cycled along a path by the River Crane on her way to work, and he had smashed her in the face to render her all but unconscious: her nose was broken as were her dentures.

Gwen told Nickolls and Dr Teare that she was dragged into the woods where her clothes had been partially ripped off; that she was so helpless she could not fight him off: all of which was evidenced by the lack of self-defence wounds.

She then explained that she was raped vaginally. Then the man raped her again, leaving his spermatozoa in her rectum.

Gwen tells that she was still alive even after being half strangled to death. That her face was forced into the wet mud under the roots of the upturned elm tree and that she sucked the muck into her lungs until she drowned.

That is what Muriel Gwendoline Maitland told the medical examiners after her death.

But she also told the police about her bike ride to death, too, because every contact, be it forensic evidence or witness accounts, or the victim's personal narrative, leaves a trace.

There are witness statements later telling police that a man with a cycle had been seen hanging around for several weeks by the stile that she had to get around as she crossed over Cranford Lane into the park. She had mentioned this to her mother and a few neighbours, although she claimed not to be too concerned. She also tells us all that her own cycle was taken away from the crime scene. She is saying that her distinctive red coat was taken away (it was found in October of that year in the woods, as was her headscarf). Added to which her killer dug a hole into which he tried to hide other various items that belonged to her.

The dead woman is saying that she knew the man who killed her, and *he* knew her. That this man had been stalking her for weeks on end, and so familiar with her movements was he, that he would choose the time and place that suited him to make his kill.

This was no opportunist killer who happened upon Muriel Maitland by chance. Had he been so, then after the rape and killing he would have fled the scene as quickly as possible and not taken the time to calmly light a cigarette, take some of his victim's personal possessions, dig a hole and try to hide them a short distance away from the murder scene. Most certainly not take the trouble of stealing her wedding ring and the very distinctive red coat that he draped over the handlebars of her cycle as rode off in broad daylight to dump it into the Grand Union Canal. No, he did all of this to hide any links between himself and his victim.

In this respect we find an organised killer: one who had planned this murder carefully and one who knew where, when and how to kill and get away scot-free.

Apart from the pathologist, the coroner and a select few senior police detectives, only Gwen's killer would have known how and why she was murdered and what had happened to the cycle, coat and the wedding ring, yet Gordon Jowers knew it all because he told me; specifically even down to his own thoughts about how she was killed – which matched *precisely* with the pathologist's report.

I have been in charge of the Police enquiries concerning the ~~murder~~ death of **MRS MURIEL GWENDOLINE MAITLAND.**

To date, no person has been arrested for this crime, but the matter is still being vigorously investigated. The bicycle, coat, headscarf and wedding ring are still untraced.

We have visited approximately 3,500 homes in our house-to-house enquiries and have taken over 1,200 detailed statements from various persons.

Apart from these, hundreds of people who are employed in the Hayes, Harlington and Cranford

districts have been questioned and our enquiries
have extended all over the country.

The results are by no means complete and we
shall continue to do our utmost to trace the person
responsible for this crime.

LEONARD WOOLNER, DETECTIVE
SUPERINTENDENT 'T' DIVISION,. 24, JUNE 1957

Before I met Gordon Jowers, I learned that he had been
pestering the police for several years – all the while
making himself a nuisance by alleging that his brother
Ronald had murdered Muriel Maitland in Cranford Park
in 1957.

This sort of behaviour is not uncommon amongst
many of these types of killer who suffer anger-
management problems. In this case, I say that Gordon
Jowers had killed Gwen for the reasons I detail below,
but, harbouring a bitter and festering hatred for his
brother Ronald, this man could eventually contain
himself no longer. He would transfer all his guilt, hoping
that he could totally wreck his brother's life and gain
much satisfaction in doing just that.

However, to his obvious frustration, the police were not
buying into any of it. He was dismissed by both Hampshire
Police and the Metropolitan Police as a fantasist, attention-
seeking, mentally disturbed; indeed, even his own GP
later told me that although Jowers *was* completely sane he
had wasted much of his limited surgery time railing on
and on about his brother, whom he hated with a passion.
Therefore, with this in my mind, I arranged to meet

Gordon Jowers, give him the attention *he* thought that *he* deserved – that we would 'bond' – as I am a true-crime writer and often appeared on the TV.

Right from the get-go, I knew that Gordon Jowers was an attention-seeker, and for me this was the first red flag, and I would give him my full attention during the weeks to follow.

> He did live in a total shit hole. He used to make me cups of tea and it would taste of soap from where he would somehow put his shaving water in kettle. I once went to fill kettle and when I opened it he was defrosting liver or kidneys in a plastic bag inside kettle.
>
> WAYNE JOWERS, SON OF GORDON JOWERS,
> MESSENGER TEXT TO ME, 26 JUNE 2018

My ploy worked. I first met Mr Jowers at his home, in Cosham, Portsmouth, and a 'total shit hole' it was too. The front garden was a tip; full of garden gnomes, toy dinosaurs on shelves, plastic windmills, and items of such insignificance they would have been better found in a dump truck.

The back garden was even worse.

On the front door was a sign that stated that a vicious dog lived there – he didn't own a dog. Along the alley leading to the back garden was a reinforced gate. The battered front door opened and I was greeted by an eighty-year-old solidly built man who looked and stank as though he had not had a bath in months.

'Hello, Gordon, I am Christopher. Nice to meet you at last!'

I was led into a back sitting room – the front room being so full of clutter it was uninhabitable. Sinking into an armchair, I could not fail to notice that this man had a deep interest in true-crime. There were dozens of cassette and video recordings of serial homicide programmes by his TV.

'Goodness me, Gordon, it seems that you certainly know your stuff. Probably better than me,' I said, and he liked that very much indeed, because a fully emerged psychopath enjoys having his ego stroked. Oh, yes, sir, they like it *very much* indeed, and here I was, giving this attention-seeker all the attention his dysfunctional mind believed it deserved.

In this instance, I was using what may be described as an adaptation of the 'Reid' interrogation technique: where a suspect is led, with guile and cunning, into a beautifully crafted mind trap: one where a psychopath who believes he is much cleverer never suspects the buddy-buddy approach could be a snare he is about to walk into. Getting straight into the crime itself is a 'No-No', for this is all about leading the suspect up the garden path and to allow him to relax, thus he's thinking that he is outwitting everyone.

During this first two-hour conversation, I encouraged Gordon Jowers to tell me all about his brother (who was the reason for his pestering the police and his GP). He railed on and on and on about his brother Ronald whom he detested for more reasons than I can now recall. Not only was Ronald a stalker, a sexual serial killer but a bully who kept on turning up unannounced in Cosham and, on one occasion, when he'd gone upstairs to use the toilet had allegedly ripped the washbasin off the wall; it was allegedly Ronald who had damaged the front door as well. In fact, when I used the bathroom I could see that whoever had wrenched the basin away had done so in a fury. When I asked Gordon if he had dialled 999 requesting immediate police assistance, he replied that he had but the police never turned up. However, I have seen letters written by Gordon Jowers's solicitor, who took his complaint very seriously and wrote to Ron Jowers as a result.

Yes, it is true that Ronald had called. It is true that he had asked to use the toilet. However, it was Gordon who, taking the opportunity to blame the brother he hated, tore the washbasin off of the wall himself – transference of blame.

Getting into his stride, Gordon Jowers proceeded to inform me that when they were in their teens his brother raped a small schoolgirl – a neighbour of their family – while they were living in Strathclyde. He said that girl was so terrified she hid under her bed for two days and no one could find her.

On top of this, he accused Ronald of fire-setting: rolling up the old type of film made from highly flammable nitrocellulose (celluloid), now usually called 'nitrate film', lighting it and pushing it through letterboxes. Gordon went even further by claiming that 'Ron' had shoved a young boy under a moving milk truck, and in doing so had killed him.

My enquiries of the Strathclyde Police bore *some* fruit. They gave me confirmation that all of those historic incidents had, indeed, taken place, including the little girl hiding under her bed, but these details were never made public. Likewise, that a child – a little girl – accidentally fell under a brewer's dray and died as a result.

The two brothers almost agreed on one very important and sickening matter. They were aged around nine years old and scrounging for food at a nearby US naval facility, when, according to Ronald, Gordon was enticed to a spot by the banks of the Clyde, where he was raped by a naval rating. Gordon, on the other hand, says it was Ronald who was raped. There seems no doubt that the incident occurred as a man was arrested, charged by police and then handed over to the US authorities for punishment. As both brothers quite independently spoke of the rape (in Ronald's case I tape recorded), there seemed little point in digging deeper.

Gordon Jowers certainly had remarkable memory for events that had occurred over seventy years earlier, before his mother died in hospital – declaring that when she was dead it was Ronald who tugged her wedding ring off, breaking the finger to steal it. Somewhat surprisingly, Ronald Jowers admitted to this during his taped interview with me on 6 September 2012. This, of course, somewhat resonated with Gwen's wedding ring having also been ripped off her finger after she was murdered.

At our second interview Gordon Jowers made me coffee. While doing so he looked at me in a threatening way and said, 'I could easily poison you, or batter you to death,' and sneered. This man *was* dangerous; he had a short fuse. He had a very menacing way about him. I would go as far as to say that he had an evil streak right through him, with ice-cold blood running through his veins.

It may be difficult for the reader to imagine what it feels like to look deep into the eyes of a homicidal psychopath, one who possesses no moral compass and who can kill without any remorse at all. Strangely enough, most of the monsters I have interviewed exhibited no real 'evil' at all. But, there are a handful of them where one can immediately sense that they are deadly. I have seen this in Kenneth Bianchi, and I could see it in Jowers's eyes as we stood in his kitchen.

Maybe difficult for you to imagine, even *more* difficult for me to express in mere words; but perhaps it is more like an acrid smell that comes from them. I guess that one can smell death on people like Mr Jowers and his type. Seasoned homicide police interrogators sense this too. They can smell evil a mile away . . . and it is a giveaway to be sure.

I turned to the matter of Mrs Maitland's murder, asking him why he was so sure that Ron had killed her.

'Oh well, I know that he used to talk about her lot. I think he used to wait by the stile at the entrance to the park then follow her on her way to work. She came to our mother's house once and she got me mixed up with my brother because we are so much alike. She was shouting and screaming at me, and demanding that I give her back the porn photos I was supposed to have taken of her in my bedroom. But she meant Ron, not me. She said she was going to report it to the police.'

I asked Jowers if he had known Muriel. He replied, '…only as someone who used to walk past our front window every Saturday with her two kids. Mostly she wore a red coat.'

Then he made a slip, adding, 'She was visiting her mother in Barrack Road. She did it every Saturday.'

'Where in Barrack Road?' I asked.

'Number 89,' came the swift reply.

I was curious as to why he remembered the number of Mrs Waghorn's house after so many years had passed, but then, changing the subject, he railed on again about his brother. This is yet another common trait amongst psychopaths. They have an innate sense about when their mindset is being threatened. They like being in control, and anything that threatens this need to be in charge up-ends their thinking processes, so they revert to a default position: they try to remove the threat through evasion – by simply changing the subject, which is yet another weakness an interrogator may, or not, exploit while he observes the suspect's body language, facial expressions and avoidance of direct eye contact. Simply put, in a face-to-face interview one can spot a liar almost instantly.

With the iniquities of his brother being established in his mind, Gordon went on 'One day she came to visit Ron and they went to the cinema. She was wearing her red coat again and was all made up like a prostitute. She was a fuckin' whore. I followed them up the road and they started arguing. She walked off and left him standing there. I think he killed her because she was going to report him to the police for taking the sex photos. She was a tart. She was a blackmailer. She was addicted to sex.'

Can you see even more red flags exhibited here?

This may sound weird but my dad used to take me away to Swanage and Portland Bill for 3 to 4 days and he used to go away on his own as well. Obviously I only saw him at weekends but he used to have about 10 page 3 birds pics with tits out stuck on the inside of his van at the back where he slept (from the age of 10 I can remember). Looking back that's not something a kid should see.

WAYNE JOWERS ON HIS FATHER, MESSENGER
TEXT TO ME, 16 JULY 2018

When I brought Gordon Jowers back to the morning of the murder, he told me that while he was driving past the main entrance to Cranford Park on his way to work as an electrician – he worked on a flight simulator at Heathrow Airport – he saw Ron on his bike at 8.30 a.m. at the main western entrance to the park. Then he picked up a pencil and drew a rough map for me of where the stile was. In fact, he even drew quite a detailed picture of the whole park with the various landmarks, entrances, *and* the River Crane with the little bridge over it.

Red flag!

'You know the park very well then, Gordon?' I asked.

'Oh yes. I spent many months there bird watching and taking photographs.'

105

Then he brought out several old OXO gravy tins. Inside were rolls of celluloid film (yes, celluloid film, the type ideal for setting fires). However, later examination of the negatives by his son, Wayne, registered for photos of Cranford Park, but they did include ones of Gordon Jowers with several different women in other parks. There is no doubt that he had taken many photographs but an avid bird watcher he most certainly was not. Nonetheless, his admission that he knew Cranford Park very well was more than good enough for me.

After my first interview with Gordon Jowers, I'd sent a note to the Metropolitan Police's SCD1 – Homicide and Serious Crime Command Special Casework Investigations Team. The matter was allocated a homicide detective whose name I cannot publish for security reasons, and I prepared a short report for MetPol suggesting that Gordon Jowers might be 'credible', so the police took a renewed interest in a case that had baffled law enforcement since the fifties.

The detective and I came up with a twofold course of action. He would initiate a search for the exhibits found at the crime scene, specifically the victim's underwear. There was a possibility that DNA could be recovered. The officer also sent me a small photo of Gwen. I would then visit my local library and search for black and white photos in newspapers from the late fifties of women similar to her; cut and paste them onto a sheet with her photo as a sort of photographic line-up. Once I had done this they were numbered 1 to 8.

Those of us who recall the fifties, may remember a particular hairstyle that was favoured by many women including Gwen. (My mother, Mary, liked it too.) So I was careful to choose black and white photos of women wearing their hair in that particular fashion.

I took this 'photo line-up' to Gordon Jowers asking him if he had ever seen a photo of Gwen. He said he hadn't, then instantly, without *any* hesitation at all pointed to Mrs Maitland. 'That's her,' he said. I asked him to mark the number and sign the paper, which he did.

Red flag, yet again!

During the course of my research I contacted the South London Coroner's Court to see if they still had any documents regarding the case. A day later a clerk excitedly phoned me to say that she had found a bundle in the basement – in a pile of documents due to be incinerated. When I received the file (the police had since lost theirs), I read the autopsy report. Combined with the findings of Lewis Nickolls, listed above, there was a complete narrative of how Gwen met her death. Only very senior police detectives, Nickolls, and the pathologist Dr Donald Teare would have known of this sensitive information, none of which was ever released to the public – with the exception of Gordon Jowers, it seems.

Now I played my trump card.

'Gordon, you are obviously an expert on homicide. I can see all the DVDs over there. And you also watch all the *CSI* true-crime documentaries. You have seen me on the TV, too. Gordon, you know all about this *CSI* stuff ...

probably much better than I ever will. So, in your sort of expert opinion how do *you* think Muriel was killed?'

His answer, abridged, is below.

Umm, I think that my brother had to kill her because she was going to report him to the police cos of the porn photos he took of her. I know he took them because my mum found out and she bollocked him. I was there when she did.

If I was Ron I would have rode down that path [Old Watersplash Lane] past Molly's Pond and waited for her to ride past the bridge [over the River Crane]. Then I would have grabbed her and knocked her out and dragged her and her bike into the woods. I think that he would have raped her and in her bum. He had told me he liked it best that way. I think he would have strangled her.

'What about Muriel's coat, bike and wedding ring ... they were never found?' I asked.

If I was Ron, I would have buried some of her stuff and tried to hide the body. The red coat was very difficult to hide. Easily sell the ring for money because she only had a few bob in her purse. He would have pedalled away on his bike and with one hand pulled her bike along with him and dumped it into the Grand Union Canal [where, incidentally, it was later found].

After this quite revealing description of a dreadful homicide that had never been made public, I realised that enough was enough, for I now had all that I needed to support a final report for the police. As I climbed the stairs to use his toilet – he used a stairlift – I spotted an old army tunic hanging from his bedroom door. A quick glance told me that one of the khaki buttons was missing with part of the thread still visible.

Of note: as can be seen from the list of items recovered from the crime scene, an army tunic button was recovered. It had obviously been ripped off by Gwen during her fight for life. Sadly, at the time of writing police have not been able to locate the crime exhibits, and when Gordon Jowers's house was cleared after his death, the tunic was missing, too – possibly because while I was saying goodbye, I mentioned it in passing. At that point he took me back to his sitting room and explained that he had been in the army. That he had been a bomb disposal officer. He added that when he was demobbed he had done part-time work as a diver working for the police.

My dad was a liar. He was always telling lies. Definitely a bullshitter.

WAYNE JOWERS TO ME, MESSENGER TEXT,
MONDAY, 17 DECEMBER 2018

I am indebted to Wayne Jowers, who cleared out his father's home after he passed away. Wayne produced many documents that proved that his father had, indeed, been a sapper, in Germany, but Wayne also recalls that one day, when he had taken his father fishing off the Isle of Wight in his boat, Gordon started talking to an old man and boasted that he had been a parachutist in the Second World War but that they couldn't jump over Nazi-occupied Germany because of the heavy flak. 'When we reached our favourite fishing spot I asked my dad, "How could you be going over Germany when you were twelve years old by the end of the war and evacuated to Scotland." He got very angry and wouldn't answer. Basically ruined our fishing trip.'

What is fact is that JOWERS. G. F. H. (Regimental No. 22455697) received a 'NOTIFICATION OF CHANGE OF RESERVIST'S ADDRESS', from the Army Form D 430, on or about 26 May 1954. This is confirmed by a postcard sent from his brother, Ronald, who was in Hamburg at the time. The postcard was originally sent to 116 Twickenham Road, Isleworth, Middlesex, and then redirected to 53 Cobbs Road, Hounslow. Of particular interest to me is an undated photograph showing Gordon Jowers wearing a paratrooper's camouflage jacket and beret with the correct badge, along with countless more of him with a Bren gun and posing by army vehicles. So, maybe he was a parachutist sapper, maybe he was a diver, thus making him a formidable and determined person, one not to cross, but he was also one who certainly had first-hand knowledge of how Gwen was stalked and murdered when this information was highly restricted.

In a nutshell, only the killer of Mrs Maitland would have known these specific details.

But what about Ronald Jowers, the man whom his

identical twin brother Gordon vehemently claimed was Muriel Maitland's killer?

Born minutes after Gordon on 5 July 1932, Ron Jowers grew up to be flat-footed so was not called up for National Service. He became a professional racing cyclist, taking part in nationwide and international events.

When I interviewed him in Bristol on 6 September 2012, he firmly denied murdering Gwen Maitland, but he did know *a* Muriel Maitland who, like him, was a highly successful road-racing cyclist. She was married to another professional racing cyclist, championship winner Robert Maitland, but Ron Jowers made no secret of fancying her, which unsurprisingly caused some animosity between him and Bob Maitland. It has to be said that Ronald Jowers *was* a bit of a cad, and he calmly admitted this much during my interview with him.

Various people that I have spoken to recall that Ron was something of a ladies' man, and 'shifty'; indeed, he did serve a short prison sentence for fraud. But this does not make him a sex-crazed killer. On the other hand it is a known fact that, at the time of the murder, he used to ride very long distances on his cycle. This is something he did even aged eighty-five when sometimes he rode in all weathers from Bristol to Portsmouth and back – a round trip of 230 miles!

Unlike the very threatening Gordon, Ronald Jowers came across as quite the opposite in demeanour, though, as he freely admitted, he did steal his mother's ring – which he later accidentally dropped into the Bristol canal where he was building a boat. He also confirmed that he had taken away a lot of his mother's furniture and personal possessions after she had died. Nevertheless, he claimed that Gordon was his parents' favourite son . . . that Gordon was always beating him up; at one time using a pickaxe handle and, on another occasion, hitting him over the head with a teapot, which required him to have seven stitches.

Ronald Jowers firmly denied ever damaging his brother's bathroom basin. He denied ever having known the murdered Gwen Maitland, and he firmly denied ever being anywhere near Cranford Park on the day that she was killed. I was pretty convinced, though, that one of these two brothers had murdered Mrs Maitland, but which one?

First, I felt it important to try to understand why Gordon Jowers harboured such a bitter, longstanding hatred towards his identical twin, and this exercise comes down to trying to get inside Gordon's head. Both men had agreed that Gordon was his mummy's boy, her favourite son, so I can understand why Ron's stealing of his dead mother's wedding ring and some of her personal effects hit Gordon hard. Yet there is a time for healing and forgiveness. Ron had admitted to his brother that he had been in the wrong, but Gordon would have none of it – not even decades after the event. What's more, Ron went much further than just saying, 'I'm sorry'. He wrote hundreds of letters to his brother, often enclosing family photographs of 'the good old' days'. He sent cards and money to Gordon, to no avail. I have read countless of these letters and I can come to no other conclusion than they were genuinely well meant. As Ronald told me: 'I love Gordon very much. This is why I sometimes rode to Portsmouth to visit him. I just wanted to sit down and talk man-to-man.' Therefore, I cannot believe that for moment that it was the softly spoken, somewhat placid Ronald who tried to kick down Gordon's front door, nor that it was he who, in a fit of rage, yanked the washbasin from the bathroom wall. However, I do sense that Ron had called unannounced on Gordon and had used the bathroom, so the hateful Gordon tore off the basin in a fury then he contacted his solicitor to blame it all on his brother out of pure spite.

Now I focused in on Gordon Jowers, and amongst the many startling slips of his tongue was that at first during my talks with him he told me that Ron was often seen loitering around on his cycle by the stile at the southern edge of Cranford Park.

'Who saw him and who told you this?' I asked him. He gave no answer, but it did confirm that Gordon Jowers knew precisely where the stile was despite the fact that at one time he'd been adamant that he'd never visited the park – only later to say that he had spent much time bird watching there and had even drawn me a detailed map of Cranford Park. Added to which is this: it was Gordon who told me that he had seen his brother on his cycle at the main western entrance to the park on the morning *shortly before Gwen was murdered*. Another red flag – for this places Gordon Jowers right by the park just twenty minutes before the poor woman was killed.

Ron resolutely denied that it could have been him his brother claims to have seen.

Another interesting point relating to this case is that when Ron Jowers first learned, several years later, that Gwen Maitland had been murdered, his first thought was that it was the young woman cyclist he had known, whom he had once been keen on, and he immediately contacted her family and her husband, to learn that she was still very much alive and in excellent health. To confirm this, I contacted a relative of *this* Muriel Maitland and they told me that Ronald had been very upset.

Fascinating as all of this may seem, it pales into insignificance when one considers Gordon Jowers's claim to have only met the murdered Muriel the one time – when, according to him, she knocked upon his mother's front door and wrongly accused him of keeping naked porn photos of her allegedly taken in his bedroom.

'She mistook me for Ron,' he told me. Having looked into Gwen's back history and taking into account her impeccable moral values as a recently widowed woman struggling to bring up two little girls, I suggest that this 'knocking on the door' scenario was nothing less than Gordon Jowers trying to paint the woman blacker than black. He told me that she was a 'whore…a tart who always dressed like a prostitute. She walked past my mother's front window around the same time every Saturday and she had her kids with her,' he added spitefully.

Then comes another slip of the tongue when he told me that her mother lived at 89 Barrack Road. How would he have known this unless he had followed her to that address? But of course he was fixated on her – for in his own words he is telling us that he was watching her, stalking her from afar and – as implied by his vengeful allegations – was probably rebuffed when he tried to chat her up, after which there boiled up in him the same violent anger that he years later revealed when groundless fury against his brother Ron manifested itself in his damaging his own property.

And finally, the one thing that *we cannot dismiss* is that Gordon Jowers gave me such a precise description of how Gwen was murdered; how she had been punched and beaten. How she was dragged from her cycle into the woods. How she had been raped vaginally and anally. This information was privy only to the pathologist and a few very senior police officers, and none of this was ever reported in the public domain for the most obvious reasons. Added to which Gordon told me how she had been forced into the mud under the uprooted elm tree, that her wedding ring had been taken from her finger, that some of her personal items would have been buried nearby, and that her cycle would have been dumped in the nearby canal. All this knowledge was highly incriminating.

Gordon Jowers was fixated on the Maitland homicide, he was fascinated with anything to do with killing and his collection of DVDs and video tape TV recordings of murder was second to none.

Taking everything into account, and while I have witnessed Gordon Jowers first-hand; bitter, twisted, strong in physique, prone to sudden 'flick-of-the-switch' violent outbursts of anger; into pornography, a sneering pathological liar according to his son, even his home and living conditions, and the state of his garden, echoed the dysfunctional personality of a highly antisocial, paranoid individual. Like so many killers, who for years relive their crimes for perverse sexual reasons, he seemed to recall and relish every detail. Additionally, in this case, such was Gordon's hatred for his brother Ron, that he tried, albeit unsuccessfully, to make it appear that the murder of Mrs Maitland was on his brother. In conclusion, I have no doubt that Gordon Jowers murdered Muriel Maitland and that his brother Ron is totally innocent.

And, such was his son Wayne's disgust for his father that he dumped Gordon's ashes off a sewerage outlet pipe – probably the best way it could be!

8

Killing *Has* to
be Done!

There are killers who stalk and spend time methodically hunting down their prey, then there are predators like Lenny the Lizard, who wait quietly in the shadows until an unsuspecting potential victim passes by. The latter predators are commonly known as 'opportunist' offenders for there is no conscious planned victim selection approach to committing murder or much of an escape plan following the dreadful deed. Unlike the stalking and rape-murder of Mrs Maitland, it is all done off-the-cuff, so-to-speak – almost in a sudden homicidal impulse, for want of a better description.

To try to better describe this homicidal 'opportunist' mindset, if we were to look at the crimes committed by Peter Sutcliffe, the Yorkshire Ripper, we find a predator who went literally trawling for prostitute victims in the red-light districts of Halifax, Leeds, Manchester, Bradford and Huddersfield. In effect, Sutcliffe went out and about with the *deliberate intent* to kill. As he himself said: 'My desire to kill prostitutes was getting stronger than ever and took me over completely.' Of course, we know that he didn't kill only 'working girls' but several other young women who were not involved at all in the oldest professional in the world. Indeed, it has since been generally agreed that at no time during any of his murders did Sutcliffe get any sexual satisfaction by way of ejaculation. His thrill came from stalking a woman then coming down on her like a demented demon, using a hammer or a screwdriver to beat and stab his prey to death. Actually, all of his victims were 'opportunity' kills although his modus operandi and his pre-killing behaviour were that of a killer out on the hunt with murder aforethought. In effect, he knew where to find potential victims – in the red-light districts and dark alleyways of cities and towns, so when opportunities arose he rained down death and destruction on those poor souls.

In this respect we can find almost identical trawling for prostitute victims techniques in the cases of US serial killers, Arthur John Shawcross, Kenneth Bianchi and Angelo Buono; in the UK notably Steve Wright, the 'Suffolk Strangler', who murdered five prostitutes in Ipswich, between 30 October and 10 December 2006.

Dean Corll; a Houston electrician and serial murderer of boys was brought to light when he was shot dead, at the age of thirty-three, by an eighteen-year-old accomplice called Wayne Henley on 8 August 1973. Furthermore, the same can be said of the likes of US sex killers John Wayne Gacy, Jeffery Dahmer and Randy Kraft. Patrick Kearney, the 'Freeway Killer', killed at least forty-three young men and teenagers during the 1970s. He picked up young men in gay bars and hitchhikers before killing and raping them. Kearney pleaded guilty to his crimes to avoid the death penalty.

In Germany, the most notable was Fritz Haarman, sometimes known as the 'Vampire of Hanover' from his history of killing, raping and biting the throats of his male victims. He killed at least twenty-seven young men between 1918 and 1924, many of whom were prostitutes. He was executed by Madame Guillotine in 1925. And, the British serial killers of gays also deserve a mention here: Dennis Nilsen; Grindr killer Stephen Port, Peter Moore from Wales, and Colin Ireland among them.

Peter Kürten, the 'Vampire of Düsseldorf' or the 'Düsseldorf Monster', who committed a series of murders and sexual assaults, most of them between February and November 1929; Albert Howard Fish, aged sixty-five at the time of his trial, a father of six, house-painter and sex killer with extraordinary perversions, including sadomasochism and cannibalism; and Harvey Murray Glatman, a sadistic killer who photographed his female victims prior to murdering them. He was executed, aged thirty-one. All of them went out trawling and hunting down humans with the express need to commit homicide.

Harvey Glatman's modus operandi is of particular interest to us as in him we see a serial killer preying on a woman's own desires to be recognised as a model – that is, admired for her beauty – for flattery is a time-honoured way of luring potential victims to their doom.

Glatman had been an intelligent child but did not make friends at school and was considered 'odd'. His parents noticed morbid behaviour in him as he approached adolescence, and an early interest in porn magazines became deep and unhealthy. He was briefly imprisoned for robbery in 1945, and again in 1947, for a series of muggings, and given psychiatric treatment. After his release in 1956, he opened a TV repair shop in Los Angeles, and, by all accounts, led a quiet life. He took up photography as a hobby, but this newfound interest merely kindled his perverted lust. In August 1957 he hired a nineteen-year-old model on the pretext of being a professional photographer. He raped her, and took photos while she was helplessly tied up. Then he strangled the girl and buried her body in the desert.

Earlier in this book I mentioned the dangers of meeting people online – well, back in Glatman's day lonely hearts ads provided killers with victims aplenty and Glatman met his next victim through this medium. He took a twenty-four-year-old divorcée out into the desert, where he went through the same tie-up, rape, photograph and strangulation routine. A third victim met a similar death in July 1958, and then Glatman met a model, Lorraine Vigil, through a newspaper advertisement he had placed for models to be photographed. During Glatman's advances to her there was a struggle, and his gun went off, wounding her in the leg. His car stopped, and despite her injury she got hold of the firearm and kept it trained on her attacker until the police arrived on scene.

It goes without saying that Glatman was found guilty.

He refused to appeal, saying, 'It's better this way. I knew this is the way it would be.' He was executed in San Quentin's gas chamber on 18 August 1959.

> I did this not as a sex act . . . but one out of hate for her. I don't mean really out of hate for her in particular, really, I mean out of hate for a woman.
>
> ALBERT DeSALVO, THE 'BOSTON STRANGLER'

Into Sutcliffe's homicidal category we can more-or-less place Albert DeSalvo (1931–1973) who, for three years beginning in 1962, stalked the streets of Boston, US, *allegedly* leaving a macabre trail of terror in his wake. I stress allegedly because it now seems that he confessed to many murders he didn't commit.

Flipping the coin over, Harvey Louis 'Harv the Hammer' Carignan is a US serial killer I corresponded with over many years and later interviewed at the Minnesota Correctional Facility (MCF) in 1996. He was an *opportunist* because like Michael Ross, he did not consciously go out with murder in mind and stalk his victim, but the thought of it was always sleeping in his subconscious, so it was almost a case of him spotting a young woman in a vulnerable situation, to have instantly triggered within him an overwhelming need for sexual activity with her. That need *had* to be satisfied at all costs, no matter the outcome, if need be brutal murder. It is about happenstance. A chance encounter at a place I call 'Murder Crossroads': the place along life's highway where two lives happen upon each other by nothing more than chance. It is at this dreadful place that one life ends and the other life moves on irrevocably and forever changed. This is what I mean by the 'opportunist' killer, indeed even a rapist, who has had no previous conscious thoughts of committing a crime, yet something almost sexually primeval surfaces in an instant and the rape, sometimes the killing, *has* to be done.

But was 'Harv' a true opportunist? He is also known as the 'Want Ad Killer' (the forerunner of websites on which people place ads such as want-ads) because in his early murder days he ran a service station, and would advertise for employees. Several young girls applied for a position and ended up dead. Carignan was unusual in that, on very rare occasions, he could be described as a 'compensatory rapist' – in that on a couple of occasions he drove his victim home after assaulting her. This type of offender sometimes apologises to the victim during or after the sexual assault. He tends to become upset if the victim is crying and will order her to stop and try to calm her down. He may also make her repeat certain phrases such as 'I love you', as he's desperate to convince himself that the rape is really a consensual act.

One such American compensatory rapist, like Carignan, drove his victim home after an outdoor sexual assault, and commented that she had a very small Christmas tree outside her home. The next day he returned and deposited a large festive tree in her front yard, driving away before astonished witnesses could react.

Former FBI profiler has written of another compensatory rapist who demanded that his rape victims talk to him about domestic trivia such as paying the bills – as did Sams with Stephanie Slater, whom we will come to in a moment. This clearly fitted into the American rapist's fantasy that he and his bewildered victim were husband and wife.

The compensatory rapist tends to live with one or both of his parents, or a nagging wife. He is usually the product of a domineering mother who may mock him in private whilst defending him publicly so that she doesn't lose face. But rape is about power more than it is about desire, so the compensatory rapist tries very hard to overpower his victims' emotions. In some instances, he even wants her to climax during the rape.

This compensatory rapist is the most common type of sexual assailant. However, it could be argued that aside from the rape, he's the least likely to inflict serious physical pain on his victim, so he convinces himself that he hasn't damaged her, although in reality his victim will often suffer from post-traumatic stress – often for years to follow. In a twisted mind, such compensatory acts might be used as self-justification.

I spent many years corresponding with Carignan before interviewing him at the Minnesota Correctional Facility (MCF) Stillwater. Ninety-eight per cent of the time he'd rape then kill his victims but on at least two occasions he became compensatory and after beating the girls up, he patched up their cuts and drove them close to their homes, where he dropped them off and apologised; one might call these 'acts of mercy' that finally proved to be his undoing. One of his victims was able to furnish police with an excellent description of her attacker, his car and the stuff inside it. Subsequently he was arrested and jailed for life, yet he still 'compensates' (i.e. justifies himself) to this very day – his warped psychopathology maintaining that it was always his victims' fault that they were murdered because they all agreed to sex, even offered it on a plate to him, then afterwards they tried to blackmail him: if he didn't pay up they would report him to the police. He was therefore 'justified' in killing them.

Giving me one ridiculous excuse, Carignan claimed that after sex with a 'willing girl' she tried to extort money from him. They allegedly argued and she jumped from the car calling for help. 'In an effort to stop her and talk sense into her, I accidently picked up an iron bar and threw it at her head,' he told me. 'I was shocked when I saw that I had killed her.'

On another occasion, Harvey explained that he'd had a row with his then common-law wife who was 'sleeping with a black man'. 'We were walking along trying to reconcile our differences when she slipped and knocked herself out on a lamp pole and she was dead.' However, what Harvey omitted to tell me was that he must have accidentally lifted up a drain cover and beat her skull into a bloody mash after which he accidentally fed her to some pigs.

We can find to a lesser degree similar compensatory behaviour in the one-legged extortionist, kidnapper and murderer, Michael Benniman (sometimes erroneously spelt 'Benneman') Sams. On 9 July 1991, he picked up an eighteen-year-old Leeds prostitute called Julie Dart.

Blindfolding her he took to his electrical workshop in Newark-upon-Trent and locked her into a box which was chained to the floor. According to him, she tried to escape during the night. The following day he made her a cup of tea and got her to write a ransom letter to her boyfriend demanding £140,000. Then he hit her over the head with a hammer. He dumped the body in a Lincolnshire field.

> Before this happened, I had a boyfriend, a job and a company car. I had loads of friends and a great social life. But he [Sams] took everything and destroyed the next twenty years of my life.
>
> STEPHANIE SLATER

Some months after Julie Dart's murder, Sams arranged to view a house with Stephanie Slater on 22 January 1992; then, just as it was with Julie Dart, he kidnapped her, took her back to his workshop and placed her into a much improved coffin-type box. This time his demand for a ransom was met, so he drove Stephanie in his orange Austin Metro back near to her home where he dropped her off, all the while making chitchat about domestic issue along the way.

It goes without saying that Sams is a highly complex criminal and he was certainly an equally well-organised offender. His motive was non-sexual but one of financial gain for he is an extortionist at heart. But what about his methods of entrapping his two female victims?

Sams's former wife, Teena, gave me a lengthy interview,

one that enabled me to get right inside Michael's head. He had used prostitutes previously but in kidnapping Julie Dart he made a fundamental error: he demanded a huge ransom from her boyfriend who didn't have a penny in his pocket. Moreover, the West Yorkshire police were not in the least bit interested, taking the dismissive attitude that the ransom bid was all a scam – besides, what was the big deal in yet another alleged missing prostitute, anyway? At least according to Sams, who in one of a series of messages to the police claimed that he would not 'spend any more time in prison for killing two [prostitutes] instead of one'.

Sams, like so many organised offenders, learned from his mistakes. Having himself bought and sold properties, he was familiar with 'estate agent speak', and wearing the guise of an interested buyer he lured Stephanie Slater to a house for sale and abducted her from there, knowing that estate agents had money and would probably pay his ransom, which they duly did.

For me, as evil as he is, Michael Sams has a fascinating criminal mindset, but equally intriguing for me is how police at first bungled in tracking him down, later to pull their socks up and bring him to justice.

Sadly, aged just fifty, Stephanie Slater died of cancer in August 2017.

In the 'opportunist' category we can include John Reginald Halliday Christie (1899–1953), the serial killer and sexual psychopath who murdered at least six women and a baby.

In 1949, Christie lived with his wife, Ethel, in the

ground floor flat at 10 Rillington Place, a grimy dead-end street in the Ladbroke Grove area of Notting Hill Gate, London. On the top floor lived a simple semi-illiterate van driver, Timothy John Evans, aged twenty-four, and his not unattractive wife, twenty-year-old Beryl. They had an eleven-month-old daughter, Geraldine.

I would be labouring the issue here to fully document the life and crimes of Christie because his case has been well covered: scores of books on him have been published, in 1971 the motion picture, *10 Rillington Place*, was released, starring Richard Attenborough as Christie, and John Hurt as Evans, and, more recently, a number of TV documentaries have been produced. Needless to say, on 30 November 1949, Evans walked into a Merthyr Tydfil police station to report that he had found his wife dead in their London home, and added that he, and he alone, had put her body down a drain in Rillington Place. The Merthyr Tydfil police contacted their colleagues in London, and, soon after, officers were lifting every manhole cover in the street. In fact it took the strength of three constables to lift every lid – and nothing was found. The bodies of Beryl and the baby were found in a washhouse in the backyard – they had been strangled.

Evans made a statement in which he confessed to the killings, but later accused Christie. For his part, Christie was called by the prosecution as a witness at Evans's Old Bailey trial in 1950, and, thoroughly grilled by the defence barrister, Malcolm Morris QC, he denied any responsibility. Evans was sentenced to death and hanged on 9 March 1950 at Pentonville Prison.

Christie moved out of 10 Rillington Place on 20 March 1953. On 24 March 1953, a tenant called Beresford Brown moved in and soon discovered a papered-over kitchen alcove. Peeling back the covering, to his mega shock and horror he found three dead bodies. Police were summoned and a fourth rotting corpse was discovered under the floorboards of another room, and the remains of two more in the garden. On the morning of 31 March, Christie was arrested near Putney Bridge.

Pausing for a moment, it is now worth looking a little closer into Christie's modus operandi, and the masks of normality he wore to entice his victims into his murderous web. Of course his motives were sexual – he admitted strangling one of his victims during intercourse, and this was probably Beryl Evans. Outwardly a respectable but unpopular man, he was a habitual liar, and had served prison sentences for theft. In his teens he was known as 'Reggie-no-dick' on account of his sexual inadequacy. He was, despite his criminal record, employed as a special constable in the War Reserve Police.

Aside from Beryl, her baby daughter, and his wife, Ethyl – whom he killed to get her out of the way, to keep her mouth shut because she held suspicions that her 'Reg' was not all he seemed to be – his other victims were women he met in pubs and who were down on their luck, several being in need of an abortion, as was Beryl Evans. Pregnant a second time, she had decided that an abortion would be the only way to avoid worsening her and her husband's serious financial problems, and Christie convinced her that he possessed some medical knowledge and could do the deed; that he was a former police officer whom they could trust, made it easy for him.

Christie was tried at the Old Bailey for his wife's murder. Giving his evidence he related how he had invited women to his house and having got them partly drunk, sat them in a deckchair, where he rendered them unconscious with coal gas. He then strangled them and raped them, all in all making him a necrophile. He was hanged on 15 July 1953 at Pentonville Prison.

So, here we find three masks of normality Christie wore: a former police officer whom one might suppose was beyond reproach; an outwardly respectable property owner with lodgers (he was actually subletting illegally), and a man who allegedly had some 'medical knowledge'. Without any doubt, in the main he was an opportunist serial killer who came across most of his victims by happenstance in pubs and lured them back to his seedy house where, overwhelmed by his perverted homicidal impulses, he killed them. It cannot be said that in the majority of Christie's homicides he went out with a determined intention to find a victim and commit murder. Rather, it is if he had spun his web and waited for potential prey to walk into it.

Beryl Evans and her baby are buried at Plot G179, a common grave in Gunnersbury Cemetery, Acton, London.

Timothy Evans was effectively, although not technically, given a posthumous pardon in 2004. He is buried in St Patrick's Roman Catholic Cemetery, Leytonstone, Greater London.

9

The Crypto-Sex Killer: Peeling Back the Mask

He who fights with monsters should look to it that
he himself does not become a monster. And if you
gaze long into an abyss, the abyss also gazes into you.
FRIEDRICH WILHELM NIETZSCHE (1844–1900)

Every experienced serious sex crime investigator knows
that one of his most reliable allies is the criminal's
behavioural habit. Every individual tends in the course of
time to acquire certain unique likes and dislikes: certain
prejudicial ways of interpreting the world around him. In
the case of a sexually motivated offender, more often than
not, he likes certain types of victims. Perhaps we can call
this his 'victimology'. He, like all of us, has certain food
preferences, preferences for certain kinds of women or
men; and so on. Moreover, the individual's ways of saying
things, or writing, choice of words; numeral habits, as, for
instance, the tendency to combine in different forms the

same numbers; or to use in different combinations some of the same letters in aliases. These 'signatures' are the allies of the investigator. Most important of all is the criminal's modus operandi, where he or she might well have a record of previous offences (antecedents), as we will later see in the chapters on John Duffy and George Smith.

No criminal, not even a 'professional', is pliable enough to escape his own unique habits, or able to change his modus operandi to any certain degree. Indeed, the professional criminal is proud of his MO. He takes pride in the fact that it belongs to him – as did Michael Sams. It is his way of expressing satisfaction with himself and acquiring some form of status with his peers, the media and public at large. And, we can see this in the boastful letters sent to the police by Jack the Ripper, and more recently by Keith Hunter Jesperson, aka the 'Happy Face Killer' who wrote taunting letters to the press, signing each one off with a in a sort of 'catch me if you can' way. However, some of the serial sex killers featured in this book leave no habit or MO clues as ordinarily defined, for his observable ways (his 'signature') are, most often, at variance with his criminal methods. Why should this be?

The compulsive sex criminal differs from all other criminals in respect of the fact that the psychosexual nature of the compulsion that drives him to commit the crime negates any personal sense of pride. Pride in achievement, whether criminal or otherwise, however, does have sociological significance. The sex criminal – rapist or killer – alone commits his act without any sociological linkage. Even the most bungling thief, burglar or robber expects some personal advantages from the crime. He may hope that his enterprise, or the gain, will enhance the ego and give him a position, however small, a little better than the one he enjoyed before the crime was committed – again Michael Sams is a good example, with his demands for ransom money. In other words, detestable as the crime may be, the desires that motivate the criminal are in a similar general class to those that motivate law-abiding citizens – ego, satisfaction, personal enhancement and status. This is true even though the criminal holds the law in utter contempt. It is this basic commonality, or a desire for self-improvement, and the fact that most criminal acts have some social linkage that encourages an application of the rules of 'common sense' and 'experience' to criminal investigation, which is the bedrock of a copper's gut feeling.

There are many varieties of sex offenders. In this book there are some whose criminal acts are so revolting, and who are driven by motives that sit so completely outside the range of normal human imagination that they seem only the stuff of nightmares – and yet they are real. I am considering the sexual sadist whose cravings drive him finally to the murder and mutilation of the object of his desires – the Jack the Ripper type, those like Ted Bundy, Arthur Shawcross and others. And, yes, stalking formed part of the modus operandi of a number of such criminals.

There are many levels of sexual sadism and there are probably many more sexual sadists moving unhampered in our societies today than most of us could guess at.

Fortunately, the great majority of these are satisfied with mild inflictions of pain such as biting, slapping, pinching and even simulated S&M forms of punishment – each to his own, one might suggest. And, it has to be said that, given an understanding and reciprocating mate, or access to an acquiescent prostitute, these relatively mild sadistic types may reach old age without conflict with the law. However, as the records show, some of these do occasionally cross the threshold and commit sado-sexual homicide.

The brutal sex killer that concerns us here may have no record of sex criminality, nor an identifiable modus operandi, and his first sex crime is likely to be horrible – possibly a botched one. It is hard for the ordinary person to grasp the black nature of a sado-sexual serial killer, and the problem is even more difficult if the murderer has committed no *known* previous offence because he hasn't yet been caught. However, all such murderers are unique in one respect: they have lived, often for many years, in a world of cruel and grotesque fantasy – the phrase I coined many years ago being: 'A world where pink elephants fly, lead balls bounce and fairies reign supreme.' Dig deep into any serial killer's head and all this proves to be true; moreover, if we could actually see the fantasies on which the imagination of such killers has played, their behaviour would not be so surprising after all – that is, if you dare to look into the abyss and then jump in.

A difficulty arising from investigating such types, either through detective work or through hours of analysis and study carried out by psychiatrists and psychologists, is that the motivational content behind the crime has been built up over a period of time, most often beneath a 'gentle' and oft-times pietistic timidity. A slowly evolving metamorphosing from the quiet, innocent sweet child who develops a dark side to becoming a monster, may be a way to put it.

Earlier, I mentioned the steam boiler with a faulty safety valve. The pressure builds up until the whole thing explodes. And how often do we hear the mothers of these convicted killers after their son's sentencing protesting vehemently along the lines of 'Oh no, no, no! My son could never have done all of that. He always has been, and still, is such a wonderful lad.'

The trained homicide investigator is accustomed to studying crime scenes, criminal modi operandi, criminal antecedents, known associates, movements, places and motives; however, the police *cannot* work their way into the mind and intentions of the sex killer by assuming his identity, even less by playing the role of the suspect. What is more, it is difficult, if not impossible, for the investigator to get substantial help from law-abiding citizens, for they merely judge by outward appearances and are psychologically ill-equipped to see behind the masks and thin veneer of social respectability that most, if not all, sado-sexual serial killers wear. They cannot believe that, for example, such a quiet, mild-mannered man, well-spoken man of the likes of John Reginald Christie, Dr Harold Shipman, or Ted Bundy, the student with his arm in a sling dropping his text books in an alleyway, would turn out to be a notorious serial killer whose deeds defy belief.

Why? Nobody could make me believe that Dennis, a very gentle guy, could commit such crimes. I knew him from church. He is one of the most religious men I have ever known.

A NEIGHBOUR OF SERIAL KILLER DENNIS RADER

So, for most of those diagnosed as psychopathic the very use of their fantasy scenes and schemes has not only protected their exteriors from suspicion but has preserved their assumed morality, until finally, under the right stimulating circumstances, and sometimes with alcohol or the use of drugs, the pressure breaks into murder.

Even after some twenty-five years of interviewing and corresponding with serial killers and mass murderers, I am still amazed to discover how safe these individuals have felt, over many months, sometimes many years, protected by their little worlds of fantasy, for many of those I have interviewed face-to-face, or corresponded with at length, or both, will swear on God's earth that they are innocent, as did George Joseph Smith from the gallows, whom we will meet shortly.

Arthur John Shawcross, Kenneth Allen McDuff, Henry Lee Lucas, John Wayne Gacy and William George Heirens, amongst many others, spent hours upon hours trying to press upon me their innocence when the evidence against them was overwhelming. Their personalities completely took them over in a Dr Jekyll and Mr Hyde sort of way, and even while serving life sentences, or are about to be executed, so ingrained is this twisted alter ego, an almost fake multiple personality persona emerges which the offender actually believes is true. Nevertheless, in all of the killers I have met, it became obvious that they had gained a great deal of sexual satisfaction in their sex killings through absorbing their fantasies: the selection, stalking and hunting down of their prey, the sexual satisfaction in the raping, torturing and killing, the post crime behaviour and, in many cases, gleefully taunting the police and media, until it was killing time again.

Just like the addict who is hooked on drugs, all their fantasies – these sexual addictions – are played out over and over in the sex killers' minds, the fantasies becoming more grotesque until there comes a time, and an occasion, when their desires can no longer be contained within. And it is this cyclical pattern of deviant behaviour that becomes the hallmark of serial rapists and murderers: the cooling-off period in between the events. Once again, this is like the aforementioned steam boiler, this time with the valve blowing to release the built-up pressure and closing again until it blows once more. Serial killers and rapists experience the same psychosexual pressure building up, whether subconsciously or not. Then they explode to commit their dreadful inner-rage-driven crime, after which the pressure and tension evaporate. They 'cool down', until the next time, the next time and then the next.

Indeed, we often see similar behaviour with people who have anger-management problems. Narcissists are particularly prone to this type of sudden outburst of ire, which, to those around them, appears to have come from nowhere. They explode, and then quickly they calm down, often going out of their way to express remorse and contrition. We see this in road-rage incidents too.

On the basis of my own investigations into the minds of psychosexual serial murderers, I am convinced that all the killers I have come across have, somewhere along the road, suffered a tremendous loss of confidence. In spite of an acceptable outward show of normality (their mask) they revealed to me histories of deterioration away from the world of fact into unreality. They often tend more and more to avoid social engagements and interaction with their neighbours and workmates, which leads to them seeming quiet, meek and withdrawn, someone who would not hurt even a mouse. In many cases they are described as 'loners', finding increasingly frequent excuses for avoiding the company of 'ordinary' people, as for instance those of their own age. What is more, they often tend to show a decreasing interest in the broader aspects of community welfare, though not unusually such a person may *appear* to be profoundly religious – thus not the sort who would ever commit such heinous deeds; a wolf in sheep's clothing might be one analogy to explore. These types are completely able to keep their behaviour and sadistic fantasies hidden, thus going unnoticed by even close members of their own family and particularly from their partner, if they have one; only when the game is up, is it learned that the mild, even timid, individual they knew was responsible for some unimaginably horrible crimes – as evidenced by the likes of Reginald Christie; Jerome Henry Brudos; John Wayne Gacy; Herbert Baumeister;

Andrei Chikatilo . . . and, of course, who would have ever expected that the good doctor, Harold Frederick Shipman, would become one the most notorious killers in criminal history with some 230 murders under his belt?

Doctors, nurses, clergymen and people from all walks of life can evolve into sex beasts yet go about their daily lives without raising any suspicions at all – and yet so many of these 'decent types' secretly spend much of their fantasy-driven free time trawling the internet, searching out explicit porn. All of these types, *without exceptions*, wear some outward camouflage, be it the tweed jacket and brown brogues of a traditional country GP, the crispy white uniform of a bustling nurse, the glittering fame of stardom, the vestments of a priest, or the uniform of a cop.

Social position, occupation, intelligence and formal education – none of these can offer much in the way of identifying a serial rapist or killer at large. Over and over again such evil monsters are so well shielded beneath a commonplace exterior as to make it extremely difficult for them to be identified, arrested and brought to justice.

This is how dangerous these people truly are, and John Francis Duffy was one of them.

10

John Francis Duffy

Day and night we went out on hunting parties,
cruising along singing to Michael Jackson songs,
tossing a coin to decide who should be first to
rape before killing them.

JOHN DUFFY

This chapter concerning stalking with a conscious mindset to rape then kill is of great interest to us because it
involves two serial rapists and killers working together as
a 'tag team'; however, we will focus on John Duffy to start
with, the reasons becoming obvious later – and because
we know more about him than his accomplice – for it was
first believed that there was only the one offender until,
much later, long after Duffy's imprisonment in 1998, an
accomplice called David Mulcahy was brought to justice.

NOTE: At this stage, I am obliged to state that at the
time of writing, and as controversial this may seem to be,

I am in correspondence with Duffy's accomplice, who, himself, is serving a life sentence. There is a rising concern that David Mulcahy just *might* be innocent.

'Every contact leaves a trace' holds that the perpetrator of a crime will bring something to the crime scene and leave with something from it, and that both can be used as forensic evidence. Indeed, if you were to walk into a room for the first time and then leave, you will deposit something of your visit behind – perhaps a hair from your head, a finger or palm print, a fibre from your clothing, your DNA, and then take away with you something so small – it could be dust, dirt or debris – that it's not visible to the human eye. Enter Dr Edmond Locard (1877–1966), the 'Sherlock Holmes of France', who indeed once met Sir Arthur Conan Doyle when the latter was in France.

After preliminary schooling at the Dominican College at Ouillins, Locard attended the University of Lyons from which he graduated as Doctor of Medicine and also Licentiate (the holder of a certificate of competence to practise a particular profession) in Law. A handsome young man with firm features, a strong nose and mass of well-groomed dark hair, he was fortunate in being taken under the wing of criminology's great pioneer, Professor Alexandre Lacassagne (the founder of forensic ballistics), who was, at the time, Professor of Forensic Medicine at Lyons, and whose assistant Locard became. He held this post until 1910, when he resigned in order to establish the soon-to-become influential Police

Laboratory which started out as two rooms at the Lyons Police Department.

A methodical man, Locard began to expand the ideas Lacassagne applied to forensic medicine to cover other scientific disciplines and methods, and in time his laboratory became the official laboratory of the Technical Police for the Prefecture of the Rhône. It was while here that Locard advanced the theory upon which most areas of forensic science are founded – the theory that 'every contact leaves a trace', of which a simple example might be: A drunk driver crashes his car into a gate before speeding off. The impact will have transferred flakes of paint from the car to the gate and vice-versa.

But this book is not about Locard's principle, is it? Or *is* it, because in so many ways I believe that this book *is* about Locard's principle in a lateral sort of way – enter 'offender profiling' and Professor David Canter's assertion that a criminal leaves evidence of his *personality* through his actions in the commission of a crime.

At this point we are not talking about human hairs, traces of blood, fibres, fingerprints, shoe prints, tyre-tread patterns or any of the countless other physical traces that may be found at a crime scene, but about the offender's behaviour, which as Professor Canter says, reveals attributes exclusive to that person, and also patterns that are typical of the group to which they belong.

To take another simple example, one which hinges on circumstances: crimes typical of the unemployed are more likely to be committed during working hours than those typical of people who are in employment. This is not the general rule but one that makes for consideration.

> At the core of rape is bizarre sexual activity. It is remarkably difficult for the offender to hide and mask certain aspects of their sexual behaviour which are indicative of the sort of person they are. There are a great variety of rapes. We look at how the attacker approaches the victim, what goes on during the attack, and what happens afterwards. From all the factors taken together, we try to build up an overall picture.
>
> DAVID CANTER

Thus, it goes without saying that where there are multiple rapes, a common modus operandi might well be established that proves a sole rapist is at large – catch him for one rape and the remainder becomes game-set-and-match! I think therefore that I can safely say that here we find Locard's principle extended somewhat from the *physical evidence* to the *behavioural evidence* that offenders bring to a crime scene and take away with them.

Now back to stalking and hunting humans.

John Francis Duffy was born in Northern Ireland on 29 November 1958, the second of John and Philomena Duffy's three children, and, incidentally, was christened 'John' after the newly elected Pope John XXIII.

The lad enjoyed a seemingly normal, healthy childhood; he joined the choir at a local church, and served as an altar boy. Aged twelve, he started at Haverstock

Secondary School, where, despite some shyness, he enjoyed swimming and judo; he joined the Scouts and the Army Cadets. As we will soon learn, judo and the army would feature consistently throughout his killing time. It cannot be said, however, that young Duffy was academically minded by a long chalk, for his classwork was weak; as a result, when he left school his only hope was to seek work using his hands.

While at Haverstock School, Duffy fell in with another pupil, David Mulcahy, and the two remained inseparable friends long after their school years.

If Duffy's school record was feeble, his employment track record was on the weak side, too. In April 1975, he was enrolled as an apprentice carpenter with a London firm. Although he earned himself a City and Guilds craft certificate in carpentry and joinery, he was a skiver and always taking sick days. Even while at work his mind seemed to wander, which didn't impress the firm, so when he finished his apprenticeship in 1978, he was not offered a full-time job.

Duffy spent the next two years working for a building firm before joining British Rail as a carpenter, based at the vehicle and furniture department at Euston station, and it was this employment, on top of his interest in judo and the army, that allowed him to travel the rail network, to build up an extensive knowledge of the system in and around London, thus developing his emerging MO for the future. Nevertheless, it is said that a leopard never changes its spots, and once again his work was rated as poor. Furthermore, his colleagues found him solitary and aggressive and he once had to be restrained after attacking a fellow worker.

> He could be really nice and then he would be like a raving madman. He had scary, scary eyes.
>
> MRS MARGARET DUFFY

Around the time Duffy joined British Rail he met his wife-to-be, Margaret Byrne. They were married at Camden Register Office in June 1980, and, as a portent of things to come, the ceremony was conducted in secret because Margaret's parents disapproved of Duffy from the outset. Indeed, so secretive was this marriage that she continued to live with her parents until some three months after they'd exchanged rings.

> No matter what they say about my John, I will never be able to believe he is guilty of those terrible things . . . not my John.
>
> MRS PHILOMENA DUFFY, AFTER HER SON'S
> SENTENCING ON 26 FEBRUARY 1988

Initially, the Duffys' marriage seemed uneventful and happy enough, but in the spring of 1982, Duffy, who had dreamed of having a child, was told that his low sperm count would prevent this. His ego now shot to pieces, he resigned from British Rail, and vented his boiling frustration on his wife. In August she left him after a series of verbally and physically violent arguments when. Once again, we remember the exploding boiler referred to earlier.

She would later tell police that he liked to tie her up before having sexual intercourse. Once, he boasted openly to her that he had raped a girl, and presented her with a personal stereo stolen from his victim. He would later also tell his wife it was her fault he was raping women – not his – because she had not become pregnant.

The first of two estrangements was short-lived, for a month after leaving him, Duffy's wife returned to their small first-floor two-bedroomed council flat in Barlow Road, Kilburn, in an attempt to patch up their differences.

Now with Margaret holding down two part-time jobs, working long, unsocial hours and at once doing all of the household chores and cooking, bone-idle Duffy started wasting his days alone at home watching horror and kung fu movies. These reignited his interest in the martial arts, and he embarked on a punishing army-type fitness regime, running everywhere and pretending to be the kung fu star Bruce Lee. It was about this time that he began to exhibit violent tendencies.

After a year out of work, John Duffy applied to do the Knowledge and become a London cabbie, and we can see where this is going to end up, can't we?

For my overseas readers, please allow a quick debrief on the Knowledge, which is the stringent teaining all London 'black cab' drivers go through to obtain their licence, and it *is* the hardest taxi-driver test in the world for it is like implanting an atlas of London into your brain. This is an almost superhuman mental effort; one that requires you to memorise every possible route through the city as well as landmarks and points of interest, big and small. This intensive course takes years, applied intelligence and dedication to the challenge.

Semi-intent on becoming a London cabbie and obviously now living on a planet a long, long way from our own, Mr Duffy bought armfuls of maps and clocked up several hundred miles scooting around on his wife's moped in a half-hearted attempt to study the streets of London. All was at his – or, rather, his wife's – expense. He attended just one test, whereupon his enthusiasm waned.

Back on the bottom rung of his life of Snakes and Ladders, Duffy was again drifting, filling his days with rented kung fu videos, and pounding the London streets in his tracksuit. Police were to say later that: '. . . during his training sessions he was planning the intricate geometry of the sex attacks and the vital escape routes through London's railways and Underground', but I don't actually buy into this theory at all. Let's face it, while he may have known the difference between a mortise and a tenon, a half-lap, dovetail or a basic butt joint, various fasteners, bindings and glues, any 'intricate geometry' would have gone straight over his head.

When police searched Duffy's flat after his arrest, however, they did find a copy of *The Anarchist's Cookbook*, a 1960s urban guerrilla manual, which listed ways to incapacitate, silence and, if necessary, kill. This book also stressed the importance of escape routes – and Duffy's knowledge of the rail network stood him in good stead in this field.

On Thursday, 1 July 1982, Duffy and, allegedly, Mulcahy, attacked and raped a twenty-three-year-old woman near Hampstead Heath railway station. Over the next four years eighteen more young women would be attacked, three of them being raped in Hendon on the same night, who told police that two men committed the offences, but were unable to help identify the men.

In response, the police set up 'Operation Hart' to hunt down the perpetrators. Launched by Detective Superintendent Ian Harley, its name an acronym of 'Harley's Area Rape Team', the operation, which eventually cost an estimated £3 million, was based at Hendon in north-west London, and involved officers from Scotland Yard, the Surrey and Hertfordshire forces and the British Transport Police.

Sunday, 29 December 1985: Alison Day, aged nineteen, from Upminster was murdered in east London. Described as a 'girl with a heart of gold', she was on her way to meet her fiancé at the printing works where he was employed. The platform at Hackney Wick station was deserted as the orange-coloured sodium lights flared in the gloom. She pulled up her sheepskin-coat collar as she stepped from the train and would never have noticed Duffy's hard, penetrating eyes following her from the shadows.

On Wednesday, 15 January 1986, Alison's body was found. Police divers recovered the remains from a nearby canal leading to the River Lee. Her killer/s had stuffed discarded cobblestones into the pockets of her coat to make the body sink. The only clues found were tiny fibres from Duffy's clothes. It is not difficult to envisage what had happened, however; Duffy must have hustled her across the deserted station footbridge and then dragged her into a rat-infested garage block nearby. There, with her hands tied behind her back with a strip torn from her shirt, the killer had garrotted her with a tourniquet made from a piece of her shirt and a piece of wood to twist it – creating a device known as a 'Spanish windlass'. Now the Metropolitan Police in east London set up their own investigation and called it 'Operation Lea'.

Thursday, 17 April 1986: Fifteen-year-old schoolgirl, Maartje Tamboezer, the eldest of three children of a Dutch Shell Oil Company executive, left her home in the Surrey village of West Horsley to cycle to nearby East Horsley to buy some sweets. As fate would have it, she was due to leave for a school holiday the next day and had planned to visit a shop nearer her home, but someone had told her that the shop at East Horsley had a better candy selection. Going against her mother's advice, to avoid heavy traffic on the busy A246 between Guildford and Leatherhead, she rode along a lonely footpath running through a dark spinney alongside the main London railway line.

Early the following morning, two men out ferreting discovered Maartje's body in thick cover. The girl had been so badly mutilated that at first they did not recognise the remains as a human corpse. She had been bound by the wrists, raped, and strangled with a tourniquet. Before making his escape, her killer/s had set fire to her upper body and genitals in a frantic effort to destroy any evidence. Maartje's cycle was found propped up against a tree. Nearby, police made an unusual discovery: a length of very distinctive bright orange nylon cord. This had evidently been deliberately tied across the lonely track, forcing the girl to dismount and thus giving her killer his chance to pounce.

Homicide detectives were able to piece together Maartje's horrific last moments during which she had been dragged at knifepoint into the nearby woods, bound by the wrists, raped, beaten, and finally knocked unconscious. She was then strangled; the killer using her own scarf tightened round her neck using a length of branch to twist it – as with Alison Day's killing. As well as the nylon cord, the murderer had left other tell-tale clues: semen traces and an unusually small footprint. At autopsy, it was revealed that a bone in Maartje's neck had been broken in a way suggesting a karate chop. A promising lead came from a railway guard and also a passenger on the 6.07 p.m. train from Horsley to London. The guard recalled a smallish man wearing a blue parka jacket rushing onto the platform as the train was about to leave. In his hurry he barged into two women. A young woman on the same train reported how the same man had gazed at her fixedly several times before she got off the train at Bookham. She described him as having 'laser-like eyes'.

This homicide prompted Surrey Police to set up 'Operation Bluebell' and to examine thousands of discarded rail tickets in a desperate, yet fruitless search, for the man's fingerprints.

*

Returning briefly to Locard's principle, already we can see that every contact Duffy most certainly made with Alison Day and Maartje Tamboezer had left physical traces: with Alison, minute fibres from Duffy's clothes were found on her clothing; with Maartje, a bright orange cord was left behind. The killer's semen was discovered as belonging to someone with blood group A. There was a very small shoeprint. And, there was another very important clue: Maartje's hands had been bound with a distinctive type of brown string called Somyarn, made not of the usual cord or thread, but of softwood pulp paper by the kraft process with the long fibres providing the strength. The manager of the factory where it was produced was able to narrow the sample down to a particular batch discontinued in 1982. Significantly, one of the company's major customers for that string had been British Rail. Find the ball of string, detectives reasoned, and the chances are that the owner is the railway rapist/killer.

Aside from the physical evidence Duffy had left behind at these two homicide scenes, he was also inadvertently, subconsciously, telling us quite a lot about himself, too. As Professor Canter says: 'It is remarkably difficult for offenders to hide and mask certain aspects of their sexual behaviour which are indicative of the sort of person they are,' and Duffy was now leaving 'invisible clues' all over and around his crime scenes.

To begin with, the railway guard and a young woman train passenger were able to describe a possible suspect as being 5 foot 4 inches with small feet, and they were also alert enough to help provide police with an artist's impression of a man with a pockmarked face and ginger hair, which was soon being circulated during Operation Hart, added to which both of the murders had actually been committed very close to the railway network. The karate-style blow to Maartje's neck, although taken in isolation, might have meant little, yet this resonates with Duffy's fascination with kung fu and interest in judo. There was a modus operandi developing here, somewhat pointing not to the white-collar type but a blue-collar worker or someone unemployed, which, taken with the physical evidence of Duffy's contact with his two victims – he was unconsciously leaving behind and taking away with him much of his twisted psychopathology – helped form a profile of the perpetrator.

Sunday, 18 May 1986: Married just a month previously, twenty-nine-year-old Anne Lock had just returned from her honeymoon in the Seychelles. On the evening in question, she had been working late. At 8.30 p.m., having left the South Bank offices of London Weekend Television, where she was a secretary, she took a train home to Brookmans Park, near Potters Bar in Hertfordshire, where she arrived at 10 p.m. She walked quickly along the now-deserted railway station towards a nearby shed where she had left her locked bicycle, but found her way blocked by a bench that had been dragged across the path like a barricade. Once again, a trap was sprung, this time a bench blocking her path, whereas with Maartje Tamboezer it had been a length of orange string pulled tight across the track.

Anne's attacker/s marched her at knifepoint along a lonely path skirting the main King's Cross-to-Scotland railway line and into a field where her hands were tied behind her back and one of her socks was stuffed into her mouth. The other sock was tied around her jaw. What happened next is unclear, but it seems almost certain that she, too, was raped. Just as in the Maartje Tamboezer homicide, Anne's body was set alight in an attempt to burn away any trace evidence. On Monday, 21 July – nine weeks after her disappearance – Anne's body was found by a gang of track-maintenance workers on a weed-covered embankment near Brookmans Park. Cause of death was suffocation.

The mysterious disappearance of this beautiful young woman only days after returning from her dream honeymoon in the Seychelles sparked massive publicity. On the assumption that Anne had become the railway killer's third victim, detectives from London, Surrey and Hertfordshire combined in yet another police operation, codenamed 'Operation Trinity'. It was to become the largest British manhunt since the poorly implemented Yorkshire Ripper inquiry of the late 1970s. Indeed, Trinity was the first such investigation to utilise basic computers and an early version of HOLMES (Home Office Large Major Enquiry System), which, updated, is still being used today.

Police began with a list of 5,000 sex offenders, all of whom had group A blood type, or whose blood group was undetermined. Every suspect was researched by a team of detectives who compared their names with indexes covering descriptions, ages, methods of attack and any known links to railways. This initial list of suspects was whittled down to 1,999 men whose description and other details fitted the pattern of the man who now was now dubbed by the media the 'Railway Killer'. On this list, at number 1,594, was John Duffy, a slightly built Irishman, who until fairly recently had worked as a carpenter for British Rail. Indeed, his name had appeared on the list of suspects because in August 1985 he had been arrested for raping his now ex-wife, Margaret. She had claimed that after she and John had separated for the second time in June 1985, he had raped her when he called unannounced at the flat in Barlow Road to collect his mail. 'On this occasion he stuffed a handkerchief down my throat,' she told police, adding between tears, 'I thought he was going to kill me.' A sock was stuffed into Anne Lock's mouth.

According to Margaret Duffy, that August (1985), John had turned up at the home of her new boyfriend, pulled a knife and attacked him. She had courageously attempted to intervene, but Duffy hit her over the head. Afterwards, both she and her lover had needed hospital treatment for their injuries. Of course, Mrs Duffy had reported this serious assault to the police but because the matter was viewed as a domestic one, the officers did not believe that the offence was linked with the then rape inquiry conducted by Operation Hart. Nevertheless, Duffy was questioned about Margaret's rape allegation, and charged separately with assault and maliciously wounding her boyfriend. Suspecting that Duffy might try to attack his ex-wife again, police opposed bail when he appeared before magistrates at West Hendon and held him in custody for a fortnight. However, in September he successfully applied for bail to a judge, Recorder Peter Kingsley Archer, Baron Archer of Sandwell, QC; a former solicitor-general who should have damned well known better, and against all strenuous police objections, allowed Duffy to walk out of the court. A few days later, Duffy attacked and raped a twenty-year-old woman in Copthall South Fields, a six-hectare nature reserve in the London Borough of Barnet.

Whittling through their list of now 1,999 suspects, detectives now zeroed in on the man with laser eyes; soon learning that aside from the problems he'd had with his ex-wife the previous year, on Saturday, 17 May 1986, the day before Anne Lock's disappearance, Duffy had been arrested at North Weald railway station on suspicion of loitering. He was found to be in possession of a sharp butterfly knife (similar to a flick knife), which he claimed he used during his weekly visits to a martial arts class near his home in Kilburn, north London. Although Duffy was soon released, the Operation Hart computer had logged his arrest.

During what amounted to a lengthy cat-and-mouse game between police and Duffy, he was admitted to a psychiatric hospital for a month, then discharged only to rape a fourteen-year-old schoolgirl on Tuesday, 21 October. Traumatised as the girl was, she was able to give the police enough information to help identify him. Not long after, Duffy was stopped apparently stalking a woman through a local park. The order for his arrest was issued on Sunday 23 November 1986.

> You are a predatory animal. The wickedness and beastliness you inflicted on young girls hardly bears description.
>
> MR JUSTICE SIR DONALD HENRY FARQUARSON, sentencing Duffy on 26 FEBRUARY 1988

On 26 February 1988, the jury of six men and six women sitting at Court No.1, Old Bailey, convicted John Duffy of two murders and five rapes. Because of lack of evidence he was acquitted of Anne Lock's murder; nevertheless he was handed down a minimum sentence of thirty years. He is currently serving his time at HMP Full Sutton, East Riding of Yorkshire.

Enter stage left David Mulcahy, and at this point, I am anticipating that in the near future I will have a number of police officers anxious to have me shot for quite possibly kicking over their tin of beans.

In 1997, about nine years after Duffy's conviction for multiple rape and murder most foul, he had an epiphany – a moment no doubt brought about as the result of many sleepless nights of soul-searching, heartfelt contrition – which he unloaded onto a prison counsellor: he would grass Mulcahy up.

The general substance of what Roman Catholic Duffy would deem as a 'confession' *appears* to have already been known to police for years – that Mr Mulcahy had been an accomplice of Duffy's in multiple rape and homicide but they had not been able to prove it. There was not sufficient evidence to prosecute; indeed as far as Mulcahy was concerned Locard's principle didn't exist. Indeed, Duffy had already squealed on Mulcahy to a psychologist soon after his arrest then zipped up and had not said anything since.

Armed with this belatedly and remarkably full confession, the police placed Mulcahy, a married father of four, who had been under surveillance for several months prior to his arrest. DNA testing – which was not yet available during the initial investigations – *allegedly* conclusively proved his involvement in the rapes and murders; unfortunately, this evidence has now been conveniently destroyed because it was deemed by some bright spark to be 'health hazard'!

Nonetheless, Duffy appeared at the Old Bailey as a witness against his alleged 'lifelong friend' in 2000. He gave detailed evidence over two weeks and the prosecution painted Mulcahy as the chief perpetrator. As the result of this, and the alleged DNA profiling techniques, which actually proved to be worthless, Mulcahy was convicted of three homicides and seven rapes with a thirty-year incarceration recommendation. Like Duffy, it is doubtful that he will ever be released.

But herein lies a possible rub, and the very reason why I might face a virtual police firing squad anytime soon, because I just don't get it . . . I don't get it that Mulcahy was the prime mover at all.

For decades it was argued by all and sundry, Jack and

Jill and all, that Angelo Buono was the prime mover in the LA-dubbed 'Hillside Strangler' serial homicides which took place between October 1977 and January 1979, and that Kenneth Bianchi (whom I interviewed in the Washington State Penitentiary, Walla Walla) was just a weak-willed sidekick. Following three years corresponding with Bianchi and an interview with him, I completely debunked the notion that Buono was the instigator; indeed, the shoe was on the other foot, and I exposed this in my 2005 book *Talking with Serial Killers 2*, published by John Blake.

Ignoring viable press claims that Duffy was paid an alleged incentive of £20,000 to drop Mulcahy in the shit, I find two different and quite distinctive personalities at large here. Yet, it is *here* that issues of MO, criminal signatures, organised or disorganised offender/s and Locard's principle come into play – or at least they do for me.

To start with, why this sudden sea change in Duffy's mind, and why did he wait nine years to spill the beans?

Turning to MO for a moment – which one of these two serial rapists had an intimate knowledge of the British Rail network? Of course, it was Duffy.

Which one of these two men had martial arts training and who was reading literature such as the *Anarchist's Cookbook*, the now-banned guide on how to silently kill, how to make a Spanish windlass, how to plan an attack and make good one's escape afterwards – Mr Duffy step up to the front, please.

Turning specifically to the murders of Alison Day, Maartje Tamboezer and Anne Lock, and recalling Duffy's comment: 'Day and night we went out on hunting parties, cruising along singing to Michael Jackson songs, tossing a coin to decide who should be first to rape before *killing them* [my italics],' despite one of the largest police manhunts in UK criminal history, there appears to be no evidence of any car, belonging to either man, being spotted anywhere near the locations from which these women were taken. In fact, following the murder of Maartje, did the police not have two witnesses who described Duffy to a tee rushing onto a train, barging other people aside, only to sit with laser-like eyes glaring at the young female opposite him? So where was Mulcahy when all of this was going on . . . leaving Duffy to hop onto a train while Mulcahy drove back home to his wife and kids?

Indeed, the only witness who apparently saw another man with Duffy described the accomplice as being 'black', while Mulcahy is white.

I once met Professor of Applied Psychology David Canter while he was working on his offender profiling studies at Surrey University. We had agreed to meet up one evening at his campus home to discuss the US serial killer, Kenneth Bianchi, and we ate takeaway fish and chips. And, of course it was David who was able, with all of the police data available at the time of the rapes, and the Alison Day, Maartje Tamboezer and Anne Lock homicides, to advise law enforcement that the *killer* most probably lived in the Kilburn – Cricklewood area of north-west London. Professor Canter also deduced correctly that *he* was a married man, probably in a *childless and turbulent domestic relationship, a loner* with little social interaction with women.

He would also likely to be a *semi-skilled worker* in a job that brought him into contact with the public. At the time of his arrest, Duffy turned out to be a carpenter with Westminster City Council. Professor Canter's profile was accurate on thirteen out of seventeen points.

But do we see any reference to an accomplice specifically regarding the three homicides here? Therefore, it might seem impertinent of me to suggest that if Professor Canter — who is recognised as one of the world's leading authorities on offender profiling — gets it correct with a thirteen out of seventeen score, then as regards MO, offender signatures and Locard's principle, something doesn't appear to fit at all.

Nevertheless, we now know quite a bit about John Duffy's narrative, so I think it would be fair to look a little deeper into Mulcahy's history too, beginning with, 'Is he a psychopath?' and I say he is not. I am basing this observation on what we *do* know about the rapes and murders, a great deal of background research and *exclusive letters* written to me by Mulcahy from prison. I also enjoy the full cooperation of his legal adviser.

David was born at Hampstead General Hospital on 23 May 1959, to John and Joan Mulcahy. His siblings are Patricia, born 1958, and Susan, born 1967.

At various times, the Mulcahys ran off-licences and were pub owners, and, or, landlords of the Prince of Beck, 161 Earls Court Road, Kensington, and The Washington, at 50 England's Lane, just south of Hampstead Heath. Their home was in Parkwood Road, Wimbledon.

Although his early days are still a little sketchy at the time of writing, David Mulcahy attended Dundonald Primary School, Wimbledon, later Haverstock Secondary School, in Chalk Farm, which is, again, just south of Hampstead Heath.

In a letter to me dated 24 July 2019, he briefly described his parents:

> My mother was a loving, caring person who went out of her way to support me in all ways. My dad, although loving, was more of his generation and thought men should be men, so he kept his feelings close. He would, however, be there for me whenever I needed him. Both were fairly strict. Right is right. Wrong is wrong. That's it. Show respect to receive respect.

At his trial for rape and murder, several of Mulcahy's former schoolteachers said that he was a good student with a good attendance record. He denies this, saying: 'I wasn't. I got bored easily so I played truant. I still somehow managed to get good exam results in the final exams.'

Mulcahy makes no bones about his criminal antecedents either, for his crimes started when he was about eight years old when he was caught stealing sweets from a shop. A copper gave him a slap around the ear and took him home to receive another hard slap from his father.

Aged twelve, this young lad was arrested for driving a car without a licence. He was banned from driving until he was old enough to start driving lessons. Almost immediately after he'd passed his test, he was banned again and didn't get his licence back until he was thirty. In his teens he started stealing cars and taking the contents. Indeed, on one occasion in 1976, aged seventeen, he fired an air rifle through one of his parents' pub windows. He was arrested and charged with assault – he puts it down to a 'childish prank'.

In 1981, Mulcahy started to commit commercial burglaries; one was a West Hampstead building site, the other on a garage. He was arrested and tried for the building-site job. He received a suspended sentence and given a hefty fine. Actually, if truth be known he also attempted a residential burglary. He climbed through a window but he 'lost his bottle' and left without taking anything; he was arrested for neither the garage burglary nor the housebreaking and entering.

Around 1989, now aged thirty, David Mulcahy started what he calls a 'building company', but when he ran short of funds, he says, he issued a false invoice and received a fine. But it is his involvement with Duffy that is more important to us here.

The two lads met while at the Haverstock Secondary School. 'He [Duffy] was short for his age, as I was, so I guess it brought us together,' recalls Mulcahy in a letter to me dated 4 July 2019. He writes, 'But, hey, it was school so you just made friends with whoever would talk to you. Even at this stage I would say he was only a secondary school friend. I hung around with a small group who were all into cars. Duffy was not into cars at all, thus he was on the edge of our group.'

According to Mulcahy, as time went by the two

started to hang around together, in fact it was Duffy who introduced Mulcahy to a young Afro/Indian woman whom he dated, and when the relationship became more serious, in 1977, they moved away and he didn't see Duffy again until the early eighties. They married on 19 June 1979, at Euston Town Hall, and moved into 4 Park Dwellings just around the corner from Duffy's parents, in Hampstead. The couple had a son, Gary, on 2 November the same year, followed later by a daughter.

As Mulcahy tells us, Duffy would often turn up at the Park Dwelling flat to hide from his own parents when he had told them he was at work although he wasn't. Apparently this went on for a few weeks, but Mrs Mulcahy found his presence eerie and uncomfortable, especially when her husband was not there. So the Mulcahys put a stop to it. Duffy didn't take this very well and disappeared off of the radar for a few months.

For his part, David Mulcahy says that after his son was born, he tried to settle down and become a good father and husband, adding, however, that that 'would be a lie, but I did try'. He continues, '. . . but I was still a kid [he was twenty] myself and didn't take as much responsibility as I should have.'

These were difficult times for the Mulcahys. His wife couldn't work because she had a child to look after; he worked as a general labourer to put food onto the table, and because his wife was Afro/Indian there were a lot of racial problems in the area that affected the couple. Then, in April 1980, their flat was petrol bombed.

In May 1980, the Mulcahys were relocated to 9 Eaton

Avenue, Hampstead, losing contact with Duffy for a period; later learning that he had secretly married a woman, Margaret, not even informing his parents for months.

While there is no doubt that Duffy was bone idle, the same cannot be said of Mulcahy, who, in 1982, started to attend the Colindale Brick Academy, on the Colindale Campus at Barnet and Southgate College. He wanted to learn a trade, and this was the place to start. Skills taught here are: brickwork; carpentry and joinery, plastering, wall and floor tiling and courses in plumbing.

From here on in things get a little hazy. It appears from Mulcahy's letters that he found employment as a plasterer for Westminster Borough Council, based at Chippenham Road, in Queens Park. It also seems that Duffy was a carpenter at the same place, with Mrs Mulcahy now working between 6 p.m. and 11.30 p.m. at Travellers' Fare in Euston Station.

David Mulcahy says that also around this time he and Duffy tried to start up a business together but ended up fighting and that put an end to it and their relationship for a while. At at this point, Mulcahy volunteers in one of his letters: 'I spent most nights at home because I worked days and my wife worked evenings. So we took turns to look after the children. I did go out at weekends if I wasn't working, but mostly street skating.' Then, rather astonishingly, he adds, 'I can't deny I did go out stealing on occasions with Duffy, but, and I can't say this strongly enough, *there was no sexual or violent element to my crimes* [my italics].

On Duffy, Mulcahy has this to say:

As for Duffy himself . . . if I had been asked the day before my arrest [2 February 1999] I would have said he didn't do the crimes.

I can, with hand on heart, say I never saw anything at the time, or even looking back, that would have made me suspicious or have any reason to think he was a monster.

He was a mummy's boy, frightened of his parents and their disapproval. He would even when warned go to their house every day.

He was work shy. There was no work ethic in him. He would sit and watch videotapes all day rather than go to work. He was always a little sly. My Gran didn't like him because he would hide away his sweets so he could eat them all himself. To me he was just a greedy kid.

When his wife gave evidence of what he had done to her, I couldn't believe it. We had been out [together] as all couples do and I never saw anything strange.

The side I heard about him in court of the things he did to the victims and his wife didn't fit with the Duffy I knew for all those years.

That last paragraph, if true and honest, is revealing, while at once we might recall the dread words of Ted Bundy.

Society wants to believe it can identify evil people, or bad or harmful people, but it's not practical. There are no stereotypes.

We serial killers are your sons, we are your husbands, we are everywhere. And there will be more of your children dead tomorrow.

As stalkers come and go, in John Duffy we find not so much a stalker in the true sense of the word; in that he spotted a victim and followed them, watched them, learned their habits and their comings and goings before setting his trap – he was more Bundyesque in his MO. One might say that Duffy was an opportunist offender: organised in some ways yet disorganised in others. We could say with more precision that he was of the 'snatch and grab' type.

If, with what little we *do* know about this twisted, insignificant little man taken into consideration, we know that he was born lazy, he was work shy and, to all intents and purposes a loner. And, we only have to look at his pathetic attempt to become a London cabbie to see that he was a loser.

He was a labourer, not really even a blue-collar worker. So, I suggest here is a man who would be incapable of pre-crime planning to any reasonable degree, but he used his knowledge of the railways, of how young women came and went, often during the hours of darkness, to locate prey.

This is a man with time on his hands, so questions to be asked must include how did he know that Alison Day would be getting off of a train at Hackney Wick, on 29 December 1985?

How did he know that Maartje Tamboezer would be

cycling along a track between a railway line and bluebell woods on 17 April 1986? In this case, Maartje's decision to take this route was a spur-of-the-moment idea, yet he certainly had time to set string across her path to bring her to a stop.

How did Duffy know that Anne Lock would be alighting from a train at Brookmans Park station, on 18 May 1986? Had he seen her earlier in the day as she locked up her cycle, and then waited for hours and hours until she arrived back to collect it? What if she had been in company?

Then we have to ask ourselves, were two men involved in all of this almost incomprehensible planning, if 'planning' it actually was? It appears that Professor David Canter thought that only one man was responsible for all of these rapes and murders because nowhere can I find any offender profiling pointing towards David Mulcahy.

And, I find it somewhat odd, if we believe the police, that Mulcahy had been in the 'frame' for some time, when they didn't have even have a smidgen of evidence with which to arrest him, least of all to charge him with serious sexual offences.

My information tells me that Mulcahy *only* became a 'person of interest' because he was associated with Duffy – had been since their school days – and both men had a criminal history.

To conclude this chapter, I must stress that I am not going marshmallow soft on David Mulcahy at all. But what I will emphasise is, if Duffy had committed his crimes in certain states of the US, he would be a current or terminally recent resident of death row.

In the meanwhile, I would like to direct you to a posting: www.davidmulcahy.com, which includes extracts taken from a forensic science report, dated 25 March 1999. Make of it as you please for it is all gruesome, if not fascinating whodunit, whatdunit, howdunit stuff, and something to get your teeth into. But, having now reviewed the information published on this website, something smells distinctly fishy here because it seems that much of the evidence against Mulcahy comes from the mouth of, effectively, a jailhouse snitch.

Who says that murder most foul isn't riveting material for a bedtime read? . . . Not me!

11

George Joseph Smith:
A Very 'Fatal Attraction'

The true habitual offender commits a crime by impulse or monetary aberration. Mostly he looks for criminal chances as systematically as a salesman looks for buyers.

Dr Harry Söderman (1902–1956)
Crime & Detection. May 1967

Harry Söderman was a Swedish forensic scientist. In his native Sweden he went by the nickname 'Revolver-Harry' (for his doctoral research work which included studying characteristics left by individual firearms on fired bullets) and he was a pioneer of modern criminology in Scandinavia; he revived Interpol after the Second World War and was the first director of the National Forensic Science Institute (now the National Laboratory of Forensic Science) in Sweden between 1939 and 1953.

Smart guy, was Harry!

Cited in the quarterly journal *Crime & Detection*, Söderman, went on to say:

He [the habitual criminal] fights no battle within himself. Business is business. He sees in crime a profession – or, at least a way of life – like any other. He may, at the start of his course, have been a chance offender but, constituted as he is, he has only to go to prison to have all of his bad instincts stimulated and confirmed by the easily gained wealth and free life of that obscure world of crime which he could have only partly known before his sentence.

He does not stop to count costs; he muses very little on the drawbacks of the life of crime. A dissipated interlude of a few days or even weeks is paid for by years inside penitentiary walls. Such an offender almost always passes the greater part of his adult life in prison, and his death, inside the walls or out, is generally as wretched as his life has been poor and cheerless.

How better can one sum up George Joseph Smith?

We usually imagine that stalking a victim is a physical exercise – one of selecting one's prey then following, watching and waiting for an opportunity to strike. Think of Ted Bundy and the many killers like him, who, in much the same way as predatory animals spot potential targets wandering away from the herd, and then strike. But what if the killer is using bait to tempt an innocent, unsuspecting victim: perhaps as does the fly fisherman casting over a pool with a colourful fly? There are labour-saving, cost-effective human dynamics at work here; simply put, there is little to no chance of the offender exposing himself to those around him because it is all achieved using stealth and a few props – in the case of George Smith, what amounts to a bath of tepid water, a pen and paper, with any possible risk factor being reduced *almost* to zero.

Over the passage of time the modus operandi and signatures of both organised and disorganised offenders have changed little, so this chapter takes us back to pre-First World War days and the reader will soon be able to compare what happened in the George Joseph Smith case to the 'Lonely Hearts Killers' who stalk the internet today, for Smith won the hearts of lovelorn women then plunged them to their deaths.

Dubbed the 'Brides in the Bath Murderer', Smith still ranks amongst the most infamous criminals of all time. Greedy, self-obsessed, totally unscrupulous, he cast a mesmeric spell over gullible women whom he left heartbroken, penniless and, in three cases, dead.

Over a hundred years have passed since George Smith was at large, so it would be easy to dismiss him as a Victorian silk top-hatted aberration with his frock coat and spats. Back then he would have been classified as a 'murderer', for the terms 'mass-murderer' and 'serial killer' had yet to enter the lexicon of crime. Today we would call him a serial killer – one who kills three or more times with cooling-off periods between the killings, or 'events', as they are labelled.

The reason why I have selected George Smith for a

dedicated chapter in this book is because after studying literally hundreds of historic and contemporary cases I find that he epitomises the consummate stalker and hunter of female prey. Using various aliases, so many variable disguises and masks of normality, he was able to flow through genteel Edwardian society, courting then bigamously marrying at least seven times, swindling and killing at least three women almost undetected. In this regard we may safely call him highly versatile, organised, adaptable to his surroundings, a chameleon – albeit in human form.

Throughout his criminal narrative, unlike the majority of serial killers whose motives are perverse sexual gratification, Smith's motive – like Michael Sams's – was greed, specifically financial gain, and we can see this writ large throughout the following pages. And we will delve into his criminal signature too, for this alone makes for fascinating study.

Aside from all of that is the utterly immoral way in which he treated women in general: he was utterly heartless, and that is an understatement.

So, let's see where Smith came from, and how his early days formatted him into becoming what we call today a serial killer, and although much has already been written about this dreadful man, for the first time I am examining his psychopathology in much greater forensic detail.

George Joseph Smith was born at 92 Roman Road, Bethnal Green, London, on 11 January 1872. His father, George Thomas Smith, was an insurance agent, peddling policies for pennies-a-week to the East End poor. He died when George was still a child, leaving his widow, Louisa, to bring the boy up single-handedly. She was a weak-willed woman who ignored the Victorian dictum that sparing the rod would spoil the child. In the absence of any kind of discipline at home, her son was soon running wild in the street.

To put things into perspective, a modern analysis has placed Bethnal Green as the second poorest London parish at that time with the population caught in a downward spiral of poverty. Life expectancy was low. Of 1,632 deaths recorded just a few years previously, 1,258 (77 percent) were of mechanics, servants and labourers who had a life expectancy of sixteen years; 273 were of tradesmen, with a life expectancy of twenty-six, and just 101 deaths were of 'gentry' and 'professional people', as one might expect enjoyed a better standard of living and diet, and who had a life expectancy of forty-five.

At the age of only nine, young Smith fell foul of the law. It is not clear exactly how this came about; it may have been a typically childish offence – stealing an apple from a barrow, or breaking windows – nevertheless, whatever it was, it had a profound effect on his life for he was packed off to a reformatory situated on Stone Street in Gravesend. Here he remained until he was sixteen.

Such a drastic measure – robbing a boy of seven years of his youth – says much about Victorian values. The nine-year-old son of a middle-class family would very probably have been excused, or received a clip around the ear, at worst a thrashing. But it was this lad's fate to belong to the lower classes, thus he could expect no leniency. The authorities would have considered that his best interests would be served not by being put across the knee and given a good hiding, but by being placed behind stone walls under lock and key with fifty other young miscreants of similar circumstances.

Around the 1850s, government, charities, and faith communities had constructed a rudimentary welfare net for children who had committed crimes by sending them to reformatories or military training ships, as was the case with young Smith. Children who were at risk of committing crimes because of neglectful or criminal parents were sent to industrial schools rather than workhouses because they were deemed at risk of becoming delinquent, but Smith drew the short straw.

Life behind the grim walls revolved around 'healthy, character-forming manual labour' with some rudimentary schoolwork thrown in. There was no remission system – as in adult prisons – and discipline was enforced by corporal punishment; these were violent and abusive places to grow up in.

We know, of course, that during these times many children suffered horrendous physical and sexual abuse, and this went on through Edwardian times and beyond. In 1910, the magazine *John Bull* published an article entitled 'Reformatory School Horrors', claiming that three boys had died as a result of excessive punishments and neglect. The newspaper particularly condemned the 'cold water' punishments of 'malingerers', one of whom 'was taken out into the courtyard in wintry weather, where he had 52 buckets of cold water thrown over him'. Other punishments included birching, caning, deprivation of food and clothing.

Victorian society may have seen harsh treatment as a part of bringing reform and a successful life to institutionalised children. Many of the reformatories and industrial schools set up by the state and charity sector during Victorian and Edwardian times ensured that most of the children who passed through them were comparatively safe and secure, harsh as the establishments might have been, and were ensured a modicum of education and employment and a better future than they might otherwise have had. The recidivism rates were 76 per cent lower than they are nowadays. For those who were irrevocably damaged by their early institutionalisation, however, of course their childhood experiences may have haunted them into adulthood. Tragically for Smith's later victims, he became one of them, although I somewhat doubt there can be any mitigation for his later crimes.

Actually, young Smith survived the grinding regime with something approaching equanimity. He used his time to gain more than a grasp of the 'three Rs'. From the chaplain he learned something of biblical cadences and vocabulary, which in later years he would echo in his windy letters to lawyers and outraged in-laws. Nevertheless, reformatory life also seeded in him other, less wholesome, characteristics: a huge ego; an overwhelming self-centeredness and an oppressive air of self-pity.

On returning to Bethnal Green to live with his mother, Smith soon resumed thieving, but was caught almost at once and sentenced to seven days in an adult jail. At the age of only sixteen, however, he was already hardened to such an ordeal. The regime of oakum-picking and sewing mail sacks held no terrors for him. He viewed such punishment with contempt, for once out of jail, he supplemented his wages from a series of dead-end jobs by filching money from his family. Then, in 1891, aged seventeen, he received six months' hard labour for stealing a bicycle.

Smith once boasted to his only lawful wife, Caroline Thornhill, that he had served for a period of three years in the Northamptonshire Regiment, but there is no record that he did. To one of his many boarding-house keepers, he mentioned that he had once been a gym instructor – there was no truth in that either. He was a consummate liar.

In July 1896, he was sentenced to twelve months' hard labour at North London Sessions for larceny and receiving in the name of 'George Baker'. He served his time at Wormwood Scrubs in West London. Then three things happened at once: Smith embarked on a career as a hardened criminal; cheating; welshing and creating for himself a series of fictitious identities, fashioning not just a double life but a series of several and separate lives. He also discovered his uncanny power over women. More particularly, he discovered how easy it was for him to persuade them away from hearth and home to thieve for him.

Not unlike Dickens's Fagin with his band of boys, Smith's scheme was to place his women in service with well-to-do families. Their task was to use this position of trust to pilfer money and valuables and hand them over to him. Another revelation to him was the heady world of property. For the first time in twenty-four years, and flush from the proceeds of his nefarious schemes, he had money put by for a rainy day. From his self-improving studies at the reformatory, he was aware that money was synonymous with power and, from 1897, when he was twenty-five, onwards, he set about obtaining as much of it, through as little effort, as he possibly could.

He was like a mad dog.
CAROLINE THORNHILL'S FATHER ON GEORGE SMITH

Smith had a plain face and a plain name, but his arrogance and deviousness were far from ordinary. Men, unlike women, were repelled by him: Caroline Thornhill's father disliked the Cockney on sight for he hardly cut a dashing figure, he had only the roughest of educations and never seemed to lose the whining, squeezed-out vowels of his native East End. Indeed, most men found him a vulgar nonentity. 'Just like any butcher,' was one detective's blunt appraisal. But by now George Smith had spent most of his life in and out of jail, imprisoned for theft and receiving stolen goods. In 1897, after another brush with the law, he stepped through the gate at Wormwood Scrubs Prison and drew his first breath of freedom for nearly a year.

Initially Smith travelled to Leicester where he opened a bread shop at 25 Russell Square under the name of George Oliver Love. His white baker's coat (he had used the alias 'Baker' before), his military bearing and bristling ginger moustache, became his 'ghillie suit', his fake mask, for he looked every inch the respectable turn-of-the-century shopkeeper, earnest and anxious to oblige. Nothing about his appearance, or his history of petty crime, betrayed the ruthlessness he was to display over the next years, for his greed was to drive him on to become the most reviled murderer of his day. However, at some point from behind his counter, Mr Love's beady eye fell on eighteen-year-old Caroline Thornhill, a friend of one of his shop girls. Within a matter of weeks he had wooed her, then, on 17 January 1898, to the shock and horror of her parents, they married.

At around the same time, his bakery business went bust, so 'George Love', with his bewildered new wife in tow, returned to London, promising her a belated honeymoon. But it turned out to be nothing of the sort. On their arrival in the capital, he set her to work as a housemaid. While most of England was celebrating Queen Victoria's sixtieth year on the throne, Smith, alias 'Baker', alias 'Love', had other things on his mind: how he was going to maintain a life of womanising and laziness. And this point it is worth pausing for a moment to look at marriage and sex for the Victorian middle-class woman as this particular subject truly does show Smith's victimology at work.

Lie back and think of England.

QUEEN VICTORIA (ALLEGEDLY), COUNSEL TO A
YOUNG WOMAN AFTER SHE HAD EXPRESSED FEARS
BEFORE HER WEDDING NIGHT

Most middle-class women during the Victorian era married by the time they were twenty-five: the ideal age to commit oneself to matrimony being five years earlier, which Caroline Thornhill was now approaching. If women had not managed to attract a husband by the age of thirty, they were well and truly on their way to being left on the top shelf, so to speak.

At the time, marriage for the woman was usually very much a case of giving up the little independence she had in order to become her husband's 'servant'. It was also a means of getting financial security. An 1843 article in *The Magazine of Domestic Economy* advised: ' . . . to sell one's independence for gold is repugnant to all correct feeling. It is too often done, notwithstanding that unhappiness is the secret if evident result.'

The husband-to-be did not, however, go into marriage offering all material goods and getting nothing in return because the bride's father would often give his daughter a dowry amounting to no more than his eldest son-in-law's future income for one year. In other words, Caroline's father literally paid George Smith to take his daughter off of his hands. It was something that he'd live to regret.

In Victorian times, as distasteful as it would be today, a woman, once married, found she had no rights. Property and independence were forfeited. She had to obey her husband, and if she failed to do so, she could even face a beating. Many women were no more than 'possessions' for their spouses to treat as they sought fit. And their possessions – or, at least, their money – belonged to the husband. Such attitudes continued into the early twentieth century, and George Joseph Smith was not slow to see the financial advantages to marriage.

With Caroline now ensconced as a housemaid in an upper-middle-class home, Smith soon realised, however, that the meagre earnings of a servant girl were insufficient to support the kind of lifestyle he had in mind. Drastic measures were called for. Caroline was to start stealing from her employers: jewellery; silver; anything valuable; anything in fact that could be pawned. And, true to her Victorian matrimonial duties, Caroline Love received her orders meekly, obediently and without question, but soon she would come unstuck after their illicit activities took them from London to the fashionable, and wealthy, resorts along the south coast.

Using forged references provided by her husband, the couple flitted from town to town as Caroline moved from job to job. From glittering Brighton to the more sedate Hove, from Hove to Hastings, from Hastings to Eastbourne where their scheme went awry. A pawnbroker became suspicious when she tried to hock some silver cutlery stolen from the house where she worked. Waiting for her to come outside with a wad of notes was Smith – then along came a constable, for, unlike today, a police officer could be found on almost every street corner. Ever the dutiful husband, George Love himself bolted when he saw the game was up, and was safely on a train to London by the time his young bride was being locked up for the night in a police cell.

A teary-eyed, twenty-year-old Caroline appeared in the police court at Eastbourne the following morning.

Although it was said in her defence that she was completely dominated by her husband (the real instigator of the theft), she was sent to prison for a year. The shock and the ignominy brought her to her senses with a jolt, and she resolved to cut herself loose from the clutches of her cowardly husband. But 'George Love' had plans of his own. With his wife behind bars and safely out of the way, back in London he took rooms at a boarding house, and in order to live there rent free, he also took the unusual step of bigamously marrying his landlady. 'He had an extraordinary power over me,' she explained later. 'The power lay in his eyes. When he looked at you, you had the feeling that you were being magnetised.'

Treacle is sweet, but revenge is sweeter.

CAROLINE THORNHILL: TO HER HUSBAND AFTER HIS
ARREST ON 11 NOVEMBER 1900

It was karma. What goes around, comes around, for as you sow so shall you reap, and this was certainly the issue when Caroline was released from prison in the summer of 1900, for surprisingly she received a letter from her wayward husband begging her to return to him. But this would have been the last thing on her mind. She was seething with bitterness, so naturally she ignored the invitation and set about trying to pick up the pieces of her shattered.

But she had still not seen the last of him.

On a mild, sunny afternoon in November 1900, Caroline spotted her husband strolling down Oxford Street without a care in the world.

She called a constable. She told the officer that she wanted to press charges, and 'Love' was arrested on the spot. In January 1901, two days before his twenty-ninth birthday, Smith, alias Love, was back in Hastings to face a charge of receiving stolen goods – the goods for which his wife had already served a year behind bars.

Of some interest to the reader might be the MEPO 6 Habitual Criminal Register, containing the Metropolitan Police records of habitual criminals, which describes Oliver George Love, alias George Smith, alias George Baker, as: '5ft 7¾ inches tall, fair complexion, brown hair with dark green eyes. He had unspecified marks on a forearm, right hand, right nipple and on his back. His address at the time of his arrest was 23 Bridgewater Road, Croydon.' George Smith, alias Love, was sentenced to two years' hard labour. When he emerged from Lewes Gaol, it was to find that Caroline had emigrated to Canada. He would not see her again until she gave evidence against him at his trial for multiple murder most foul.

After his release from prison, Smith returned, briefly, to his London landlady and he started beating her up. 'He came home and thrashed me till I was nearly dead,' he reported later, so this liaison ended as abruptly as it had begun.

For several years, George Joseph Smith (abandoning 'Love') stalked the south of England wooing, wedding and walking out on a string of women whom he fleeced, to leave behind a litter of closed savings bank accounts. The man who was later to become the 'Brides in the Bath' murderer was, however, at this point merely sharpening and polishing his modus operandi. He, like so many emerging serial killers, was learning what worked and what didn't, and we can see this writ large through most if not all serial murderers' narratives.

The year 1908 finds this organised offender flush with £90 – a considerable sum in those days – swindled from an unsuspecting spinster in Brighton. At this juncture, he hotfooted it to Bristol where he opened a second-hand furniture shop. He then hired as housekeeper a woman called Edith Pegler, whom he married within the month.

Smith then explained to his newlywed that the business required him to travel around the country, and he managed to cover several philandering expeditions on the way. George and Edith seemed an ill-matched couple. He was now thirty-six, and quite the dapper entrepreneur in his silk topper, frock coat, a gold fob watch chain across his waistcoat and grey spats on his boots. For her part, she was twenty-eight; the homely type with a round innocent face, blue eyes and swept-up hair and almost drab in comparison with George.

Sometimes they led a nomadic life, travelling together around London and the Home Counties. There were periods spent back at their Bristol shop; and occasions when Smith was away for weeks on end, travelling alone on ill-defined 'dealing' expeditions, and, just like Caroline Thornhill, Edith had no say in anything at all.

Much later, Smith would explain away one of these extended absences by saying he had been to Canada where he had sold a Chinese idol for £1,000. Edith knew better than to ask questions. The truth, of course, was that

George Smith was living not a double life but a multiple one. Throughout his married life with Edith, one that was bigamous in any case, he maintained a bizarre lifestyle of meeting, illegally marrying and robbing a number of unsuspecting women.

One of Smith's bigamous interludes, typical of his MO and well-plotted philanderings, concerned a delicate little creature called Miss Sarah Freeman. Smith spotted her strolling along a seaside promenade while he was on a 'business trip' with Edith. Almost immediately packing Edith back off to their shop in Bristol, he introduced himself to Miss Freeman as 'George Rose', a bachelor and dealer in antiques. It took this oily conman all of four months to get Sarah up the aisle – a long siege by Smith's somewhat hastier standards – but they were finally married by special licence and, pausing only to collect Miss Freeman's belongings from her room, the couple caught a train to London.

'He knew I had fifty pounds in cash before I married him, but nothing else,' she later recalled. 'We got to lodgings at Clapham and when there I told him I had other money, as he saw my bank book while I was unpacking.'

As might be expected, Smith, alias Rose, lost no time in suggesting that Sarah should withdraw her money from the bank to set him up in business. Accordingly, within a week, his wallet was bulging with over £300 of his new bride's money and it was now the time to play his favourite, cruel card. He suggested an outing to London's National Gallery, where he sat Sarah on a bench and excused himself, saying he had to visit the lavatory.

When, an hour later, he had not returned, Sarah asked the cloakroom attendant to check for any sign of her husband. The attendant returned, shaking his head. When she arrived back at their lodgings, 'Mrs Rose' found that her husband had been back and stolen all her money, jewellery and clothes. Generous to a fault, he left behind a handful of pennies.

Smith had in fact previously pulled this vile trick on a middle-aged widow from Worthing. Having accepted his proposal of marriage in the summer of 1908, Florence Wilson cheerfully handed over twenty gold sovereigns and two large white £5 notes – almost all she had in the world. 'I'd better take care of the money for you,' said Smith, scooping it up. 'You haven't got a pocket.' Smith then suggested a visit to the popular Franco–British Exhibition at White City. He left her sitting on a seat, saying he would be back shortly. 'He went away, as I thought, to get a paper,' a dismayed and tearful Florence told the police, '. . . and I haven't seen him since.'

Although Sarah and Florence had lost everything, they had least escaped with their lives. They were among the lucky ones, for George Smith's next victim was the ill-fated Bessie Mundy.

Beatrice 'Bessie' Constance Annie Mundy: baptised in Warminster on 9 July 1875, Bessie was thirty-four and living in the Clifton suburb of Bristol when she met George Joseph Smith. Since the death of her Warminster bank manager father in 1904, she had led a solitary life living as a paying guest or at boarding houses. Her sole income (about £8 a month) came from her share of her father's estate. The executors were her uncle, Herbert Mundy, and her brother, George. The legacy amounted to over £2,500 (circa £212,000 today) but the capital was tied up in such a way as to give her the right to dispose of it only *after* her own death.

For his part, Smith felt otherwise.

Bessie appears to have been a romantically inclined, simple woman, but soon what dreams she may have had were shattered, for after only a few weeks of marriage – the ceremony had taken place on 26 August 1910, in Weymouth – her husband, a Londoner calling himself 'Mr Henry Williams', and describing himself as 'picture restorer and the son of a commercial traveller', had, on 13 September, suddenly walked out of their lodgings at 14 Rodwell Avenue, Weymouth, taking with him all of her cash. Worse still was the note he had left her.

> Dearest,
> . . . I have caught from you a disease which is called the 'Bad Disorder'. . . I don't wish to say that you have had bad connections with another man and caught it from him. But it is either that or not keeping yourself clean.

Never one to let grass grow under his feet, even before the wedding ceremony at Weymouth Registry Office, Smith had succeeded in learning the secrets of Miss Mundy's financial affairs. They had been to a solicitor whom Smith had instructed to apply to the Mundy's family lawyer for copies of the father's will, the settlement and quite obviously, the list of investments. On this, and similar occasions later, it was Smith who did all the talking, for Miss Mundy always appeared perfectly willing to leave the conduct of her affairs to him. This was the way it was back then.

By the time the documents arrived, Smith had changed his solicitor. He next wrote to Bessie's uncle suggesting that the sum due on the investments should be sent by money order and not cheques. Eventually, £135 2s.11d. – the accumulated interest on the investments – was sent, and this amount Smith received from the solicitor in cash.

Smith then returned home alone and asked the landlady of the lodgings where they were staying if a telegram had arrived for him. She gave him one that he had sent to himself. Looking pensively at the telegram he told her that he had been called to London on 'urgent special business', and asked her to let his wife know that he would return on the following Monday. He added that his wife would get her cheque at midday and that she would pay the rent and anything else owing.

In the afternoon a registered envelope arrived enclosing two letters from Smith: one to the landlady and her husband, the other to Miss Mundy. The first stated that he did not know when he would be back and asked them to look after his wife. The second letter, quoted above, informed Bessie that she had made him ill with a venereal disease, that he was going to London to seek treatment, which would be very expensive, and that he would be away a long time. He also told her what to do in the event of her uncle calling and asking about the money which had been received and which Smith had gone off with. She was to say she had put it in her leather bag, had gone to the beach, fallen asleep, and had awakened to find the bag had been stolen.

'If you do not carry out every word of my advice you will cause a lot of trouble,' added Smith. 'The whole affair will be in the police court, and you may bring disgrace upon yourself and your relations.'

Bessie was then instructed to take the letter, tear it in pieces and throw it away. All the details were repeated two or three times and underlined, as if the writer were informing a child. That was what Smith thought of the intelligence of Miss Mundy. Apparently she obeyed his instructions. She also continued to endure loneliness, which was to end only in disaster.

Eighteen months later, on 14 March 1912, Bessie was strolling along the esplanade at Weston-super-Mare. In a week or two, the sandy beaches would be teeming with Easter holidaymakers, but now the town was empty and bleak.

Suddenly she stopped short. In front of her was a lone figure standing at the promenade rail. She approached, scarcely knowing whether to believe her eyes. 'Henry?' she ventured. The man turned quickly. It was indeed the man she knew as Henry Williams, who was, in fact, George Joseph Smith.

'My dearest Bessie!' he cried. 'I've been searching the country for you. It was all a terrible mistake . . . I can explain.' There was much explaining (lying) to do. Why had he abandoned her? Where had he been? What had he done with her money? Of course Smith hadn't been searching the country for her at all; he had known full well where to find her.

'Williams' took her by the arm, sat her down on a promenade bench and begged forgiveness. They talked for two hours. His explanation was straightforward. Lying his back teeth out, he said that he had thought, mistakenly, that he had contracted VD. He had decided to do the honourable thing and left home, rather than risk passing it on to her. As for the missing money (£150), well, he had spent twelve miserable months searching for her in 'every town in England'. One of her relations (he was not definite as to which), had mentioned Weston-super-Mare. Instead of calling a constable and having him arrested, Bessie forgave him and they returned to her lodgings. The landlady, Mrs Sarah Tuckett, an acquaintance of Bessie's aunt, was sceptical about George Williams's story, seeing through the man immediately, and wired Bessie's aunt. The reunited couple moved out at once.

The following day, Smith fired off an indignant letter to Mrs Tuckett, essentially accusing her of interfering and wishing to cause strife, adding: '…the past is forgiven and forgotten. Life after all is not finished yet … I trust there are many many years of happiness before us.'

Smith now played a bold move. Together the couple visited a solicitor and fed him a carefully concocted story, in the details of which Smith had already coached Bessie. The money he had previously stolen from her was now a 'loan' advanced by her to pay debts he had contracted before he had met her. He had been mistaken about his 'illness' and was once more reconciled to his wife, and they hoped to live 'happily ever after'.

Although considering this a somewhat curiously lopsided arrangement, since 'Mr Williams' was virtually penniless, while his wife was worth over £2,500, the solicitor received these details in good faith and passed them on to Bessie's brother, Herbert. Moreover, Smith himself wrote to her uncle, stating that, 'with the help of the higher powers which have reunited us twice, Bessie shall have a comfortable settled home with me.' Apparently this fairy tale was believed, and the couple went to live together at Herne Bay in Kent, where they rented a small house at 80 High Street (now No, 159). Outside, he fixed a brass plate: H. WILLIAMS, ART DEALER. PICTURES, CHINA, COINS AND ANTIQUE FURNITURE, ETC BOUGHT.

But the 'many many years of happiness' were not to be. Smith soon set about achieving the object he had in view, which was to obtain possession of the whole of Bessie's property. He made inquiries of a solicitor, and even took counsel's opinion as to the possibilities of having the settlement revoked. The advice given was that it was probable that the trustees could defeat his aims (which proved to be correct), so he proceeded to adopt another, more summary, method. He persuaded Bessie to make a will, and he did the same, each bequeathing their sole possessions to the other – that, unlike her, he had as good as no possessions does not seem to have worried her.

Although the house was pleasant enough, they had been living for some time without a bath. In those days, unless one was better heeled, baths were few and far between. So, in July, when he saw a second-hand bath at an ironmonger's, Adolphus Hill, in the High Street, for the price of £2 he expressed an interest in buying it. Two days later, he sent Bessie there to knock the price down to £1 17s, 6d., which she did, and it was delivered shortly thereafter, before any money had changed hands.

The following day, Williams took Bessie to see young Dr Frank French at his surgery. Here, Williams explained that his wife had blacked out during an epileptic fit. The inexperienced doctor was puzzled. Bessie seemed perfectly well and had no history of fits. He suggested a sedative of bromide of potassium which he made up there and then. But in the early hours of Friday, 12 July, Williams was back at the surgery, hammering on the door and shouting that his wife had had a second fit. It was a sticky night, and the doctor found Bessie in bed in her nightdress. Her hands were moist and clammy, but Dr French put this down to the weather. Again the doctor was perplexed. People with fits often bite their tongue, but Bessie's tongue showed no bite marks. He took Williams back to the surgery and made up a second bottle of sedative.

That afternoon, Dr French again saw the couple at his surgery. Bessie seemed in perfect health, complaining only of being rather run down, indeed, even Smith agreed she looked much better. That evening, she sat down and penned a letter to her uncle, saying, 'I had a bad fit . . . I have made my Will and left all to my husband. That is only natural as I love my husband . . .'

Dr French was getting dressed the following morning

when at 8 a.m. a short note was delivered. 'Do come at once. I am afraid my wife is dead.' Dr French hurried the few hundred yards to Williams's house, where, in the middle of an upstairs room stood a bath, three-parts full of tepid water. Bessie's naked body was lying in it, face up, mouth and nose submerged. The legs were straight out from the hips, the feet being against the narrow end of the bath. A bar of soap was clutched in her right hand. Williams explained that he had gone out to buy herrings for breakfast. Upon his return, his wife was dead.

The verdict at the inquest was death by misadventure, but ...

... If, however, anyone who had taken the trouble to measure the bath and then compare it with the measurements of the deceased woman, a different conclusion might have been reached. Assuming the husband was fond of his wife – and there is no evidence as to the contrary, but a great deal of evidence that he was – it was a terrible blight.

MR WILLIAM RUTLEY MOWLL, CORONER FOR EAST
KENT, AT BESSIE MUNDY'S INQUEST

With poor Bessie drowned aged thirty-seven, Smith was quick to move on. Before her family had a chance to intervene, he had her buried in a public grave. He sold their furniture back to the original seller, and asked the ironmonger to take back the bath – which he had in any case not got round to paying for – and inherited all Bessie's money (in the region of £150,000 today).

Somewhat ironically, the site of the rented house, 80 High Street, at which 'Mr and Mrs Williams' lived, and where poor Bessie met her end, since renumbered no. 159, the property long ago demolished – is now occupied by a shop called Custom Kitchens & Bathrooms Ltd. Bessie was buried in an unmarked grave in Herne Bay Cemetery, which is also the final resting place of Detective Inspector Edmund John James Reid, who, as head of the CID in the Metropolitan Police's 'H' Division at the time, led enquiries into the Whitechapel murders of Jack the Ripper in 1888.

Alice Burnham: in 1913, the plump and lively twenty-five-year-old daughter of Charles Burnham, a wealthy Buckinghamshire fruit farmer, was working as a private nurse looking after an invalid in Portsmouth. She was also a supporter of the suffragette movement.

For his part, Smith had recently purchased seven houses in Bristol, for which he'd paid £2,180 out of the proceeds of Bessie's money, and here we find him strolling nonchalantly along Southsea's promenade, on the lookout for single young women. Posing as 'a bachelor of independent means', now in his forties, and exuding a certain winning worldliness, he introduced himself to the ladies along the seafront as George Joseph Smith. He had not been in Southsea long when he met Alice, and within a matter of days he had swept her off her feet, marrying her, bigamously, on Tuesday, 4 November 1913 in Portsmouth. Several days later he had his new bride's life insured for £500, had wheedled money out of her savings account into his, and then, in early December, persuaded her to make a will in his favour. Almost immediately thereafter he began to bombard her relations with peremptory demands for the delivery of the money her father was holding on her behalf.

Wishing to leave Southsea for somewhere far from the location of Bessie's demise, Smith had chosen to take his new wife to Blackpool, but in his haste neglected to book accommodation in advance, so when the couple arrived they had to trudge the cold streets in search of somewhere to stay. Smith – for reasons known only to himself – was particularly concerned that his new bride should enjoy the luxury of a bath. He stressed that because she was a nurse she was very particular about her personal hygiene. After a while, they were directed to a Mrs Crossley's lodgings at 16 Regent Road (the property still exists very much as it was back then, now called, somewhat grandiosely, the Royale Hotel). Here, during the evening of 10 December, they took a week's let on a bedsitting room with the use of a bathroom for the sum of ten shillings. That first night they went out. Regent Road joins Church Street and from there it is a short walk to the Promenade passing the Winter Gardens en route. At the Promenade the pier and Blackpool Tower are within easy walking distance. The next day they went out to buy chops for lunch. In those days guests would buy their own food with the landlady preparing it. George bought chops. They had lunch at 1p.m. and as Alice felt slightly unwell they went to see a Dr Billing who prescribed for her headache and stomach cramp. They returned to their lodgings with butter and milk for their tea and, in the evening, they went to the cinema. Alice then wrote a postcard home telling her mother that she was suffering from bad headaches.

On Friday, 12 December, the couple had a breakfast of bacon. They bought stewing steak for lunch, which they had at one o'clock. They went out and returned at 5 p.m. for tea. Alice went for her bath while Margaret, her daughter Alice and her son-in-law Joseph (also Crossley) sat down for a meal.

By now, all of her money, amounting to something over £100.00, had passed into Smith's possession who had promptly insured Alice's life for £500 under an endowment policy. His carefully trap was ready to be sprung.

This is the greatest and most cruel shock that ever a man could have suffered. Word cannot describe my feelings.

GEORGE SMITH, IN A LETTER TO ALICE
BURNHAM'S MOTHER

As the Crossley family were eating their meal in their kitchen one of them noticed a big patch of water on the ceiling. It grew larger and dripped down the wall. They knew that Mrs Smith was having a bath in the room above, and there was some discussion as to who should go up and investigate. At that moment, George Smith came in and placed a paper bag on the table. 'I've bought these eggs for our breakfast in the morning,' he said, and went upstairs. Moments later, he appeared on the landing shouting to Mrs Crossley to fetch the doctor. 'My wife cannot speak to me,' he exclaimed. Dr Billing was called, and he found Smith in the bathroom supporting Alice's head as she lay in the tepid soapy water. Both men then pumped her chest in an effort to revive her but it was too late. She was gone.

Although it was not measured at the time, the bath in which Alice met her death was 5 feet 3 inches long, and 2 feet 3 inches across at its widest point, and, as the doctor noticed, her head was at the narrow end. She was a rather stout woman, and to him it was quite impossible that she could have sat in the bath and drowned as she was found. At the other end, which was wider and sloping, there was some of her hair. This indicated that her head had been there previously. Despite the doctor's reservations, an inquest was hurriedly convened, and within thirty minutes just as hurriedly concluded: 'The deceased suffered from heart disease, and was found drowned in a hot bath, probably through being seized with a fit or faint. The cause of death was accidental.'

The next morning saw George Smith arranging the cheapest possible funeral at Layton Cemetery. At 11.30 a.m. he sent a telegram to Alice's family advising them of the sad news. Her mother and brother Norman immediately started a journey to Blackpool to see if they could arrange a more fitting interment. This came as a bit of a shock to George Smith because the undertaker, John Hargreaves, said that it could be arranged but would mean postponing the funeral from Monday to Tuesday.

On the Monday, Hargreaves took the coffin to the mortuary at Layton Cemetery and placed Alice in it, screwed down the lid and a brief service was held at the cemetery's chapel, after which George Smith hurried off to get a train, having promised Alice's mother that he would send on Alice's clothes . . . then he stepped out of their lives.

Smith had not had a happy relationship with his in-laws. Charles, Alice's father, had taken a particular dislike to him from the outset. He regarded him as a spiv and a fortune hunter. Alice loved her family but was firm in her desire to marry George. She claimed to her family that she had met George at a Congregationalist Service, which was completely false. Nevertheless, Charles Burnham was so seriously alarmed by Smith, he hired a detective to look into him, and he tried to withhold money to which Alice was entitled. Smith was not conciliatory. When his father-in-law sent him a letter asking about his background he wrote back:

Sir
In answer to your application regarding my parentage etc. My mother was a Buss Horse, my Father a Cab Driver, my sister a Rough Rider over the Arctic Regions. My Brothers were all gallant sailors in a Steam roller . . . Your despised Son-in-law, G. Smith.

It will come as no surprise to the reader to learn that once again the drowned bride was given the cheapest possible funeral and her body, like Bessie's', put in a pauper's grave with no headstone of flowers. Her estate – willed entirely to George Joseph Smith – was worth £600, and he returned to Miss Pegler in Bristol. This time his excuse for being away for so long was that he had been to Spain, had picked up a lot of jewellery for which he hoped to get £200.

It is a measure of Smith's psychopathic traits that he was incapable of grasping natural human feelings or emphasising with people. Mrs Crossley, no admirer of his, refused to let him stay in the house with his dead wife: 'Because I won't have a callous man like you in the house', because, she said 'he did not seem to worry at all'. He went on to upset her son-in-law when he dismissed the minimal funeral arrangements he'd made with the words 'When they are dead they are done with.' And the formidable-sounding secretary of the owner of the house rented by Smith and Bessie Mundy, Miss Rapley, who had been in the job a long time and had seen all sorts of humanity – and was generally deemed unshockable – *was* shocked when in the middle of an outburst of unconvincing grief and tears for Bessie, Smith suddenly remarked, 'Was it not a jolly good job I got her to make a will?' For his part, he seemed unable to comprehend that he'd said anything unacceptable.

Smith's next seaside conquest was a servant girl called Alice Reavil. He spotted her listening to the band in Bournemouth's Winter Gardens. It was September 1914, a few weeks after the outbreak of the First World War. 'We had some conversations,' Alice later recalled, 'in which he admired my figure.' Less than a week passed and she agreed to marry him, believing him to be 'Charles Oliver James' with a private income from '. . . some land in Canada'. The wedding took place in the Woolwich Register Office, and once again this was Smith's cue to act.

Announcing that he planned to open an antique shop, Smith persuaded Alice to draw all her savings out of the post office in order to help finance it. She later told police, '. . . in all I received £76 6s. and some coppers. He picked up the notes and I had the cash – the odd six shillings. I never saw the notes again.'

She also handed over £14, the proceeds of selling the few small items of furniture she owned. That evening, Smith ordered all their belongings to be loaded onto a barrow and removed from their lodgings, telling Alice that they needed to move to new accommodation the next day. The following morning, he took his new bride for an outing to a nearby park. They sat down a bench. Then Smith excused himself, saying he needed to go to the lavatory. Alice never saw him again. 'I was left with only a few shillings and the clothes I was actually wearing,' she later explained.

Margaret Elizabeth 'Peggy' Lofty, at the time of her meeting George Joseph Smith, her marriage and her murder was thirty-eight years old.

Born on 12 November 1876, at Monk Sherborne, Hampshire, the daughter of the late Reverend and Mrs Lofty, she had held down a number of jobs as a lady's companion in Bristol. A broken love affair in the summer of 1914, with a man whom she discovered was married, had left her depressed, so she moved to Bath to live with her mother and sisters. She met Smith in Bristol where he was masquerading as an estate agent. He introduced himself as 'John Arthur Lloyd' aged thirty-eight (he was forty-two).

No doubt you will be surprised to know that I was married today to a gentleman named John Lloyd ... He is such a nice man ...

MARGARET LOFTY IN A LETTER TO HER
FAMILY, 17 DECEMBER 1914

The wedding ceremony had been performed on 17 December 1914, at Bath Register Office. They gave their address as Dalkeith House, 4 Stanley Road West, in Bath – Bath of all places . . . perhaps a coincidence, perhaps a sardonic choice by Smith. When the service was over, however, the couple left Bath and travelled by train to London where they found rooms at 14 Bismarck Road, in Highgate. The property has long been demolished and was replaced by what is now called 'The Archway'.

At about 7 p.m. on the couple's full day, the landlady, Miss Louisa Blatch, boiled up a huge copper of water for 'Mrs Lloyd's' bath. 'I heard someone go upstairs,' she said later. 'I was ironing in the kitchen when I heard the sound of splashing. Then there was a noise as of someone putting wet hands or arms on the side of the bath ... then there was a sigh.' Miss Blatch pressed on with her ironing. Then came another sound – the sound of music, swelling and filling the house. It was 'Mr Lloyd' seated at the organ in the sitting room, playing a hymn. She recognised the melody at once; it was 'Nearer My God to Thee'. 'I thought it sounded beautiful,' she remembered.

The music stopped, and Miss Blatch heard the front door slam. A few minutes later, the doorbell rang. It was Mr Lloyd, grinning sheepishly and saying that he had forgotten he had a key. He indicated a paper bag, saying he had slipped out to buy some tomatoes for his wife's supper. 'I'll go up and ask her if she'd like them now,' he said, starting up the stairs and calling out Margaret's name. But there was no answer. In the bath, her lips blue and swollen, Margaret, the bride of just one day, lay drowned.

This alibi of going out to buy something just before the discovery of a dead body was repeated in all the murders; with Bessie Mundy at Herne Bay you will recall it was fish – herring to be precise.

With Alice Burnham at Blackpool, it was eggs.

Now with Margaret Lofty, in London, it was tomatoes. The day after the death, the 'widower' deposited a small parcel at the Highgate Hill branch of the South Western Bank. It contained the will of Miss Lofty along with an insurance policy on her life to the tune of £700.

After yet another haggle with an undertaker about the price of the funeral, Smith managed to knock nearly a pound off the original quotation and buried Margaret in a common grave for the princely sum of £6 10s. Snatching up the receipt, he muttered: 'Thank goodness that is all over.' When the undertaker asked him if would like to see the body before the coffin was closed, Smith replied 'No. Get on with it. Screw it down.' A day or two later he attended the opening of the inquest, but the hearing had to be adjourned because one of the witnesses was ill. Directly after, Smith returned to Bristol to join Edith Pegler for Christmas. He was characteristically mean in his choice of gift for Edith, presenting her with one of Margaret Lofty's dresses, straight from her trousseau.

According the website 'Find a Grave', Margaret was buried on Wednesday, 23 December 1914, in a common grave with about a dozen other people. There is no marker and, indeed, the precise location has been lost to memory. However, it would have been 'Plot 0/20045' on the north side of Withington Road, just east of the junction with Randall's Path and Lower Road.

This proved to be the last of Smith's 'marriages'. On 27 December 1914, the *News of the World* carried the following report.

FOUND DEAD IN BATH
BRIDE'S TRAGIC FATE ON DAY AFTER WEDDING

Particularly sad circumstances under which a bride of a day met her death were investigated at an Islington inquest on Margaret Elizabeth Lloyd, thirty-eight, wife of a land agent of Holloway.

The husband said he was married to the deceased at Bath. After travelling to London she complained of headache and giddiness, and he took her to a medical man, who prescribed for her. The following morning she said she felt much better, and during the day she went out shopping. At 7.30 that evening she said she would have a bath, and she then appeared cheerful.

A quarter of an hour later witness [John Lloyd] went out, and returned at quarter past eight, expecting to see her in the sitting room. As she was not there he enquired of the landlady, and they went to the bathroom which was in darkness.

He lit the gas, and then found his wife under the water, the bath being three parts full. The next day witness found a letter among deceased clothing but there was nothing in it to suggest that she was likely to take her own life.

Dr Bates said death was due to asphyxia from drowning. Influenza, together with a hot bath, might have caused an attack of syncope.

This story was seen and read by thousands of families all over Britain. But in two particular homes the report sounded a particularly ominous note of alarm.

At his fruit farm in Buckinghamshire, Mr Charles Burnham, father of the late Alice, read it over breakfast. So did a Mr William Haynes, two hundred miles away in Blackpool. In a moment, Mr Haynes, friend and neighbour of the Crossleys, was knocking at their door. All were struck by the similarity of the brides' demise and, it is believed, both Joseph Crossley and Mr Burnham sent cuttings of the inquest report to the police.

Alerted by letters and enclosed newspaper cuttings from Blackpool and Buckinghamshire, the Metropolitan Police at Scotland Yard appointed Detective Inspector Arthur Neil to investigate the suspected link between the cases of Margaret Lofty and Alice Burnham.

On a snow-covered New Year's Day, 1915, the inquest into Margaret Lofty's death resumed and the jury returned a verdict of accidental death. Three days later, her husband – still posing as John Lloyd – called at a solicitor's office in Uxbridge Road, Shepherd's Bush, London. Armed with the dead woman's will, her life insurance policy and the marriage certificate, he instructed the lawyer to obtain probate (the official certificate stating a will to be genuine). From the upstairs window of a pub across the road, detectives kept watch. They continued to do so for nearly a month, for 'Mr Lloyd' was calling almost daily in his anxiety to collect the proceeds of his late bride's will and insurance.

> Smith? I'm not Smith. I don't know what you are talking about.
>
> SMITH TO DI ARTHUR NEIL ON BEING ARRESTED

On Monday, 1 February, as Smith left the solicitor's office, DI Neil stepped forward. 'Are you John Lloyd?' the officer asked.

Smith, alias Lloyd, replied, 'Yes.'

'You were married to Margaret Elizabeth Lofty at Bath on December the seventeenth?'

'Yes, quite so!' Smith said.

DI Neil then arrested Smith on a holding charge of making a false entry on his marriage certificate. The charge read: 'Causing a false entry relating to marriage between himself as John Lloyd and Margaret Elizabeth Lofty, at the Registry Office, Bath, on December 17 last.'

You may as well hang me at once, the way you are going on. Get on, hang me at once and be done with it. I have done no murder. It's a disgrace to a Christian country, this is. I am not a murder, though I may be a bit peculiar.

GEORGE JOSEPH SMITH AT HIS TRIAL

The trial of George Joseph Smith opened at the Old Bailey on Tuesday, 22 June 1915. After what is commonly called 'a sensational trial', he was found guilty of murder on Thursday, 1 July. His appeal was dismissed on Tuesday, 27 July.

Smith, protesting his innocence all the while, was inconsolable during his last days, and his ginger-brown hair turned white. But when he wrote to his faithful Edith Pegler for the last time, on 9 August 1915, this extract shows him at his most self-serving and morally bigoted best:

. . . I have not asked for a reprieve, nor made a petition and do not intend doing so . . . My property I give to you. Don't be alone on the last day, when I shall have left this weary ark behind, where perjury, malice, spite, vindictiveness, prejudices and all other earthly ills will have done its best and can harm me no more. My time is occupied in solemn and deep meditation. May an old age, serene and bright, and as lovely as a Lapland night lead thee to thy grave . . . now, my true love, goodbye until we meet again.

Yours, with immortal love, George.

There was no black flag or tolling of the bell when he was executed at Maidstone Prison on Friday, 13 August, that same year. He refused to make a confession. On the contrary, his last words as he plunged to his doom, were: 'I'm innocent.'

Thus died one of the most evil killers ever known in the UK. While at Maidstone Prison, his behaviour was exemplary, and he was very popular with the officials. The chaplain spoke very highly of him and did all in his power to persuade him to confess – pleas that fell upon deaf ears. The governor also had a good opinion of him, and said that he was above the average intelligence, and an 'interesting talker'.

At first he would have nothing to do with religion but Smith was eventually confirmed by the Bishop of Croydon; however, when he was given a Bible and a prayer book, he handed them both back and said:

'I don't want this and I don't want that. Send them to the detectives at Scotland Yard. They have far more use for them than I have.'

According to the hangman, John Ellis, George Joseph Smith died 'game, without the slightest fear'.

In itself the history of Maidstone Prison, where a total of fifty-eight hangings took place, between the prison's opening, in 1819, and 1930, is a riveting subject. Visitors now learn that the execution building was later used as a dog handler unit and the condemned cell area is now the reception centre. The gallows were taken down and placed in oiled cloth and kept in a cellar area under one of the cellblocks – apparently remaining there to this day.

GEORGE JOSEPH SMITH: A VERY 'FATAL ATTRACTION'

In 1885, builders carrying out renovation work in the prisoners' visiting hall uncovered human remains around the building, apparently of executed prisoners who were buried in boreholes. And, of course, Maidstone Prison has its resident Grey Lady ghost too. Over the years, several of the officers have been startled by unexplained happenings and sightings of the ghostly figure, several doors that were open suddenly slamming shut, although there'd be no wind, no other natural conditions present that would explain what had happened, and I have no inclination to spend a night there to try to find out why.

> He mentioned to me once – just after last Christmas – that he would not have much to do with bathrooms if he were me, as they were dangerous.
>
> EDITH PEGLER, AT SMITH'S TRIAL

Aside from the drug cartels and their bosses who order murders, rarely do we find a male serial murderer killing just for financial gain, but this seems to have been Smith's sole motive, even though multiple bigamy might at the time have suggested otherwise. The only financial-gain offender that I have had personal experience of is John Martin Scripps, who rather horribly murdered at least three people, then appropriated their funds. His last three murders were carried out in Singapore and in Thailand. He was arrested by Singapore police, tried and condemned to death; I interviewed him while he was in prison before his execution in 1995.

The other highly unusual feature of Smith is that, as far

as I can determine, he is the first serial killer in history to use a bath as a means to commit homicide. (Scripps chose a more grisly method, and having knocked out his victims with a stun gun, used a a hammer to kill his prey and then butchered the bodies.) In Smith's case, for the police at the time the puzzling aspect to what was almost certainly a crime was the lack of evidence of a struggle. Sir Bernard Spilsbury, the renowned pathologist, was consulted, and the bodies exhumed. In all three cases, the victims seemed to have been in generally good health, and death seemed to have been almost instantaneous – this, allied to the lack of evidence of a major struggle, led some to consider that the victims had been hypnotised into acquiescence – until experts pointed out that it is not possible to hypnotise someone into doing something that would endanger their life.

After considerable thought, Spilsbury came up with a plan, and under his guidance Inspector Neil persuaded a woman of his acquaintance, an experienced swimmer who was accustomed to having her head under water, to take part in an experiment. Dressed of course in her swimming costume, she climbed into a bath full of warm water; Neil then tried pushing her head under water and although the woman knew he had no murderous intentions she immediately began struggling violently and it was clear that this struggle would leave signs. After a few more attempts and having allowed the woman time to recover, he tried again. But this time, as Spilsbury had suggested, Neil suddenly and unexpectedly took hold of her feet and pulled sharply. The woman's head immediately slid quietly under water. As all present stared at her, they realised that she was not moving and hastily lifted her out and onto the floor. It took Neil and a doctor over half an hour to revive her. When she came to, she told them that the only thing she remembered was the rush of water before she lost consciousness. Spilsbury's theory was proved, and on this evidence Smith was convicted of the three murders.

Since then there have been a number of cases where men have been convicted of killing their victim by drowning in a bathtub, notably the murder of twenty-four-year-old Sarah Widmer committed by her husband, Ryan, on 11 August 2008, at their home in Hamilton Township, Ohio. Widmer was sentenced to fifteen years to life imprisonment and at the time of writing he is appealing his conviction.

This case is particularly interesting and fuller details of his account of what happened can be found on the internet, all of which bears a striking resemblance to the excuses made by George Smith.

According to Dr D. Rhoades, Advocate Lutheran General Hospital in Park Ridge, Illinois:

Those with seizure disorders need to be especially cautious when taking baths... For those with seizure disorders, drowning is the most common cause of unintentional injury or death, and the bathtub is the location where most of these accidental drownings occur.

KATE ELLER, WRITING IN *HEALTH ENEWS*, 2018

As previously noted, in the early twentieth century fitted bathrooms were still the exception in many lower-class homes. Even where baths were in place, they often lacked built-in plumbing and had to be filled with pans of hot water. For many people, a weekly wash meant sitting in a tin bath in the back of the kitchen with little if any privacy – all of which would not have suited Smith's method of killing one bit. The Herne Bay bath was 5 feet long, but it narrowed to 13½ inches at the tap end. The Blackpool bath, with a width at the narrow end of just a foot, was an even tighter fit – hardly large enough to accommodate the buxom Alice Burnham even at a tight squeeze, and this alone *should* have aroused strong suspicions from the outset.

Having now established that George Smith's sole motive was one of financial gain, now is the time to examine his victimology: the study of victimisation, including the psychological effects on victims, relationships between victims and offenders – for this tells us much about this killer's MO: his victim selection, his hunting grounds and where he was most comfortable and thus best placed to snare his prey. The seaside resort was well suited to Smith's motive (finding and 'marrying' gullible women of means) because for both sexes the annual seaside holiday was a release from the daily grind and rigid convention – before the First World War more for the well-to-do than today.

Seaside resorts – back then called 'watering places' – had become fashionable in the mid-eighteenth century. The whimsical Sir John Floyer and Edward Baynard, London-based medical practitioners, published praises of the cures effected by seawater bathing: asthma, cancer, consumption, deafness, ruptures, rheumatism and madness were just some of the 'diseases' and ailments it could banish. Carried away with enthusiasm, the distinguished medical men almost burst into this verse, with:

> Cold bathing has this cure alone:
> It makes old John to hug old Joan ...
> And does fresh kindness entail
> On a wife tasteless, old and stale.

The prospect of renewed sexual vitality has always been the surest guarantee of any cure's success. Bathing machines were introduced in 1735 and, by the 1770s and into the twentieth century, many glittering seaside resorts, such as Brighton, Bournemouth, Southsea, Weston-super-Mare, Hastings, Eastbourne, attracted thousands of visitors, with the more prudish using these strange contraptions.

While it has to be said that the Victorians may have created Britain's seaside towns, it was the Edwardians who gave them their distinctive, raffish air. From Brighton, with its Regency terraces and sugar-cake hotels, to the rough-and-ready delights of Blackpool, the combination of sea, sand and sex proved irresistible to the vast hordes of turn-of-the-century pleasure seekers. The railways had put the big cities and towns within easy reach of the seaside. Trains were fast and cheap: in 1901 it took about 55 minutes to make the 50-mile journey from Victoria Station to Brighton – and things have not changed today, with 55 minutes still the shortest time. Thus, the resorts expanded, and competed for custom. People packed the beaches to sit, swim, or watch a Pierrot (a type of French pantomime) or Punch and Judy shows. A penny at the turnstile purchased admission to the piers. At Weston-super-Mare, for example, there were two piers offering such attractions as a switchback, shooting gallery, flying machines, bioscope (an early form of cinema) and helter-skelter, as well as a bandstand and souvenir shops.

For reasons only known to George Smith, he chose these seaside resorts as his hunting grounds; most probably a decision he made when he first took Caroline Thornhill to Hastings where he pressed her into domestic service with the sole aim of having her pilfer anything of value she could lay her hands on. And it would have been at Hastings where he first saw 'big money' floating around. During the nineteenth and the first years of the twentieth century, many young men were emigrating to the colonies, there to make their fortunes; and then, come 1914, many were conscripted or volunteered to fight in the First World War, so there was a scarcity of eligible young men. Seaside resorts therefore saw comparatively high numbers of lonely spinsters taking in the sea air. With Caroline in jail, no longer was stealing from the wealthy an option open to Smith – he had to quickly change his modus operandi if ever his dreams of becoming rich were to be achieved. So he went on the prowl along piers and promenades for marriageable youngish ladies of independent means. Marrying money (however little there was) and then absconding with the new wife's 'fortune', worked for a bit, but, as Smith found with Bessie Mundy, there could be major snags … and then it occurred to him that taking out life insurance on his bride could add to his potential income, so a further change to his MO – ensuring he was their beneficiary should they die – was implemented.

The evidence against George Smith was overwhelming for there were no less than thirteen coincidences linking the deaths of Bessie Mundy, Alice Burnham and Margaret Lofty:

Death occurred in a bath, shortly after moving into premises.

All three bathrooms were unlocked.

The women made their wills in Smith's favour shortly before their deaths.

Smith stood to benefit, either from life insurance or from money and property willed to him, or combinations thereof.

The women had called in debts and realised the proceeds of savings and bank accounts shortly before their deaths.

Each had visited a new doctor in a strange town, complaining of mysterious ailments.

Each wrote to relatives a day or so before drowning, mentioning their ailments.

Smith alibied himself by going out to buy food for future consumption.

It was always Smith who discovered the body, then left it in situ until someone else had seen it too.

Each was a sham marriage.

Smith benefited financially by their deaths.

He buried his 'wives' as quickly and obscurely
as possible. After each murder he immediately
returned to Edith Pegler giving excuses as to his
whereabouts that could never be verified.

Smith's sex appeal was much discussed at the time of his trial. In court, the wife of one of the lawyers confessed privately that she found the defendant attractive, and the famous-in-his-day criminologist Harry Brodribb Irving (1870–1917), sitting alongside two fashionably-dressed women, was amazed to hear them vying with each other in praising the prisoner's charms. Some of the newspapers commented indignantly on the scenes at Bow Street Police Court, when Smith was almost mobbed in the dock by a crowd of eager women. At the Old Bailey, police were given special instructions to discourage women from attending the trial of this seductive killer.

For numerous women there was a 'fatal attraction' about George Smith – many of whom were mesmerised by his dark green eyes. His technique was not so much one of stalking his intended prey, for his was more of going out on 'fishing expeditions' and he knew where the women literally swam in shoals – by the seaside, of course. His was a 'numbers game' – he might approach and doff his silk topper to many a young woman; he was well dressed and complimentary, charming to a fault, yet, while many women might have returned his pleasantries with merely a demurring nod, the odds were in his favour that one of these little fishes would soon bite, his bait being the attractive, glittering lure of 'hope' cast out on a line of smooth chat. In this respect we can see how many young women were attracted to him as moths to a deadly flame.

Smith was obsessed with the idea of making money at the expense of other people, but he was unskilled in handling it. Even when he reaped the proceeds of murder – he received £2,500 in Bessie's killing alone, which was more than the average working man earned in a decade – he managed to squander it in a series of incompetent business and property deals. In the course of his criminal career, he acquired a total of nearly a dozen properties. He should have been a wealthy man, but he mismanaged his affairs so badly that he made a loss on each of them – over £700 in all. Smith's trouble was that he was out of his depth in complicated financial matters. He failed in the buying and selling of property, so he bought an annuity designed to yield over £70 a year. But when he changed his mind, he found that the money could not be released, so he turned to insurance fraud, collecting on the death of Alice Burnham and planning to do likewise in the case of Margaret Lofty. In the end, murder only produced a negative profit for George Joseph Smith. His venal mean-mindedness, arrogance and stupidity, sealed his fate.

12

Internet Homicide: Spinning a Web

O, what a tangled web we weave when
first we practise to deceive!
Sir Walter Scott (1771–1832),
'Marmion: A Tale of Flodden Field', 1808

I want to start this chapter on a high note, so congratulations, because according to *The Economist*, 12 April 2014, [I paraphrase] the 'UN Office on Drugs and Crime Report', '. . . if you are reading this book then you are not one of the circa 427,000 people whose lives have not, as yet, ended as a homicide statistic,' therefore, the other unfortunate half-million are all of those around the world slain every year, and who won't be reading this book, ever.

By my calculations, and I have never been spot-on with maths, this means that the average person, like you and me, has roughly a one-in-16,000 chance of being bumped off each year – with the odds increasing, or decreasing depending on where one lives or who one associates with.

The first trick to not prematurely finding yourself in a pine box is *not* to live in Africa or the Americas, where murder rates (one in 8,000 and one in 6,100 respectively) are more than four times as high as the rest of the world. Indeed, if you're dead keen to stay alive, I would suggest Liechtenstein. That little place rarely sees a murder in decades, though to be fair its population could easily fit into a football stadium.

The second top tip is to be (or become) a woman because your chance of being murdered, believe it or not, will be barely be a quarter what it would be if you were a man. In fact, steer clear of men altogether: nearly half of all female murder victims are killed by their partner or another (usually male) family member.

Now let's assume that you truly want to sit back, grow older, wear a bib and suck your meals through a straw. Well, from the age of thirty onwards, murder rates fall steadily in most places, but not everywhere. Europeans are more at risk in middle age than in youth. European women cannot let their guard down even in retirement: those aged over sixty are more likely to be killed off than those aged between fifteen and twenty-nine.

But, what if you *are* murdered? The chances are that no one will be convicted anyway. Worldwide, only 43 per cent of murders result in someone being locked up, for the murderer will escape justice while you have become ashes-to-ashes, or buried in a hole in the ground. The good news, however, is that serial killers are extremely few and far between. US media estimates suggest that there are in the region of 300 serial murderers active at any one time, but our American cousins are always inclined to exaggerate because the FBI say that this figure is closer to somewhere between 50 and 100 – well they would, wouldn't they?

I just don't get this at all – I mean this clamping down on gun crime in the US, thing. They bitch and moan about the church and school massacres one minute, yet allow kids to buy an arsenal of high-powered weapons – *then they want to arm the teachers*. Give me a fucking break, please! Imagine the scenario:

Good morning children and remember our motto: 'PROTECT & SERVE', so here is your new firearms tutor, Red. Ya'll remember that he and his five buddies were all over the world's media last week when our 'Boys in Blue' blasted an innocent man to death with 27 shots of red-hot .45-cal, lead when the black preacher, holding aloft a Bible, reached for a tissue to wipe his nose.

Kids, pay particular attention to the kit that Red is wearing for *your* protection today: head-to-toe black Kevlar body armour; a ski mask; .45-cal 'Dirty Harry' magnum service auto; a twelve-gauge pump; a military-issue assault rifle; 25-inch long Maglite and a large bag full of Hostess donuts. Those of you who have been to the UK will know that all of this is standard issue for Brit traffic wardens these days ...

Now, let's give Red a round of applause. He has just been promoted to captain!

Levity aside, you might want to ask yourself: 'How will I be murdered?' – not that it will matter much because, quite obviously, you won't ever be conscious after the event. However, I can assure you that in many parts of the world the majority of murders are done with a firearm – a huge sign of relief to my British readers because here, in the UK, we don't hand out guns to citizens like sweets as they do in the US. In the UK, the vast majority of killings are done with a knife, while strangulation, stabbing and bludgeoning are respectively way down the list.

But, here comes an upset. Flying in the face of the statistics produced by the aforementioned UN Office on Drugs and Crime Report, if you live in the US and are a woman, you have a slightly higher chance of being killed a man would, with serial killers choosing 51.4 per cent female victims. So, your chances of being killed by a serial murderer *are* incredibly small at less than 0.01 per cent. In fact, even with the US homicide rate of 3.9 per 1000,000, you have only got a 0.00039 per cent chance of becoming a serial killer's victim.

Now I can hear you clamouring for a few UK homicide statistics.

The bad news for men in the UK is that their murder rate is increasing according to the Office of National Statistics (ONS), the latest figures, published in March 2017, standing at about 709 a year. This is much faster than for female victims where the numbers have remained broadly even with fewer than 100 a year. And, because the UK has far tighter firearm controls than the US, the most common method of killing is by knife or other sharp instruments, with these implements accounting for 30 per cent of homicides. And, this brings up another question: what implements or means of extinguishing life account for the other 70 per cent? Alas, the ONS doesn't even touch on this grim subject but I bet using a bath to kill, as did George Smith, features nowhere.

There, that's the good news done and dusted, so let's move onto the World Wide Web.

The world's population is circa 7.7 billion counting upwards by the millisecond, and, circa 2.32 billion people are active worldwide users of Facebook every month as of 31 December 2018.

December 2016 saw 1.15 billion mobile daily active users (Mobile DAU), with an increase of 23 per cent year over year, while 1.52 billion people log onto Facebook daily and are considered active users (Facebook DAU). And, this of course is just Facebook. Instagram is a mobile social network that allows users to edit and share photos as well as videos. In 2015, there were more than 77.6 million active Instagram users in the United States alone. This figure grew to 110 million in July 2019; for the UK it was 23 million.

Why do I mention any of that at all? Well, sit down in a comfortable chair, pour yourself a stiff drink and wait and see.

While the reasons men – and a few women – commit homicide have remained pretty much the same for several hundred years, as have the methods of stalking and the hunting of prey remained constant, though over the millennia and centuries there have been modifications: now, for instance, we have the World Wide Web; a place, out there in cyberspace, where very dangerous individuals live and breed in a sort of fantasy world of their own making. But it has a print predecessor – newspapers and magazines with their pages of classified ads – where a form of hunting for victims similar to that employed in cyberspace, has existed for a very long time.

Lady cook (31) requires post in school. Experience in school with forty boarders. Disengaged. Salary £66. Miss I. Wilkins, 21 Thirlmere Road, London, SW16

IRENE WILKINS, *MORNING POST* PERSONAL
ADVERTISEMENT, THURSDAY, 22 DECEMBER 1921

From Victorian through Edwardian times and, with some variations, up to the present day we have had the newspapers' and magazines' small ads – classified advertisements and personal ones, from 'Situations Vacant' or 'Wanted', 'For Sale' to 'Lonely Hearts' columns through which to seek what we may want or, possibly, grant to others what they want … and, of course, today we have the internet and all it has to offer. To see an example of such advertisements being used to find and trap prey, let's flip back the calendar to the 1920s 'Want Ad' killer chauffeur Thomas Henry Allaway who lured strongly built, 5-foot-4-inch Miss Irene Wilkins to her death, in Bournemouth, in December 1921.

To Miss Wilkins's advertisement, Allaway immediately replied by telegram:

MORNING POST COME IMMEDIATELY 4.30 TRAIN WATERLOO BOURNEMOUTH CENTRAL CAR WILL MEET TRAIN EXPENSE NO OBJECT STOP

Delighted with such an immediate answer, Miss Wilkins sent off a reply to say that she was, indeed, coming. She left her house at 3 p.m. to catch the 4.30 p.m. from Waterloo. The unfortunate woman had but a few hours left to live.

At 7.30 a.m. the following morning, a labourer was walking down Ilford Lane, a mile or two to the north-east of Boscombe, when his attention was drawn to some cows acting oddly. Curious about their unusual behaviour, the labourer decided to investigate, and, upon taking a closer look he found the body of a woman in the corner of the cow's field.

A post mortem revealed a number of blows on the victim's face, which, as the then young barrister (later to become an eminent judge) Christmas Humphreys wrote in his 1931 book *Seven Murderers*, 'were probably caused by a human fist, while the more serious of the wounds had smashed the skull beneath, thus causing death ...' probably by the use of a hammer. 'Death was due to haemorrhage and shock caused by the wounds to the face.'

As a side note: various website accounts state that Irene was raped during this attack. This is incorrect, however, and his motive will have to remain a mystery. Allaway was executed by hanging at Winchester Prison on Saturday,

19 August 1922. To this very day, the field where Irene was murdered remains much the same as it was back then. There are still cows in it but not the same ones!

FERNANDEZ AND BECK

Raymond Martinez Fernandez (1914–1951) and Martha Jule Beck (1920–1951) were an American couple, who used lonely-hearts columns to entrap their victims. It is believed that they could have killed as many as nineteen women and a baby girl during their murderous spree from1947 to 1949, although only three have been verified, one of them the little girl.

In modern criminology lexicon they would be labelled a 'homicidal tag team', for one could not have committed multiple homicides without the other being involved as an accomplice, much as were Rose and Fred West, and Hindley and Brady. Fernandez and Beck were oddballs and social misfits and they committed murder solely for financial gain.

For his part, Fernandez, a Hawaiian-born Spaniard, had apparently led a normal life until he was badly injured in a shipboard accident when a hatch cover fell on his head, as a result suffering brain damage, which seems to have changed his personality and behaviour considerably. Ask anyone how it feels to have a cast-iron hatch cover drop on their head, and they will probably start dribbling, mumbling incoherently then scribble a note saying that it hurts. In Fernandez's case, he started telling people that he had been a British Intelligence agent (think James Bond);

and he developed a belief in his own supernatural powers, claiming that he could hypnotise people at a distance and compel women to fall in love with him. This probably originated in his having become an adherent of voodooism while serving a year in prison for having bizarrely tried to walk off a ship with a large number of items taken from the ship's storeroom, an action probably also ascribable to his brain injury. The accident also caused him to lose all his hair, so he took to wearing a toupee in an attempt to restore his former good looks and sex appeal.

Using lonely-hearts columns, Fernandez seduced women and then swindled them out of their savings. In fact, confidence tricksters do much the same today, advertising themselves on dating sites and other online forums, so not much has changed at all!

For her part, and it *is* a large part, for she was an *extremely* large woman, Martha, then aged about twenty-five, was as neurotic as one can be. She later alleged that during adolescence she had been raped by her brother, and her enormous weight didn't help her state of mind either – on the scales at well over 200 pounds. Nevertheless, she qualified as a nurse and by all accounts was a good and hardworking one and was moderately successful in any employment she took on. On the other hand, she comes across to us as 'sexually overactive because of her glands', and she formed several disastrous relationships, going through two botched marriages before signing up with an equally unhappy band of lonely hearts club members.

Fernandez picked Martha's name from the lonely-hearts list of prospects for two reasons. She was, unlike most addicts of such clubs, merely twenty-six years old. She had also given her maiden name as 'Seabrook' – and he regarded this as a good omen as a believer in voodoo, for, coincidentally, William Seabrook was the name of the author of *The Magic Island*, his voodoo 'bible'. So he sent Martha his, to our ears over-oily, standard letter – one of dozens he sent out each week merely changing the name of the recipient where applicable.

Dear Martha,
 I hope you will allow me the liberty of addressing you by your Christian name. To tell the truth, I don't quite know how to begin this letter to you because, I must confess, this is the first letter of this sort I have ever written.
   Would you like to know a little about me? I'm 32 and I've been told I'm not a bad-looking fellow. I am in the importing business from Spain, my mother country. I live alone here in this apartment, much too large for a bachelor, but I hope some day to share it with a wife.
   Why did I choose you for my debut friendship letter? Because you are a nurse and therefore I know you have a full heart with a great capacity for comfort and love.

Your friend,
Raymond Fernandez

A month later, Martha came, by his invitation, to New York and, it was a sorely disappointed Raymond who received her at the 139th Street apartment, for not only did Martha seem a poor bet financially but her appearance was repellent with her treble chin, mop of dark, unwashed hair and heavy makeup hardly in line with the fashions of the day, although she usually wore black in an effort to make herself seem slimmer than she was.

Skinny Fernandez had drawn the short straw. Almost immediately he tried to break off the relationship, but she refused to let him off the hook. To her, with his long, sallow Spanish face, thin moustache, and receding hairline concealed by a toupee like a seedy, dance-hall gigolo, Fernandez was the handsome lover she had dreamed about all her life. He was the very embodiment of *all* the romantic heroes, the Prince Charming she'd read about in the true-love magazines she devoured with a passion.

> I bashed her [Janet Fay's] head in with a hammer in
> a fit of jealousy. Then I turned to Raymond and said:
> 'Look what I've done.' Then he finished the job off
> by strangling her with a scarf.
>
> MARTHA BECK, TO POLICE UPON HER ARREST,
> MARCH 1949

Sadly, the word count for this book does not permit fuller details on the crimes committed by Fernandez and Beck; however, I am sure that the interested reader will find ample material about them elsewhere. Suffice to say that this murderous couple's MO was simple enough. Fernandez, sometimes under the alias of Charles Martin, would use lonely-hearts clubs as places to fish for victims.

As soon as a woman took his bait he would reel her in with his over-the-top charm offensive then move into her home with his phony sister, Martha Beck, in tow. Each victim was beaten and/or strangled to death, and any money or property she possessed fell into the hands of Fernandez and Beck. Their last victim was a twenty-eight-year-old widow called Delphine Downing who had a little daughter, Rainelle. Delphine had shown signs of being uncooperative and was fed sleeping pills to quieten her down. Then Fernandez shot her in the head. To silence the hysterical Rainelle, Beck drowned her in a washtub.

Fernandez and Beck were both found guilty of first-degree murder, and during the long months they spent on death row at Sing Sing (Ossining) Prison, New York, awaiting the outcome of their appeals, they corresponded regularly. One of Martha's most treasured possessions was a letter from her Latin Romeo saying: 'I would like to shout my love for you to the world.' Their appeals were rejected and the date for their execution, by electric chair, was fixed for the night of Thursday, 8 March 1951. Both seemed calm and unrepentant. Fernandez entered the execution chamber in the company of a Roman Catholic priest at 11.12 p.m. 'I'm going to die,' he said calmly and absolutely correctly, adding, 'That is all right. As you know, that's something I've been preparing for since 1949. So tonight I'll die like a man.'

After his body had cooled down and been removed from 'Old Sparky', Martha Beck followed him twelve minutes later. It had been decided beforehand that she should go last because she was less likely to break down in the face of impending death. Her last statement to the world was a rambling attack on everyone who had judged her:

> What does it matter who is to blame? My story is a love story, but only those tortured with love can understand what I mean. True, I am fat, but, if that is a crime, how many of my sex are guilty?
>
> I am not unfeeling, stupid or moronic. The prison and the death house have only strengthened my feeling for Raymond, and in the history of the world how many crimes have been attributed to love? My last words and my last thoughts will be: Let him who is without sin cast the first stone.

In its seventy-five years of operation, a total of 695 men and women were executed by the electric chair in New York State, with 614 at Sing Sing alone. From 1914, all executions were conducted (pun unintended) at Sing Sing prison using 'Old Sparky', which is a generic name for all electric chairs – other labels in other states include: 'Yellow Mama', 'Gruesome Gertie', 'Sizzling Sally' and 'The Hot Seat'. New York's last electrocution took place on Thursday, 15 August 1963, when Eddie Lee Mays was strapped down and 'burned alive' by the 'Electrocutioner'. For a brief period, the State of New York adopted lethal injection but completely abolished capital punishment in 2004.

As for New York's Old Sparky? Well, it still exists today. I know because during the making of one of my

TV documentaries I was allowed to sit in it. And, at that moment, my producer, Frazer Ashford, told the warden that there was something wrong with the chair. 'What's that?' was the reply. 'Ah . . . it's not switched on, is it?' exclaimed Frazer, which says a great deal about working with TV producers, does it not?

Proof of motive is never necessary in the proving of a crime, for absence of any discoverable of motive is of little consequence in deciding whether or not the prisoner committed the crime, for the most astute jury of our peers is helpless in deciding the mental processes which actuate the criminal. However, where a motive *can* be established, and proved, however, it is at least a factor of importance to be taken into account.

In an earlier chapter, I listed the five main motives of criminal actions and if one were to look back to the time when reliable criminal records first started to be kept we would find that the motives for committing any type of crime, including murder, have remained constant, being: to avenge some real of fancied wrong; to get rid of a rival or obnoxious connection; to escape the pressure of pecuniary or other obligation, as in a debt, for instance; to obtain plunder or other coveted objects; to preserve reputation or gratify some selfish or malignant passion – with committing sexual homicide applying to the latter. Indeed, one would be hard-pushed to find any murderer whose motives cannot be included among what amount to Money, Hatred and Sex, or any combination thereof.

I think that we can also safely say that – whatever the

motive – the methods used by criminals to select, stalk and hunt down victims, and to commit murder have also remained constant throughout the decades. These days, however, their sinister endeavours are made far easier to plan and (in part) execute, as they can be carried out sitting comfortably in a chair and using the internet.

'Internet homicide' loosely refers to a killing in which victim and perpetrator met online, in some cases having known each other previously only via the internet. Also 'Internet Killer' is an appellation found in media reports for a person who broadcasts the murder online, or who murders a victim met through the World Wide Web. Some commentators believe that reports on these homicides have overemphasised their connection to the internet, however, taken into the historical contexts described in the cases cited previously in this book and the aforementioned statistics above, I suggest that cases of internet homicide can only increase, not decrease, in the months and years to come.

In 1995, Craig Newmark launched Craigslist, an online equivalent to the classified ads pages in papers and magazines, which since its modest early days a quarter of a century ago, it has achieved remarkable success with at least sixty million users in the US alone, becoming the thirty-third most viewed website in the world; operating in seventy countries in fourteen languages and yet with only fifty employees, it is *the* cyber-place to sell, buy, rent, hire, share, meet, swap, discuss, find, serve, connect, give away, announce, work, collect, care, perform, learn, marvel, mentor, befriend, fall in love . . .

Craigslist gives very clear advice as to how users can protect themselves from harassment or abuse whilst using their website.

Harassment, publication of personal information
If your personal information has been posted on craigslist, use our online form to report the issue.

Abusive email
If you receive an abusive email from an address that ends with 'reply.craigslist.org', for example, 'rcc9la26d7534400a6a03514c34f9200@reply. craigslist.org', locate and use the last link that appears at the bottom part of that message:
'Please flag unwanted messages (spam, scam, other)'.

If you are receiving email directly from another individual (i.e. you can see the sender's email address), it may be advisable to forward details of the messages, including the full email headers, to the sender's email account provider. If you feel the harassment is significant enough, it may make sense to report the issue to law enforcement as well. In addition, it may help to set up a block against the sender's email address in your email client.

Abusive postings
You can flag abusive postings using the flagging links provided.

Despite this, Craigslist, like all other websites, has been misused by predators. Social media, various forums, chat rooms, dating sites, all should be used with caution. Just a few examples of internet-generated rape, attempted murder and homicide follow.

DAVID RUSSELL

Why won't you die ... you've ruined my life for ever.
DAVID RUSSELL, TO MARICAR
BENEDICTO, 1 APRIL 2011

A twenty-year-old McDonald's worker, David Russell, posed as the tattooed rocker Oliver 'Oli' Sykes (lead singer in the Sheffield-based metal band Bring Me the Horizon) when he met a Californian teenager, Maricar Benedicto, on Facebook and they built up a friendship based on their shared love of heavy metal. When Maricar worked out that he was not really Oli Sykes, she gave herself the pseudonym 'Ruby Townsend', which was that of Sykes's girlfriend, and they continued to correspond. In due course, Russell suggested that she should visit him. She was nineteen and trusted him, so she flew to the UK to meet him.

Russell met Maricar at Northampton railway station at 1.30 p.m. on 1 April 2011, and they took a taxi to a wooded area off Harlestone Road. Telling her that he had fond childhood memories of the Harlestone Firs forest, he led her into the trees, where he seated her on a fallen tree; saying he had a secret gift for her, Russell proceeded to blindfold her, then stood behind her and slit her throat.

The terrified girl tried to escape but Russell came after her, hysterically shouting 'Why won't you die? You've ruined my life', stabbed her several times with a serrated breadknife, hit her in the face with a log and head-butted her. Miraculously she survived, largely because she had the sense to tell him that she had given his details to immigration officials when she arrived in the UK. Russell panicked and fled, leaving his blood-soaked victim to find her way to the nearest house and get help.

The police were quick to pick Russell up, back at his home, and charged him immediately. At his trial, police revealed that an examination of his computer showed that just the day before the attack Russell was searching Google with phrases such as, 'How to kill someone and get away with it', 'best knife to kill', and 'how to knock someone unconscious'. Russell's motive remains unknown, and why he felt Maricar had 'ruined' his life is only a matter for conjecture.

Following a retrial in 2016, Russell's initial sentence of seventeen years in prison was reduced to a minimum of fourteen years.

After the trial, the investigating officer was at pains to issue this warning:

> . . . people should always be cautious and if they are going to meet up with someone, make sure they let people know where they are going and who they are meeting. Always meet in a public place and keep in contact with friends and relatives whether in the country or abroad.

To that I would add that when meeting an online acquaintance in the flesh for the first time, you should check and double-check their ID, get a few photos, and, as the police officer advised, be sure to inform family or close, trusted friends, or some official authority (in Maricar's case, immigration officers) who you are meeting, where and when.

PHILIP MARKOFF

Philip is a beautiful person inside and out . . . he could not hurt a fly.

MEGAN MCALLISTER, FIANCÉE OF PHILIP MARKOFF

Born 12 February 1986, Markoff was a second-year medical student at Boston University when he was arrested for the murder of masseuse and former call girl, twenty-six-year-old Julissa Brisman, whom he met through a Craigslist ad.

The son of a dentist, he attended Vernon-Verona-Sherrill Central School, where he was on the bowling team, youth court and a member of history club. Unlike David Russell, Markoff seemed destined to become a highflyer and went on to the State University of New York, University at Albany, where he received a bachelor's degree in biology. Here, he met fellow pre-med student, Megan McAllister. Three years later they became engaged and their wedding was arranged for 14 August 2009, but their plans were terminally halted when they were arrested on their way to a casino during a traffic stop south of Boston. Police, following an email trail to Markoff's computer, found several thousand dollars in their possession. Markoff was accused of murder, armed robbery and kidnapping.

Julissa was one the legions of young women around the world who advertise sexual services online – at the very least a risky business – and, in her case, she advertised on Craigslist. Late in the evening of Tuesday, 14 April 2009, she was found unconscious with multiple gunshot wounds in a room at the Copley Marriott Hotel, 110 Huntington Avenue, in Boston. She later died in hospital from her injuries.

The motive for the killing, it seems, was not of a sexual nature but one of financial gain. Police say the confrontation between the victim and her killer seemed to have begun as an attempted robbery and ended when Brisman fought the zip ties that bound her. This was substantiated when detectives learned that a previous attack had taken place on 10 April 2009, when a twenty-six-year-old masseuse, who also advertised her services on Craigslist, was attacked, bound, and robbed of both her debit card and $800 in cash. Rhode Island Police believed that the perpetrator was the same man who tried to rob a woman, offering 'lap dance services', at a Holiday Inn later that same month.

On 15 August 2010, jail officials found Markoff, at the age of twenty-four, dead in his cell. He had slashed multiple arteries and tried to suffocate himself with a plastic bag. He had also swallowed toilet paper to prevent efforts to resuscitate him.

When we talk about stalking, it is clear that Markoff had sought, you could say, hunted, potential victims online (investigating police had found plenty of evidence of online activity linking his computer to Craigslist and other social media), specifically trawling for victims with financial betterment in the forefront of his mind.

LISA MARIE MONTGOMERY

It looks like my daughter's stomach has exploded.
BECKY HARPER, MOTHER OF BOBBIE STINNETT,
ON 911 CALL

Born 27 February 1968 and on her third marriage Montgomery – who had had four children from previous marriages, and could not have any more for medical reasons – came up with a grisly plan to acquire another child … A rat terrier enthusiast, she met a young woman who bred these dogs (for my UK readers, these dogs somewhat resemble tall, long-legged Jack Russells) in an online chatroom devoted to that breed. She soon learned that the woman, twenty-three-year-old Bobbie Jo Stinnett was eight months' pregnant, and on the forum, and in emails, Montgomery fabricated the story that she, too, was pregnant, and then arranged to meet Bobbie on the pretence of wanting to buy one of her dogs. On 16 December 2004, Montgomery strangled the pregnant woman with a pink neon rope in her home in Skidmore, Missouri, and cut the infant prematurely from Bobbie's womb (she had watched caesareans being carried out online). Miraculously, the baby survived and remained in good health. She took the baby home, claimed to her husband – who had believed she was pregnant – that she had gone into labour while on a shopping trip, and attempted to pass the infant girl off as her own child. The police investigating the crime, however, were quick to trace Bobbie's online and email activities to Montgomery, and she was arrested the following day.

Although her defence put up numerous psychiatric conditions in mitigation, none of these washed. She was sentenced to death on 4 April 2008. No. 11072-031 Montgomery is currently being held at the Federal Medical Center, Carswell in Fort Worth, Texas.

ROBERT 'BOBBY' FREDERICK GLASS AND SHARON RINA DENBURG LOPATKA

I kind of have a fascination with torturing till death.

SHARON LOPATKA, POSTING ON
THE INTERNET BEFORE HER DEATH

This unhinged couple liked each other to the degree of a consensual killing, and yes, you have guessed correctly – they met in an online pornographic chat room, and again you have guessed right, for they exchanged hundreds of lurid text messages, *and* some 900 emails, in which they shared their darkest sexual desires, during which forty-five-year-old Robert Glass agreed to fulfil thirty-four-year-old Sharon's fantasy – of being tortured to death.

Into the subject of necrophilia in a big way, she met

scores of equally distasteful types online with whom she discussed her macabre dreams of being killed in the most horrible ways. Indeed, on one occasion she met a man in New Jersey who'd agreed to do as she asked, but when he realised that she was 'for real', she couldn't see him for dust.

At first blanch we might view Sharon as being mentally subnormal but she was far from that. Born to Orthodox Jewish parents, she was part of a school sports team and a member of her the choir and described by her classmates as 'as normal as you can get'. On leaving school she married Victor, a Catholic, to her parents' dismay. This was seen by her friends as a 'way of getting away' from her religious parents. An internet entrepreneur in the days when the internet was unfamiliar territory to most of the world's population, Sharon operated a number of small successful online businesses, running websites selling all manner of things, from copywriting services to psychic readings to home-decoration guides; most of her online sales/marketing business was legitimate, but she also, and more profitably, dabbled in porn. Using more pseudonyms and persons than police could count, she was a frequent visitor to chat rooms such as fetishfeet.com and sexbondage.com – both of which obviously were not intended for those interested in organically grown vegetables or knitting.

For his part, 'Bobby' was no mental slouch either. For the better part of sixteen years he had worked as a computer analyst for the government of Catawba County, North Carolina. He had been married, with two young daughters and a son. But this marriage all fell apart in May 1996, when his wife, Sherri, noticed that he was spending much more time online than he was with her. Taking a peek at his PC, she saw what he was spending his time on, under pseudonyms such as 'Toyman' and 'Slowhand'.

Quite naturally, what domestic bliss that had existed was shattered when Sherri delved deeper and the proverbial shit hit the fan. Armed with printouts of the licentious emails and postings that she found, she scooped up her children and walked out, then hauled ass down to her attorney's office with the outcome being obvious.

> If my body is never retrieved, don't worry: know that
> I'm at peace
>
> SHARON LOPATKA, FAREWELL NOTE TO HER
> HUSBAND, VICTOR, 13 OCTOBER 1996

On Sunday, 13 October 1996, Lopatka arrived at Glass's home in rural Lenoir, North Carolina. She stayed with him three days during which time he killed her, hopefully in the manner she had so excitedly anticipated. Her remains he buried in the woods behind his house.

Glass was arrested. He pleaded guilty to voluntary manslaughter and sexual exploitation charges – the fact that *she* was equally culpable appears to have been a moot point. Glass was also sentenced to an extra twenty-seven months on federal charges of second-degree minor exploitation, to be served consecutively, all of which amounted to having a very light book thrown at him, not that he would be around too long to appreciate it.

He died of a heart attack in prison on 20 February 2002. It has been claimed that this case was the first of its kind where a murder suspect was arrested by a police department mainly thanks to the retrieval of evidence from email exchanges. There have been other cases that have preceded it, and there *will* be a lot more examples in the decades to come. This is a given!

As for the stalking and hunting down aspect of the Glass/Lopatka case, which primarily is what this book is all about, I would suggest that this is more or less like a gazelle wandering into a hungry lion's den with a highly illuminated poster hung around its neck, advertising: 'Hi, guys. Are you hungry tonight?'

It is here that I am trying to make a point – which is that in all the time before the advent of the internet, as far as I can determine, no one had ever advertised in a newspaper asking to be tortured to death, for I am sure that any editor with half a brain would have pulled the ad and telephoned the police who would have immediately called the men in white coats to bring with them a straitjacket. Today, however, grotesque figures like Glass and Lopatka infest the dark corners of the World Wide Web – each to his/her, own, I suppose. But I also suppose that if people want to swim in a moral sewer then occasionally one might expect to find him- or herself in deep shit!

ARMIN MEIWES

And on this note, let us turn briefly to the case of Armin Meiwes, aka the 'Rotenburg Cannibal' or the 'Master Butcher'. In this internet-generated homicide, we see echoes of that 1991 bums-on-seats movie *The Silence of the Lambs* starring Anthony Hopkins as Dr Hannibal Lecter, and its 2001 sequel *Hannibal*, However, unlike the character Paul Krendler (played by Ray Liotta), part of whose brain was gently fried with shallots and fed to him, Meiwes and his voluntary victim, Bernd Brandes, mutually agreed that the latter's penis be cut off, also fried 'Hannibal-style', for them *both* to savour the flavour.

> I am looking for a, young, well-built 18- to 30-year-old to be slaughtered and then consumed.
>
> ARMIN MEIWES, ADVERTISEMENT ON THE
'CANNIBAL CAFÉ' FORUM, 2002

Born 1 December 1961 in Kassel, West Germany, and with chilling echoes of the Glass/Lopatka case, during 2001, computer repair technician Meiwes was scoping the dark areas of the internet in his search for someone to cannibalise. His favourite haunt was the 'Cannibal Café', a website for those with cannibal fetishisms – 'vorarephilia' – a paraphilia involving erotic desires to be consumed by or to consume another person, refined into 'soft vore' or being eaten alive and whole, or 'hard vore', with killing and gore. Fortunately it is chiefly practised by role-playing, shared fantasies, images and stories.

As might be expected, Meiwes initially received many enquiries from the dysfunctionally inclined, but they soon backed out when they realised that he meant what he said. Indeed, one man actually visited Meiwes and came close to being killed, but he saw the light after viewing the cellar with all its gruesome paraphernalia and where he would be disjointed, so he left almost as fast as he had arrived. Finally, however, an engineer from Berlin who had had a long-term girlfriend, Bernd Jürgen Armando Brandes, took up the offer and the two men met at Meiwes's home in Rotenburg, on Friday, 9 March 2001.

The murder itself is well documented elsewhere, including by Meiwes himself, who videotaped the whole process, but it can be summarised thus: Brandes prepared for the highlight of his evening by swallowing twenty sleeping pills, some cough syrup and half a bottle of schnapps, and his host got to work.

First, Brandes' penis was amputated with a knife – with his consent – after Meiwes had unsuccessfully attempted to bite it off. They tried it raw, but Brandes quickly gave up, finding it too chewy; Meiwes then took the severed appendage and fried it in a pan with salt, pepper, wine, garlic and some of Brandes' own fat. Unfortunately Meiwes burned it and the two men were unable to eat it, so instead, he fed it to his dog. Brandes managed to only eat a single bite of his own flesh before the blood-loss made him too weak to continue.

Meiwes then ran Brandes a bath and while the latter lay in the tub, Meiwes sat reading a novel and checking on Brandes every fifteen minutes as he bled out. Eventually, Brandes collapsed into unconsciousness due to blood loss. After long hesitation and saying a prayer, Meiwes killed Brandes by stabbing him in the throat. He then hung the body on a meat hook. The entire affair was caught on tape. Over the next ten months, Meiwes dined off

Brandes' body, parts of which he had stored in his freezer, hidden under, of all things, pizza boxes. Authorities say that all in all he had consumed over 22 kilograms of flesh.

Meiwes was finally arrested in December 2002. A college student had found a new advertisement for a victim online, as well as details about Brandes' murder. He called the police, who searched Meiwes' home and found the remaining body parts and videotape.

To all those who knew Meiwes, he came across as a sweet, and charming man who was happy to spend time helping out in his community, assisting neighbours who had problems with their cars and their landscaping needs. He would even invite neighbours over for dinner parties, so he was the perfect neighbour – or so everyone thought!

In 2004, Armin Meiwes was convicted of manslaughter, but in 2005 he was re-tried on one count of murder, as the court felt the charge of manslaughter was not enough. In 2006, he was sentenced to life in prison, for murder because, it was argued, he must have seen that Brandes was mentally disturbed.

So, once again, we find stalking and hunting for a human victim – this time to eat – using the World Wide Web.

Humans have been stalking, hunting down and eating each other for different motives and needs for millennia, as my book *Cannibal Serial Killers* documents, but the likes of Meiwes have a 'paraphilia' (previously known as sexual perversion and sexual deviation), which is characterised by intense sexual arousal involving atypical objects, situations, behaviours, and fantasies, including vorarephilia.

As mentioned previously, motives have changed little, if at all, throughout criminal history, but it is of interest to see how offenders move with the times: from the earlier days of posting want-ads in newspaper job columns, or in lonely-hearts clubs, through to the present day where the internet is swamped with websites, forums and chat rooms; additionally, whereas the newspapers of Victorian times maybe had a readership of circa 100,000, as we can see from the data published at the top of this chapter, nowadays internet posting circulation figures can run into billions.

Armin Meiwes trawled for prey using the internet. He knew *precisely* where people like him congregated, therefore, just like killers who target prostitutes in red-light districts, he, too, while sitting in his chair, used 'focused intelligence' to satisfy his perverse sexual cravings. A model prisoner, he has said he hopes to be able to deter others from cannibalism – and it is rumoured that he has become a vegetarian.

JOHN EDWARD 'JR' ROBINSON

I have never discussed this with anyone before, and I will not discuss it with you now. This is very valuable information to me. Your British readers would be very interested in my appearing before the Queen. If you send me $500 I will give you the exclusive story, which you can sell to the media and make a lot of money.

JOHN ROBINSON, LETTER TO THE AUTHOR,
FEBRUARY 2008

The above letter from Robinson – serial murderer, conman, embezzler, kidnapper and forger – is just one example of his devious mind at work. When I pointed out that this 'meeting the queen' claim, if in fact he did, was only for a few milliseconds as an Eagle Scout in 1957; that this reportage was all in the public domain anyway, and that he was trying to manipulate me, he replied, on 4 March 2008:

> You obviously have no business intellect. You are going to lose a golden opportunity. I have written to Richard Branson and he wants this exclusive story now. Your unwarranted accusation of attempted manipulation and flim-flam (as written) much says it all. Don't blow smoke. I don't have time of meaningless delays. I don't have the funds to play games.

For several years I corresponded at length with 'JR', as he likes to be called – a much fuller account of his life and crimes is published in my 2011 book *Dead Man Talking*. Included in that book are many of his letters to me; all illustrating how manipulating he is. I have touched on him earlier in this book, but, risking repeating myself, feel him to be a prime example of the worst kind of predator.

Dubbed by the media the 'Internet Slavemaster', he is the first recorded serial murderer in criminal history to specifically utilise the BDSM chat rooms and forums – like Meiwes above with cannibalism, years later – to single out his favoured prey; his victimology involving women with an unhealthy interest in becoming contractual sex slaves to their 'master' – in this case Robinson. Actually, he didn't use just the internet to entrap his victims – he preyed on some women in the 'real world' too; to begin with, he advertised for employees to work in companies he had fraudulently set up. Young women, successful applicants, were never heard of again. But as the internet became a part of life, and with the establishment of the World Wide Web in 1991, he did not look back. This was the way to stealthily zero in on a target and rain down death and total destruction – and rain down destruction he did, too. He bludgeoned most of them to death using a blunt instrument, usually a hammer.

Robinson was born Monday, 27 December 1943, in Cicero, Illinois. His murders were committed in Kansas and Missouri between 1984 and 2000, after which he was arrested on 2 June 2000. His known victim toll is eight – however, it is strongly believed by law enforcement that he is responsible for many other homicides. All of his victims were female: Paula Godfrey, nineteen; Lisa Elledge Stasi, nineteen; Catherine F. Clampitt, twenty-seven; Sheila Dale Howell Faith, forty-five and her daughter Debbie Lynn Faith, fifteen; Izabela Lewicka, twenty-one; Beverly Bonner, forty-nine, and Suzette M. Trouten aged twenty-eight.

Robinson was sentenced to death for the murders of Izabela Lewicka and Suzette Trouten. He is currently KDOC No. 45690, on death row, El Dorado Correctional Facility (EDCF), Prospect Township, Butler County, Kansas.

But, it is the highly organised Robinson's stalking and

trapping techniques which we are concerned with, and straight-off-the-bat, here we find him sitting either in his home or his office, and using no fewer than five computers to plan and execute all of his crimes. By using the World Wide Web, and aliases such as Anthony Turner, Jim Turner and James Turner and the pseudonym 'Slavemaster', he was easily able to weave his own deadly web in multiple BDSM chat rooms and, using guile and cunning topped up with buckets full of bullshit, with precision entice gullible prey into his clutches. Furthermore, these exercises were cost-effective: requiring very little financial outlay, minimal travelling, and would not interfere with his day-to-day crooked businesses, and, as one can see from his correspondence, he was extremely budget-minded, so he carried out his trawling for victims in an efficient way. Moreover, when one really starts to analyse this criminal's psychopathology he makes for interesting criminological study – quite fascinating in a morbid sort of way.

And, I also think the term 'fishing' fits with well with this man's MO, because he simply cast his line tipped with the glittering lure of a fabulous business opportunity over a lake and waited for the right fish to bite. Occasionally a fish might take an interest – to become suspicious and swim away. But, sitting at his desk, Robinson had all the time in the world and would wait patiently until someone eagerly took the bait. Then he would groom the woman and dish out his well-polished conman patter – after which she was doomed.

Due to the gruesome fact that the bodies of most of Robinson's victims – those that were discovered – were sealed in steel barrels to rot in their own juices, only Lisa Stasis received a decent burial and she rests at the State Line Cemetery, Hazel Green, Madison County, Alabama.

It was Robinson's case that prompted me to write my 2008 book, *Murder.com*, and a chapter in *Dead Men Talking*, as mentioned earlier. *Murder.com* was written with the total cooperation of US and international law enforcement and provides numerous grim warnings about men and female predators who utilise the internet to trawl through dating sites for gullible prey. Indeed, many of these dark sex forums and glossy dating agencies can be as deadly as any red-light district, perhaps even more so, as online killers, rapists, conmen and women, chancers and sex stalkers, along with all types of crooks, are out there in almost unimaginable numbers. Be warned!

MICHAEL JOHN ANDERSON

Katherine was, unfortunately, too trusting. She had found benefits on Craigslist, but in her trusting nature, she fell into this trap.

REV. ROLF OLSON ON HIS
DAUGHTER KATHERINE

In April 2009, twenty-year-old Michael Anderson was convicted on six counts, including one of first-degree murder, for shooting and killing twenty-four-year-old college graduate, Katherine Ann Olson in a suburb of Minneapolis.

At the time only just nineteen years old, Anderson lured Olson to her death using a fake babysitter advertisement posted online in October 2007, where he posed as 'Amy', a married woman, to allay any suspicions. However, when she turned up he took her up to his bedroom, and when she tried to leave, he pulled out his father's .357-calibre Magnum and shot her in the back. On 26 October 2007, her body was found stuffed into the boot of her car, which she had parked up at the Burnsville Nature Preserve

Katherine, who loved the theatre, was an outgoing young woman who lived life to the full, travelling around much of the world, from Egypt to Argentina, where she worked as a circus juggler. She had had a number of positive experiences with Craigslist, mostly nanny-type jobs, and she had worked in Turkey as a nanny. In fact, this bubbly lass's email address was 'Pelirroja loca' – Spanish for 'Crazy redhead'.

Katherine is buried at the Oakland Cemetery, Marines on Saint Croix, Washington County, Minnesota.

Michael Anderson was convicted of murder in the first degree and sentenced to life in prison with no chance of parole. MNDOC inmate no. 228994 is currently held at MCF Oak Park Heights.

It would be right for me to say that an estimated 99,995 of every 100,000 web posts are not associated with any crime whatsoever, but it is the other five you might need to worry about: various websites have enabled countless thefts, burglaries, robberies, assaults, rapes, STD transmissions, and murders. According to Jim Goad, 'People have lost their lives while innocently and good-naturedly conducting transactions involving iPads, iPhones, cars, trucks, and apartments.'

At the time of writing, an unsolved case involves a Long Island serial killer who slaughtered at least four prostitutes he met through online ads. Also, currently awaiting trial for stabbing a man to death after ensnaring him on a social media site is a self-proclaimed Satan-worshipping teenage mother from Pennsylvania who says she's killed at least twenty-two people, which would make her one of the most prolific female serial killers in American history. So now to a tag team.

RICHARD BEASLEY

I'm supposed to be dead anyway.

> Brogan Rafferty, accomplice of
> Richard Beasley

By definition a serial killer, grey-haired and slowly balding 'Good Ole Boy' Richard Beasley, a self-styled street preacher, self-proclaimed 'Son of God', will be meeting his Maker sooner than he wants to if the Ohio criminal justice system has anything to do with it, for he was sentenced to death for the killings of three down-on-their-luck men lured by bogus caretaker job offers posted online.

The murdered men were Ralph Geiger, fifty-six, David Pauley, fifty-one, and Timothy Kern, forty-seven. All were looking for a fresh start in life, the prosecutor said repeatedly during the trial, stating, '. . . the defendant has the soul of Satan, a monster who has buried three innocent men after luring them into the wilderness.' The prosecutor added with more than any Bible-thumper's relish: 'There they came, bringing all of their worldly possessions with them, to be sold off with their money pocketed and their identities stolen, and out there in the night, stood Rafferty with a pickaxe and shovel at hand.'

Fifty-three-year-old Beasley teamed up in 2011 with the teenaged Brogan Rafferty, whom he'd known since the latter was a young child, and would hold out the promise of work on his 688-acre farm to lure men there with the intention of robbing them. Each one travelled down a dark secluded road with Beasley and accomplice Brogan Rafferty and were never seen alive again.

One man did survive, however: forty-nine-year-old Scott Davis testified that he heard the click of a gun as he walked in front of Beasley at the alleged job site. Hit in an arm, he knocked the weapon aside, fled into the woods and after hiding for hours eventually managed to reach a farmhouse, where he was taken in and the police were called.

Beasley's co-defendant, Rafferty, gave the court a chilling account of Timothy Kern's final moments.

I heard a 'pop' and I turn around and Mr Kern is on his knees kind of holding the side of his head, and Beasley is saying to him 'Are you all right?' Beasley shot him again. I think he shot him three times in the head. The gentleman was still breathing, so Beasley went up and got the gun close to him and shot him again. And I said, 'He's still alive,' and he said, 'His brain's dead, there's no way. He's got four bullets in his head and I put one between his eyes.' The man literally I think had five dollars in his pocket.

Like so many offenders, large or small, they signally failed to realise that police can track down people when they've been online, by tracing their IP address. This they did on the Craigslist ad to a house in Akron, where Beasley rented a room under the name of Ralph Geiger, his first victim. After that, police tracked a mobile number Beasley had left with the landlady, and he was arrested.

A sad thing about this entire case is how Beasley's nineteen-year-old daughter, Tonya, feels about it all, when she says:

> I blame myself for everything that happened because if I had known he was using the internet to do these things I wouldn't have shown him when he asked me about the internet. It was a new technology to him, so of course I showed him all these things. He had said he wanted to sell a few of his old things that he could no longer use, and I didn't think anything of it. I thought it would just help Dad make some side money.

So, let's look at the bait that Beasley used to ensnare his prey, and just like John Robinson, he would cast his line while sitting at his PC, and it all begins with an innocent-looking ad on Craigslist:

> Wanted, a caretaker for a farm, simply watch over six hundred and eighty eight acres of hilly farmland,

feed the cows. You get three hundred dollars a week, older to elderly preferred but we consider all. Be on location a must.

It sounded perfect to forty-nine-year-old Scott Davis.

'I was actually looking forward to it. I love being in the country. I'm a country boy,' Davis told a hushed courtroom. 'There was plenty of hunting and fishing, and it sounded like a dream job to me.'

But this 'dream' job would soon turn into a horror-type scenario. 'Since that night,' said Davis, 'I've had nothing but nightmares. It just keeps coming back and back and back . . . there is a man standing in the middle of my nightmare. It's Richard Beasley. He's holding a pistol that jammed with the first pull of the trigger.'

Relating how things went after he first spotted Beasley's Craigslist ad, and after many emails and phone calls back and forth, Davis learned that the job was his for the taking, so he loaded up his trailer with everything he owned and headed off to rural Summit County, Ohio, about ten miles south of Akron, where he met Beasley and his 'nephew', Brogan Rafferty. What none of the three men could have known was that a surveillance camera catches them at a local restaurant for breakfast, afterwards recording them as Davis parks his truck and trailer and climbs into Brogan's old Buick for the long ride out to look over the alleged 688-acre cattle ranch.

Later, police learned that Beasley had made this same breakfast stop and journey on the very same road three times into the country before with three different men who were never seen alive afterwards.

'He [Beasley] was continuously coming up that he was a preacher and a pastor and that he was always going to church with his nephew,' Davis recalled.

But Beasley was being economical with the truth. It was not a case of Beasley being without previous sin: he had returned to Ohio from Texas in 2004 after serving a combined twelve years in prison on separate charges of burglary and illegal firearms possession. At the time of the murders he was using an Iver Johnson .22-calibre semi-automatic pistol with a seven-round clip.

Now driving deeper into rural countryside, Davis was keeping his eyes open and thinking how far it was going to be from there to drive back and call his mother to let her that he'd made it. Then finally, Beasley signalled Brogan to stop the car.

The following is an extract from Davis's evidence. It makes for chilling reading.

After Brogan dropped me and Richard off he got back in the car and Richard told him go up there and see what the road looks like up there. Richard told me he had stashed some equipment there in the woods so nobody would steal it. But, suddenly Beasley seemed uncertain if he is in the right place. He said to me, 'Let's go another way. Maybe I got the wrong spot.' And I think one of the biggest mistakes of my life that I made that day was let somebody behind me, that's something I don't do.

The hair just stood up on the back of my neck and I said to myself, 'Man, something definitely just went wrong,' when I heard that click. I spun around immediately and when I spun around he already had that gun back up and I am looking straight down the barrel. I looked into his eyes and all I saw was coal. They were black eyes. They were just black like a shark in feeding water. The gun had to be jammed so that right there I should have hit the ground and that would have been the end of me. I turned around and when I did he shot me right in the elbow and shattered everything in there.

At this point I was like, 'He's got a gun and I don't.' So I got up and with my whole life I ran with all I had. I kept falling down and while I'm doing this he is continuously firing at me. I just kept running and falling and running and falling and he kept popping shots at me.

I kept hearing those shots ring one after the other and I was falling down, and when you hear 'pop, pop, pop', you try to count in your head how many bullets does he have?

I hope that by now the reader will be imagining the abject terror Scott Davis was feeling back then, because I most certainly can. He is running for his life, and a terrifying manhunt is on.

I don't know if I'm being hunted by dogs, by humans, at this point I don't know what's going on.

All I know is I got somebody shooting at me. So, I'm going down through the creek to lose . . . if there was any dogs I wanted to make sure that I ran to the creek so there wasn't going to be any scent of me. I was trying to be careful with my blood there. I was looking at my blood leaking out into the stream . . .

After seven gruelling hours he knocked on the door of a house . . . 'everybody came and helped and got the police and ambulance there.'

At the trial Beasley offered the weak defence that Davis had, in fact, pulled a gun on him in retaliation for serving as a police informant in a motorcycle gang investigation. He received the death sentence. As for his co-defendant Brogan Rafferty, who was sixteen at the time of the crimes, he was too young to face the death penalty so was sentenced to life in prison without any chance of parole.

So, yet again we find a highly dangerous and organised killer out for financial gain using the internet as a tool to attract his prey – the bait of course being the offer of an idyllic job in the country and a well-paid one too. Beasley, like so many others, was playing the numbers game by simply casting his line of enticing bullshit, adding to it the respectability of being a man of the Church (his ghillie suit), and waiting for the right fish to bite.

DERRICK TODD LEE

Lee's stalking modus operandi aligned with his victimology shows that he zeroed in on random women who had two things in common – they were all very attractive and successful, and, with the exception of Treneisha Dene Colomb, who was attacked as she attended the grave of her mother, he attacked them in their homes. Each victim was sexually assaulted before he either strangled, stabbed or bludgeoned her to death. And, it is worthy of note that during his killings, Lee was arrested a number of times for what police called 'unrelated incidents' of robbery, trespassing and peeping, so with his already abysmal criminal track record why he hadn't been locked up with the key thrown away years back is a mystery.

Born Tuesday, 5 November 1968, St Francisville, Louisiana, Lee, the 'Baton Rouge Serial Killer', was sentenced to death but died of natural causes at the Louisiana State Prison Angola, on 21 January 2016, aged forty-seven, moreover, if anyone deserves the label 'Homicidal Lust Stalker' he does.

At school Derrick Lee was bullied and called 'retarded'. His first brush with the police came on Sunday, 8 November 1981. Aged thirteen, he was arrested for burglary and smashing up a candy store; on the same day he assaulted a woman in front of his own mother, and this was a portent for things to come.

Three years later, on Wednesday, 8 August 1984, he was arrested on suspicion of murdering a man, but the charge was dropped. Lee also set fire to his own car to cash in on the insurance, but of that case nothing more is known. Nevertheless, on 2 July 1988, he was arrested for an attempted robbery. The charges were reduced and soon he was back on the streets. In 1988, he married a

Jaqueline Sims and almost immediately began slapping her around the face, and on one occasion even threatened her father with a firearm.

In 1985 he attacked a woman but the charges were dropped, yet again!

On 23 August 1992, forty-one-year-old Connie Lynn Brooks Warner was bludgeoned to death with a hammer. Her body was found ten days later, but there was no evidence with which to charge Lee. Connie is buried at the Azalea Rest Cemetery, Baton Rouge. A must-read is the book *I've Been Watching You: The South Louisiana Serial Killer*, by Susan D. Mustafa, and Special Prosecutor Tony Clayton with Sue Israel.

On 1 January 1993 Lee robbed and almost killed seventy-three-year-old Melvin Foster with a stick, then, on 4 April that year, he attacked a teenage couple with a six-foot harvesting tool. Both survived. Friday, 24 September found him stealing items from a Salvation Army drop-off point. Again the charges were dropped.

In 1997 we find his crimes escalating in violence. On 1 June, thirty-four-year-old Eugenie Wickham Boisfontaine was beaten to death. Her body was found on Sunday, 7 August. Eugenie is buried at the Metaire Cemetery, New Orleans.

Twenty-eight-year-old home-help nurse, Randi Jane Cieslewicz Mebruer, was raped, beaten, stabbed – and then disappeared – on 18 April 1998; her body is presumed to be 'lost or destroyed'. Randi had gone to the local video store near her home in Zachary, Louisiana. She and her young son returned to their residence on Saul Avenue at approximately 7 p.m. Her son walked to a neighbour's home the following morning and said that his mother was missing. Evidence inside Mebruer's house indicated signs of a struggle and foul play. There was a pink plastic bag in her carport, which was stained with her blood. Investigators believe that she was assaulted inside her home and murdered. Traces of Lee's DNA were found at the site.

On 22 January 2000, Lee almost beat to death his then girlfriend, and that same day he attempted run over a sheriff's deputy with his car. In both instances, the charges were dropped.

Tuesday, 25 September 2001: he raped and strangled forty-one-year-old Gina Wilson Green. Weeks before she was murdered in her home, she told a friend and her mother that she felt as if she was being watched. DNA evidence later tied Lee to the murder.

Wednesday, 26 September 2001: Lee assaulted his first wife, Jaqueline Lee (Sims). The charges were dropped.

Monday, 14 January 2002: he raped, beat and stabbed to death twenty-year-old Geralyn Amanda Barr 'Sissie' DeSoto in her home. Geralyn's father said after Lee's arrest, 'He can talk about going to God all he wants, but he's going to burn in hell. If the policemen wouldn't have stopped him he would still be out there murdering.' Geralyn is buried at the Masonic Cemetery, Simmesport, Avoyelles Parish, Louisiana.

Thursday, 23 May 2002: twenty-three-year-old Christine Moore was killed by blunt force trauma. Her skeletal remains were found twenty-four days later.

Friday, 31 May 2002: Lee raped and stabbed eighty-three times twenty-two-year-old Charlotte Murray Pace. Charlotte, who had recently graduated from Louisiana State University, was alone when she fought for her life as her attacker stabbed her repeatedly in the townhouse she'd moved into days earlier. Charlotte is buried at the Mound Cemetery, Rolling Fork, Sharkey County, Mississippi.

It is worth noting that at the time of her murder, Pace lived only three houses away from Gina Green. Christine Moore, another LSU graduate student, had also lived in the same neighbourhood as Pace. Moore had disappeared, and her skeletal remains were found only a couple of weeks after Pace's murder.

Tuesday, 9 July 2002: Lee attempted to rape, then beat and strangled Dianne Alexander who survived to tell police that he had knocked on the door of her St Martin's Parish home asking for directions. Talking to KLFY, she said: 'I can't say how many times he hit me, all I remember was one force hit to the forehead and that was it for me.' By the grace of God, she miraculously survived because her son returned home from school. She recalled: 'When Lee heard my son pull up in his car he ran out of the back door. I had my air conditioner turned on and he turned it off so the silence would alert him if anyone would show up.' Dianne has written her own book, *Divine Justice: The Dianne Alexander Story.*

Sunday, 14 July 2002: Lee entered the home of forty-four-year-old Pamela Kinamore and raped and beat her and slashed her throat. Pamela is at the Resthaven Gardens of Memory & Mausoleum, Baton Rouge.

Thursday, 21 November 2002: he raped and bludgeoned with a tree branch twenty-three-year-old Treneisha Dene Colomb, at her mother's graveside. She was reported missing by her family on 22 November 2002. Two days later her body was found by a hunter in a field off a remote road in Scott, LA near Lafayette. Treneisha rests at the Saint Charles Borromeo Cemetery, Grand Coteau, St Landry parish, Louisiana.

25 December 2002: on Christmas Day Mary Ann Fowler disappeared. She has never been found. Her body is presumed 'lost or destroyed'. Mary was last seen standing outside a Subway sandwich shop on Louisiana Highway 415 West of Port Allen on Christmas Eve 2002. Investigators believe she was abducted from that location as her belongings were found scattered on the pavement shortly after her disappearance. Investigators also found some of her acrylic nails, which may have been torn off in a struggle with her abductor. Robbery did not appear to be the motive as her purse, keys and food were left behind, as well as Christmas presents in the back of her car. She was on her way to visit her husband, Jerry Fowler, who was in prison at the time of her disappearance. Jerry was a former Louisiana elections commissioner and was serving five years for bribery.

Monday, 3 March 2003: Carrie Lynn Yoder, a twenty-six-year-old Louisiana State University biological sciences graduate student, was taken from her apartment, raped, beaten and asphyxiated. A fisherman discovered her body near the Whiskey Bay boat launch about thirty miles west of Baton Rouge, a few hundred yards from where the third known victim of Lee's was found. She was cremated and her ashes were scattered along Weeks Bay in Alabama.

CHRISTIAN GROTHEER

I spent whole nights in these chat rooms and I saw them as my family. From my point of view the internet was the ideal way to meet people because you get talking to people very quickly and almost all visitors, male and female, are looking for sexual contact.

CHRISTIAN GROTHEER

At the time of writing, I have just finished appearing in a TV documentary on the British serial killer Joanna Dennehy for Story House Productions, based in Germany, so it would be remiss of me if I didn't include a sexually fantasy-driven German stalker/killer in this book, so Grotheer seems to fit the bill.

A twenty-seven-year-old construction worker, he says that, using the nicknames 'Rosenboy0207' or 'Riddick300', he met around 150 women in internet chat rooms – he has since been dubbed by the media 'Germany's First Internet Murderer'.

Be that as it may, he admitted that his first killing was an 'accident'; that he murdered his second victim when she called him a rapist. He drew the tag 'Riddick300' after the fictional serial killer in the science fiction/horror film *Pitch Black* (released 2000).

Perhaps one to exaggerate just a little, he claims that he spent 'tens of thousands of hours' on dating sites and went on dates with 'at least a hundred women', all of which is a remarkable sexual odyssey considering that for the better part of his week he was humping bricks around and mixing cement. Oh, wow; the youngsters today . . . just where do they get their energy from because I haven't got a damned clue!

Be that as it may, on Thursday, 5 June 2008, Grotheer stabbed to death twenty-six-year-old 'Jessica K', who went by the pseudonym 'Babylove'. According to him they got into a heated argument, during which 'I only touched her throat and she suddenly dropped dead,' he explained to the police. Her body was found fourteen days later and, at post mortem, it was determined she had been stabbed in the back. In the second case, Grotheer claimed that after he and the mother of three children had sex at her apartment, she then cooked him a meal; and then they went for a stroll, during which she accused him of rape and demanded money. At that, after he had looked into the eyes of Christ, he knocked her down and stabbed her twelve times in the back and fourteen times in the chest – her body was discovered the next day by a passer-by.

On April Fool's Day 2009, this despicable piece of work, Grotheer, was sentenced to life in prison.

JOHN KATEHIS

If you disrespect me then I will fucking break your neck.

JOHN KATEHIS

INTERNET HOMICIDE: SPINNING A WEB

On Sunday, 22 March 2009, George Weber (a famous radio broadcaster who did hourly news updates on the ABC Radio Network) was found dead in his Brooklyn apartment after his bosses became concerned that he hadn't shown up for his daily show in two days. When police entered the forty-seven-year-old's ransacked apartment they discovered that his hands and feet were bound, a massive ten-inch dildo had been forced into his rectum and he had been stabbed multiple times in the neck, his throat was slashed, and semen was dripping from his mouth. The water was still running in the bathtub and kitchen sink, and investigators believe Weber's killer used the water to clean himself after the murder. But Weber had a dark secret, for it was soon learned he used cocaine and that he frequented networking sites to look for men with whom he would enjoy rough sex.

Weber, like so many like him, was dancing with death.

On 25 March, sixteen-year-old self-confessed Satanist and sadomasochist, John Katehis, was arrested on suspicion of murder. In his defence he claimed that he and Weber had been having an ongoing relationship, got high on cocaine, and that he had stabbed Weber when he, himself was attacked with a knife – an unlikely story as at the time of the murder Weber was well and truly trussed up. In what is called a 'homosexual hate crime', this homicide somewhat falls into the subject matter of this book as it has Weber trawling the internet looking for a deviant sex partner and a deadly spider bit him back.

Of course, each to his own I will add, and if people wish to involve themselves in this type of activity, so be it. It goes without saying that the majority of these types of internet-generated relationships can develop into long-term loving affairs, free of any type of violence of any kind, but, one has to remember that like attracts like. In some cases it is like playing with fire, in other cases it is like playing Russian roulette with a revolver. You can only spin the chamber so many times before you end up dead.

NYDOC no.12A0161 John Katehis, DOB 26 July 1992, is presently serving a natural life sentence at the Sing Sing Correctional Facility, Ossining, New York.

ANTONI IMIELA

As criminal history confirms, women are at their most vulnerable when thumbing a lift, or, in many cases, climbing into a taxi late at night while intoxicated.

According to the *Guardian* of 28 December 2017, the number of alleged sexual assaults by taxi or private hire drivers had risen by 20 per cent in the previous three years. According to figures released under Freedom of Information laws, at least 337 assaults were reported between April 2016 and March 2017 in England and Wales – up from 282 in 2014–15. A number of incidents were recorded where the victim was a child under the age of sixteen.

According to *Business Outsider*, 17 November 2017, quoting data obtained from the Metropolitan Police and compiled by Transport for London, in 2016 Uber drivers were convicted of almost half of the sex offences, with over 150 rapes, and not one licensed black cab driver was charged over that period.

> He had raped people and obviously been with prostitutes. I cannot feel the same, but deep down I do still love him and I want to support him because I am sure he is ill.
>
> Anyone that is ill, I do not think they should just be discarded.
>
> CHRISTINE IMIELA, ON HER HUSBAND

Born in Lübeck, Germany in 1954, later to be dubbed by the media the 'M25 Rapist', Imiela's crimes took place in Surrey, Kent, Berkshire, London, Hertfordshire and Birmingham, and he was found guilty of the rape of nine women and girls, and the attempted rape of a girl whom he repeatedly punched and throttled.

Growing up in Newton Aycliffe, County Durham, in 1996 after serving a prison sentence for a series of robberies, former railway worker Imiela moved to Appledore, near Ashford in Kent. Five years later he began a campaign of attacks – raping four girls aged between ten and fourteen, assaulting a ten-year-old, and four women in 2001 and 2002, dragging his victims into secluded areas where he threatened to kill them. One young woman was attacked but saved by her dog.

At his trial, the jury heard how, in November 2001, Imiela had snatched a girl in Ashford, Kent, as she took down posters outside a police-run youth club, and yanked her down a muddy path and through stinging nettles.

Despite her pleas that she was only ten years old, he indecently assaulted her and raped her before leaving her to stumble half-naked to a nearby house for help.

In July 2002, Imiela struck twice in one day – first in Earlswood, Surrey, a place he was familiar with through his work – like John Duffy, on the railways – in Putney, south-west London. The thirty-year-old woman in Surrey was left with fifty-six separate injuries after she was repeatedly punched by Imiela who had grabbed her as she jogged along a riverside path, before tying her up and raping her.

Just six hours later, he struck again; this time attacking a twenty-six-year-old woman walking across Putney Heath in an almost carbon copy of the previous assault. Not content with just raping the woman, Imiela stole his victim's mobile phone and, as he walked away, used it to taunt her mother and sister about the rape.

In 2002, he was arrested while driving along the M20 when one of his neighbours contacted the BBC after watching the TV show, *Crimewatch*. He told the cops that he knew Imiela by sight. On 4 March, Imiela was sentenced to seven life terms.

You are wholly unrepentant about your life of guns, rape and general violence and, despite having served eight years of your life sentence you have not expressed one jot of remorse.

His Honour John Bevan QC, sentencing Imiela at Maidstone Crown Court, 4 March 2004

While Imiela was serving his time at HMP Full Sutton, a DNA match linking him to a twenty-nine-year-old woman was confirmed. In 1987, he'd grabbed her off the street in Sydenham, south-east London, put his hand over her mouth, dragged her onto waste ground and sexually assaulted her before threatening her with a brick. Police believe that Imiela committed many other offences, but he died of natural causes (believed to be a heart attack) in prison on 8 March 2018.

Much like John Duffy, Imiela was a 'disorganised' snatch-and-grab serial rapist who used some of his previous knowledge of the railway network in the commission of his crimes. Highly mobile, he was a sexual fantasist who, like so many snatch-and-grab serial killers and rapists, appeared to be subconsciously seeking out prey as he moved around. In other words it is as if he was always on the hunt, and when a suitable victim crossed his path he struck without warning.

13

Poison Potion:
The Black Widow

I don't want to go to prison.
I'll kill you like all the rest.
KATHLEEN MCCLUSKEY AT A DRUG-
AND ALCOHOL-FUELLED SEX ORGY

Some say that she was vivacious, with her mass of dark hair, high cheekbones, sexy, and voluptuous figure but it was the cruel mouth and penetrating eyes that should have given her away for there was a hardness about her and there can be no denying it, for Kathleen McCluskey's passions were closely entwined: she was driven by a yearning for exhibitionist sex and she enjoyed creating tinctures which would render her victims insensible.

With Mrs McCluskey, we find one of the most deadly human Black Widows in British criminal history, and just like a spider she lured victims into her web, although it has to be said in a fifty-fifty, almost agreeable sort of way.

Visitors invited into her Gray Road, Cambridge, flat were left in no doubt of her lust for sex. Photos on the walls showed her half-naked, in compromising positions with a Mohammed Shoja Assadi, a forty-seven-year-old artist and Iranian refugee. The pictures were taken while he was in his death throes from a drug overdose. He was one of four men she was accused of murdering when she stepped into the dock at Norwich Crown Court on Tuesday, 3 December 2002.

Prosecutor, Mr Nigel Graham Godsmark QC (a Circuit Judge since 2012), told the jury that the photos of Mr Assadi were taken at a sex party at his flat in Cambridge. The photographer was her then husband, James Baxter, fifty, who spent the evening of 19 August 1999 with her at Assadi's place, enjoying an orgy involving sex, heroin, alcohol and cannabis. Of some incidental interest is that James Baxter was born James Wormald. The son of a Fellow of Peterhouse College, Cambridge, he had been a head boy at Eton, and then dropped out, abandoning his studies after two years to go to Nepal as a cannabis-smoking hippie. After meeting and marrying Kathleen in 1994, he changed his name to Baxter, her maiden name. His drug addiction made him impotent, so he got his thrills by watching his wife have sex with other men.

Neighbours had heard Mrs McCluskey shouting, 'I can fuck anybody!' as she had sex with Assadi. Later another witness heard a distressed woman's voice crying, 'Wake up, wake up!'

It transpired that, during the evening, Baxter had gone to his own flat, returning with a bottle of methadone – a heroin substitute – and then crashing out asleep with his wife. When they woke up, nearly half of the methadone had gone with Assadi now stone dead.

Paramedics arrived in the early hours of the 20th, to find a now-hysterical Mrs McCluskey sprawled across the deceased's body on a settee. She had phoned for the ambulance, and she asked a woman special constable, 'What have I done? I have poisoned him, but he was greedy.'

A paramedic testified that she had to be pulled off Mr Assadi, while her husband stood by, still stoned out of his tiny mind, apparently indifferent to what had happened. 'She's my wife,' Baxter mumbled, and, pointing an accusatory finger at the dead Assadi, shouted '. . . and *his* whore.'

Sixteen months later Baxter committed suicide, gassing himself in his car while suffering from depression, and now his widow was accused of murdering Assadi, and also thirty-two-year-old care worker Marvin Brodie and one Raymond Diaz, a forty-eight-year-old unemployed neighbour, plus her second husband, James McCluskey, forty-eight, added to which she was accused of administering a 'noxious substance' to a Mr Peter Bakulinskyj, who survived. All of her victims died between August 1999 and September 2001, all were known to McCluskey and lived near her in Cambridge. Surprise, surprise, all had histories of drug or alcohol problems.

Denying all the charges, plus four alternative counts of manslaughter, the flamboyant McCluskey sat impassively in the dock as Nigel Godsmark told the court: 'The prosecution say that in each case the defendant supplied drugs to the people who died, or supplied the means of taking these drugs. Her interests also extended to what she described as tinctures or potions.'

The jury were told that Mr Assadi, like the other victims, had drug or alcohol problems, and he had met McCluskey when both went for drug and alcohol counselling. For her part, she was unemployed and a heroin addict, and shortly before Assadi's death she had been given a litre of methadone on prescription. This was more than enough to last a fortnight, enabling her to stockpile it. Mr Baxter himself was prescribed a similar amount, so one could say that the couple were well stocked up.

Assadi's death was followed in June 2000 by that of Brodie, whom she'd met through a friend. He was an alcoholic but not exactly a hardened drug addict, and after meeting him at his home in Cambridge she joined him to watch a sex video at a mutual friend's house. Several other people were present, and 'her behaviour there was uninhibited,' said Mr Godsmark, adding: 'She was making sexually explicit remarks, and at one point she said, "I don't want to go to prison" and "I'll kill you like all the rest."'

One of Brodie's friends was later to say that during that evening she went to the kitchen for a bread knife with which she proposed to cut off the clothes of one of the people watching the video. Then she asked if she could have sex with Brodie on the table while the others watched the film. Whether they did so to the letter is unknown, but she and Marvin Brodie did spend the night together. The next morning he accompanied her to her flat. Shortly afterwards a witness heard a woman's voice say, 'I can't wake him.' Six hours passed, and then McCluskey summoned an ambulance. Brodie was unconscious, and died shortly afterwards from the combined effects of methadone and alcohol.

Next to die was another friend and neighbour of McCluskey's – heroin addict and alcoholic, Raymond Diaz died in similar circumstances. Once again she called paramedics, telling them that he'd collapsed; that he had bought heroin that day and had gone to her flat knowing she had syringes and needles. Cause of death was the same as that of Brodie.

James McCluskey, whom she married in April 2001, died six months later after taking methadone. The couple's brief marriage had been stormy. When she dialled 999, she told the operator that he'd had a 'fit'.

Kathleen McCluskey's repeated calls for ambulances finally raised suspicions that murder was afoot. A police investigation was launched, and when officers searched her home in Gray Road, they found a copy of the *British National Formulary*: the pharmacists' bible that details prescribed drugs and their contraindicative effects. The picture painted was of a woman with a drugs and alcohol-based, hedonistic lifestyle who liked to make up tinctures which, in the wrong hands, could be deadly.

The morbid picture was further tainted because McCluskey had an ambivalent attitude towards men. Four had died of drug overdoses in her company over the course of two years. Bakulinskyj, who survived, complained of being given drugs that rendered him insensible very quickly. Her reaction at the time of the deaths seemed odd, either over the top or minimally dismissive.

Bakulinskyj told detectives that he had declined McCluskey's requests for sex, but he had accepted an invitation to have lunch with her and her then-husband, James Baxter, at their flat on Christmas Day 1999. He arrived to find there was neither food nor Christmas decorations, but the couple said that they had a gift for him. This turned out to be beaker filled with a blue liquid.

'It tasted very bitter and strong,' Bakulinskyj told the police. 'It was slightly unusual, but at the time I didn't really think anything of it.' He explained that he couldn't remember anything after that apart from waking up on the sofa. 'My eyes opened up but I couldn't move my body. I didn't know where I was or what I was doing.'

Pausing for a moment, please allow me to ask the reader to imagine this.

You are invited around to a couple's home for a roast turkey dinner with all the trimmings, so off you go having missed breakfast because the table will be burgeoning under the weight of the festive feast. Upon your arrival, you hang up your hat, coat and scarf, walk into the living room and find – nothing! Indeed, you are not even offered a glass of cheap wine – instead what is proffered is a drink of what appears to be antifreeze.

'Quaff that back me, old mate,' says the obviously undernourished mein host, Baxter. 'That's Kathy's home brew ... it'll knock you right off your feet!' What amazes me is that Mr Bakulinskyj 'didn't think anything of it'. Nevertheless, once he had recovered sufficiently to stand upright, the somewhat confused man was helped by Baxter back to his own flat in Cambridge. Bakulinskyj had been a methadone user for more than two years but had never experienced such an adverse reaction. Later, he said that he now believed that Kathleen and James had been trying to get him to participate in a threesome. 'She started pestering me for sex and she was very flamboyant. She came out of the bedroom naked, with these leather things on. It wasn't a pretty sight,' he told the police. 'She said, "I want to sleep with you. You know I'm going to sleep with you," but I never succumbed.'

Despite this near-death experience, a fortnight later Bakulinskyj visited the couple again. 'Kathy was very randy. She presented herself in this get-up of leather. I didn't want to look.' Instead, he explained that he looked at the provocative photos on the wall, showing her with Assadi. 'I could see I was being set up to be a sexual swinger. Whatever sins I might have, sexual deviance is not one of them.'

Adding more to this lurid account, Bakulinskyj said that Kathleen had made up to forty obscene phone calls a day to him, telling him how she was having lesbian sex. She had even made similar calls to his father and his mother, to whom she said that her son was a heroin addict and she would find him on a mortuary slab.

Two weeks into the trial, the judge, Mr Justice Moses directed the jury to clear Kathleen McCluskey of the charges relating to her second husband and Raymond Diaz. There was insufficient evidence against her in three cases, he said. It had been James McCluskey's 'free choice to take methadone,' adding, 'he wanted to take heroin, and indeed had injected himself with it.'

The trial ended on 17 December, when the jury found Kathleen McCluskey guilty of the manslaughter of Mohammed Assadi and Marvin Brodie. She was acquitted of administering a noxious substance to Peter Bakulinskyj. Her sentencing was postponed pending psychiatric reports, and on hearing the verdicts she shouted, 'This is fucking ignorance!' She was sent prison for ten years.

Kathleen McCluskey was the daughter of a Bradford hospital porter. Leaving home for the bright lights of London, aged sixteen, she had become a drug addict, funding her habit by working as a cook and a prostitute. She had told people that she was a witch, would often answer her door stark naked, and was said by a former friend to be 'sick and twisted,' worshipping Satan and inviting visitors to stroke a brass statue of 'Old Nick' which she kept in the living room.

All in all this is a tragic case, for we have a rough-and-ready drug- and sex-addicted, cold-blooded femme fatale who, although she was found guilty of manslaughter not murder, had, I am sure, homicide on her mind. I suggest 'cold-blooded' because despite the drugs and booze flowing through her veins her heart was as cold as ice – a truly evil personality.

With that being said, there has to be some culpability to be found in all of her victims. Drug addicts, alcoholics and social drop-outs, their mucky legacy proves that if you dance with the Devil you must expect the worst, for in many respects they willingly entered the Black Widow's web and suffered the consequences, as shocking as this may seem to be.

14

I'm Gonna Find Ya ... an' I'm Gonna Getcha!

It has been said for decades that there are five distinct categories of rapists and killers: Compensatory; Opportunistic; Anger-based; Date Rape and Sadistic, but I cannot believe this to be correct. Leaving out 'Compensatory', for these types very rarely kill, dismissing 'Date Rape' too, what follows shows there is frequently a mix of Opportunistic, Anger-based and sexual Sadism, all of which form parts of, or the whole of the criminal's psychopathology as he goes about committing his dreadful crimes.

The other interesting factor to take into consideration is that the act of stalking can either be a *conscious* effort to go out with the specific intent to commit rape and kill, as Peter Sutcliffe, Arthur Shawcross and Dennis Rader did when hunting down prostitutes, or *subconscious* stalking when an offender comes upon a likely victim by happenstance, and acts on the spur of the moment.

This book concerns itself with stalking; so now is the time to look at those 'opportunist' offenders' whom we can also label 'exploitatives', in that they exploit every opportunity. These types fall into the category of 'disorganised' offenders, the sadistic snatch-and-grab types such as John Duffy, the 'Railway Rapist', and Kenneth Erskine, the 'Stockwell Strangler', and Michael Ross, the 'Roadside Strangler', who enjoy the power they have over their terrified victims. These are criminals who will sexually assault, rape or even commit murder.

One reconstructed rape screened on the BBC programme *Crimewatch* showed a woman who had impulsively spent the night at a girlfriend's house. She woke at 5 a.m. the next morning, and as it was already daylight decided to walk home. An opportunist rapist saw her, dragged her into a nearby garden and raped her. It was said on the programme that the act simply could not have been premeditated, as 'neither party knew in advance that she'd be there at that particular time'. However, we can debunk that theory because the moment an offender makes the decision to commit an offence 'premeditation' exists. And, as we have seen throughout this book, while her attacker might not have gone out during the early hours with rape in the *front* of his mind, he would have been a sexual fantasist with rape in the *back* of his mind.

Another example comes straight from Michael Ross's MO, for the last time anyone could recollect seeing twenty-three-year-old Debra Smith Taylor alive was around midnight on Tuesday, 15 June 1982. She was with her husband when their car ran out of fuel on Highway 6, near Hampton, just eight miles east of Ross's Connecticut home. A state trooper came across the stationary vehicle and drove the couple to a Sunoco gas station in Danielson, where the boyfriend of one of Ross's earlier victims, Tammy Williams, had lived. The trooper recalled that the Taylors were arguing, and that Debra was so annoyed she said she would find her own way back home. After leaving her husband to his own devices, she stormed off across Danielson Town Green, to the bandstand, where she gratefully accepted the offer of a ride from a bespectacled young man who had walked up and spoken to her.

On Sunday, 30 October that year, two hunters discovered the skeletal remains of Debra Taylor in one of the large tracts of woodland east of Route 169, in Canterbury, Connecticut. The body was so decomposed that identification was only possible by means of dental records and items of jewellery. When I interviewed serial killer Ross on death row, he told me that she was 'very spirited' and put up a hard fight for her life. In fact, he enjoyed this kill so much that he revisited the corpse several times to masturbate over it. However, he was at pains to stress that he never went out solely with the intention of committing rape and murder, but he always had the thought of doing it inside his head, and the sight of a young woman walking alone was enough to set the demon inside him off.

Another category of rape/killer is one who is psychologically 'anger-based', a person who takes out the rage that he feels about his wife or partner, his work or his general situation and projects this onto his victim. Many of these offenders suffer from the 'Little Man Syndrome', have low self-esteem and are unable to hold their ground, so take their revenge out on others. As such, he is extremely dangerous. He can project decades' worth of hatred onto a woman walking down the street in front of him. He is also known as a 'displaced rapist/killer', as he displaces his feelings onto the innocent object of his desire. We can find a mix here with the opportunist offender.

These types have a strong desire to humiliate and hurt the victim, so anal sex followed by oral sex may be the preferred assault as was the case with Muriel 'Gwen' Maitland. By and large they would be opportunist, disorganised offenders in much the same way as were Gordon Jowers and Harvey 'The Hammer' Carignan, the latter telling me at interview that he hated all women with a 'passion' and that's why he bludgeoned them to death by smashing their heads in after having forced them to give him oral sex before he raped them. Harvey is also of interest to me because like so many anger-based serial killers he was able, and without a shred of remorse, to tell me that it was always his victims' fault and it was they who caused their own deaths. If that is not 'displaced' I don't know what is!

If thus far this book appears all doom and gloom, please allow me to try and lighten the load because those with an overtly sexual and homicidal resolve rarely advertise their intentions for they are 'first strike' offenders whose motives are to commit rape and kill, then try to escape justice – and they are extremely rare.

At the very outset of this book I mentioned the animal kingdom: the lion, for example, doesn't advertise his killer instincts to his prey, for what would be the point of it? Neither does Lenny the Lizard, come to that. Equally – and I know that I will get some criticism for suggesting this – nor did the likes of John Duffy or any of the other hunter killers referred to in this book advertise their intentions either, so they are the types to worry about. They come out of nowhere and as Michael Ross once said to me: 'They [the victims] were dead the moment I saw them.'

But what about those men and women who *do* advertise their stalking intentions? Well, UK law is very specific about what amounts to harassment in the Equality Act 2010, and this may be summarised as: 'Unwanted conduct related to a protected characteristic which has the purpose or effect of violating the dignity of an individual, or creates an intimidating hostile, degrading, humiliating or offensive environment for the individual.' Indeed, to be guilty of the offence of stalking, the offender must, on at least two occasions, indulge in conduct that causes the victim harassment, alarm or distress. This form of criminal behaviour is as far from the conduct of homicidal stalkers as one can get.

The 2012 Act recognises stalking as harassment that may include: 'Persistent and repeated contact or attempts to contact a victim because of some pathological fixation or another,' and we see these patterns of behaviour with 'Celebrity Stalking' time and again. But, here we see the offender 'advertising' his intentions therefore putting himself, or herself, in peril, at once giving his intended target forewarning, and unless one is unlucky enough to ignore these threats, as did John Lennon, who was being stalked and was then shot dead by Mark Chapman, there is good advice on how to deal with these people, and it is well worth considering.

The first rule when it comes to dealing with overt stalkers is to have no contact with them at all. Aside from the real world, if contacted online, or via web chat such as Facebook, Hangouts, Messenger or WhatsApp, screenshot the message and save it to a folder. Name it by time and date and *don't* lose it. One has to remember that most of these types of offenders live in a fantasy world of their own dysfunctional, psychopathological construction – the world I have mentioned previously; in which they are always inventing and reinventing themselves to become someone that they can never be. What these people *do not understand* is Locard's principle – that every crime leaves a trace. When using the internet to stalk and harass one might as well be pointing police to one's own front door.

Of course, it might not be evident that any person is going to turn into a stalker; nevertheless, it is important to be wary of online communications and to ensure that you keep your social media profiles private. So another golden rule is to be careful what information you do put into the public domain because stalking is made much easier for an offender while he is nice and cosy and sitting at his PC. If you even sense someone has taken an unhealthy interest in you and the communications are worrying you, again take a screenshot and record them, then block their profile. Once this has been done the stalker should soon lose patience and move on to someone else. What you do *not* want to do is maintain contact because this merely adds fuel to the fire, so do not feed the troll, except to tell him, or her, that you have kept copies of all of his/her messages and photos, and if you are pestered again you will report it to the police.

All of this advice might seem obvious to the reader; however, it is vitally important to watch over your kids who might know no better.

To the best of my ability, I have tried in this book to use historic and contemporary case histories to prove that human motives for stalking and the hunting down of human prey have remained *exactly* the same for hundreds of years, being, and I repeat yet again: the desire to avenge some real or fancied wrong; to get rid of a rival or obnoxious connection; to escape the pressure of pecuniary or other obligation; to obtain plunder; and to gratify some other selfish malignant passion i.e. sex!

There are 'organised' and 'disorganised' offenders. There are sex criminals who subconsciously have rape and murder in mind with their homicidal intentions only springing forth when an opportunity presents itself – a case of the victim being in the wrong place at the wrong time (for the offender, the *right* place at the *right* time), while there are other types who go out with the deliberate, conscious intention of committing rape and murder most foul.

There are men who carefully select their victims and are prepared to watch and secretly stalk their targets in real life, or on the internet, for days, weeks and months on end because they get their kicks out of this pre-kill activity in a voyeuristic sort of way.

Sometimes, it is a mix of any of the five motives listed above being present in the criminal's mind, and some of the offenders featured in this book can be 'organised' on occasions while 'disorganised' at other times. But, what they *all* have in common is this 'wearing of different masks' which conceal their true, evil entities, for if they are so able to conceal their real self from their own spouses and partners, their families, relations, work colleagues, friends (on- and off-line) and the police, they make for very dangerous human predators indeed.

We are now living in the age of the internet, so I have tried to give the reader a few examples of the inherent dangers of being too loose and fancy-free while using it, for it is riddled throughout with snake-oil salesmen and women who will stalk you, harass you, con you, extort, blackmail, rob, steal and far worse – if you really let your guard down – lure you to a lonely place to commit rape or even murder.

With all of that being said, it all comes down to 'horses for courses'. If you are up for online dating, BDSM blogs with extreme sexual content, or like Armin Meiwes who frequented cannibal chatrooms, and the countless other websites where one can indulge in every licentious pleasure known to modern man, do not expect to meet someone of your dreams. To dance with the Devil is to engage in risky, reckless, potentially immoral, even fatal, behaviour. You could easily get burned because internet homicides, as we have seen from the very few examples referenced previously *are* on the increase not decrease – but it's your call anyway.

Perhaps, and this may only be a naïve suggestion on my part, and without me wishing to be labelled a sexist, I have found that in the most part, a woman's intuition enables her to smell a rat a mile away, but, as this book tries to set out, when women place themselves in vulnerable situations, most especially at night and/or when emboldened with drink, they might place themselves at great risk when a little common sense should have prevailed.

Of course, it goes without saying that a woman should be able to dress as she pleases, do as she wishes and go about her life without fear for her welfare – this *is* a given. Sadly, however, there are male sex predators out there who abuse society's rules – that *is* a given too. Walking alone in the dead of night is a 'no-no'; always get a friend to take you back home, or at least book a licensed cab, and *never* accept a lift from a stranger no matter how nice and charming he may appear to be.

Someone picked up a tipsy Sandra Court who was staggering home from a party. She was raped, stripped naked and found dead in a water-filled New Forest stream. If her friends had booked her a taxi she would still be alive today. This was an opportunist homicide, as was that of Shirley Banks at Bristol, while the abduction of Suzy Lamplugh in south London, was organised and pre-planned. John Cannan, who was convicted of the murder of Shirley Banks, was also questioned in relation to the death of Sandra Court – and that of Suzy Lamplugh – but never charged.

Tammy Williams would still be alive if she hadn't decided to walk home alone at night after a row with her husband and accepted a lift from Michael Ross. As a matter of fact, many of Ross's victims accepted rides from this monster, including two schoolgirls: April Brunais and Lesley Shelly, both aged fourteen, from Griswold, Connecticut. The kids had earlier walked to a neighbouring town, it got dark, and their parents ordered them to walk back home as 'punishment'. Ross murdered both children in the most horrific way imaginable. These were all opportunist murders.

Several of Peter Sutcliffe's victims were thoroughly decent young woman who were walking home alone at night before he stalked them and hammered or stabbed them to death, leaving their bodies dumped like so much trash, and the same grim scenario has been played out time and again with young women being offered rides by the likes of Harvey Carignan, Kenneth Bianchi and Angelo Buono.

Why did I tie her under my truck? To grind off her face and prints, that's why!

KEITH HUNTER JESPERSON: TO THE AUTHOR
IN CORRESPONDENCE.

Dubbed the 'Happy Face Killer', Keith Hunter Jesperson gave rides to girls waiting at truck stops – and they all ended up dead, with one girl, Angela Subrize, being tied to the rear axle of his rig and dragged fifteen miles with her body ending up in bits along the side of an interstate highway. These were all disorganised opportunist murders.

Henry Lee Lucas and Ottis Toole committed more sex

murders than anyone can truly count, with many of their victims accepting rides after thumbing a lift. These were all disorganised opportunist murders.

None of Ted Bundy's victims were 'working girls', but in the majority of instances unwittingly got too close to this psychopath and were bludgeoned to death soon after bumping into him during daylight hours or at night. Why, because he wore the fake mask of 'normality' and they trusted this mask, soon to find out that they had met a sex-crazed demon.

Arthur Shawcross, Peter Sutcliffe, Kenneth Bianchi, Angelo Buono, and Steve Wright are but a few of the scores of serial killers who consciously went out with the intent to use, abuse and kill 'freelancers', and we can include our notorious Jack the Ripper amongst them. Maybe there are a few lessons to be learned here . . . just maybe?

As this book illustrates: prostitutes prove easy pickings for sexual psychopaths, most especially in the US; fortunately not so much in the UK nowadays. And the reason for becoming easy pickings is, as far as I can determine and I stand to be corrected, is that they work on the streets and often alone. Most of these 'working girls' started off down on their luck and had to earn a living one way or another, perhaps because they had children to support or a drug addiction.

However, in the Far East – most especially Thailand and the Philippines (both of which are the premier 'Sex-Sin' countries in the world) – the murder rate of working girls is almost zero because they work in areas that are well policed. These 'freelancers' work in groups, such as can be found in the red-light districts of Angles City and Burgos Street, Makati, Manila, or 'Walking Street' in Phuket, Thailand.

The women who *do* work in bars and clubs are under constant CCTV surveillance. There is none of this 'in the back of the car sex', only short-time/long-time services in hotels where the security staff know their hotel guests and they record the IDs of the girls as they come and go. Indeed, if a girl is treated badly in *any* way, and this includes verbal abuse too, she'll tell the cops and the guy is locked up in a heartbeat.

15

Hi, Handsome!

Whether one is seeking genuine love or just short-term kinky sex, or has the desire to be cannibalised, or unwittingly fleeced, it is fair to say one can find everything, and every conceivable opportunity when you go online for love, or death, maybe just a mouse click away.

Earlier, I made references to various other online communication forums, which, by far, offer up to users more good than bad. Used sensibly they can be a godsend; especially if one is into religion, whatever the faith you adhere to. But pure evil sits inside the World Wide Web too.

Over recent months I conducted some research after hearing from a middle-aged man from Florida. I have changed his name to protect his identity, but 'David' had started talking to who appeared to be an intelligent, classy young twenty-something girl called 'Linda Rose' who had contacted him out of the blue on an instant messaging app. After using this app for a few moments, she insisted that he open a Hangouts account using a new Gmail address, and send her his Gmail details so she could join him there, too. Hangouts is more 'private', she explained, saying that she no longer used Facebook because she'd been hacked by a jealous boyfriend. The photographs that she posted of 'herself' were of a beautiful, young, buxom blonde, and she explained that she lived in California with her grandmother.

A carefully spun web within the World Wide Web had been set and this spider's prey could have easily been dicing with death.

After only a day of texting each other, with the conversations becoming overtly more sexual in nature, this woman said that she had dropped her mobile phone and unless she could afford get a new one then their relationship would have to be put on hold . . . perhaps even for an indefinite period. Now hooked, Our Man in Florida offered to pay for it either by using Western Union or MoneyGram – where she could, upon presenting valid ID at one of their agencies, pick up the cash. This she refused. Better to send me gift cards, she insisted. Amazon or Steam cards she wanted. She could sell these and convert them into cash. $US 500.00 in Steam cards was soon on its way, then surprise, surprise, he didn't hear from her for a week, when up she popped again, with: 'Hi, handsome . . . sorry I have been away from you. Miss you. You are my King. I have to look after grandma and deb [sic] other people don't care abot [sic] her. Promise not to break my heart as I want marry u. I love u.'

This dialogue continued for another few hours during

which time they exchanged 'selfies' before she hinted that if she had some extra money she could pay someone to look after granny and she could visit him in Florida. Another $US 1,500 was swiftly on its way after which he never heard hide nor hair from her again, *but he did hear from one her closest friends*, who called herself 'Rose Cherry'.

Miss Cherry was as equally alluring as Miss Rose. Another piece of hot totty on legs, she told our man that her friend had been involved in a car crash and tragically had died. Although apparently heartbroken with this dreadful news, and with two thousand bucks already flushed down the drain, this new relationship soon blossomed. Miss Cherry knew all about Grandma and she said that Miss Rose had been very much in love with him.

As was par for the course, it was now Miss Cherry who was short of funds. Allegedly, she had lost her US ID and passport while on a modelling assignment in Kuwait. To prove this she sent photos of 'herself' in Kuwait (dozens of them in fact) all revealing, and revealing (excuse the pun) her to be one of the most gorgeous creatures ever to have walked God's earth. So, off went another $US4,000.

David was smitten; figuring out that it was now God's will that his first online girlfriend had snuffed it because now he had struck a seam of sexual gold, and soon his money was leaving his wallet almost as fast as he could earn it.

At first it was the four grand, then smaller amounts, a few hundred dollars here and there. Then came a request for three thousand dollars because she wanted to move to be closer to him. This, he convinced her, would HAVE to be sent via Western Union, so she agreed, however, having lost her ID, it would have to be sent to her friend who would collect it on her behalf.

So far, so good, and David wired the money in the 'friend's' name and sat back to hear from his newfound love who would confirm that she had received the cash.

She hadn't!

Her story was that her 'friend' had collected the money and kept it. She dared not call the police because the guy was mob-connected with pals in Florida. 'If we call the police he will have us killed,' she wrote.

At this, David decided to pull the plug and he blocked Miss Cherry from his Hangouts account.

For a month David ruminated. He missed his beautiful, sexy Miss Cherry, and wondered if he had been too cruel to her. Then, in a moment of what he now calls 'lunacy', he unblocked her and they began talking again. 'You were so wicked to me,' she complained. 'I believed that you really loved me. You don't know the meaning of love. Prove that you love me if you are a real man . . . send me some gift cards and then we can start again.'

David hesitated, then a bomb dropped onto his world.

Miss Cherry told him that she and the allegedly deceased Miss Rose had shared all of their secrets like sisters and that she had some sexy nude photos of him sent to her by Miss Rose before the accident.

'HOLY SHIT!'

'You have treated me very badly,' she railed. 'If my gangster friend gotta hold of pictures he'll put them all over the internet, and contact your boss because we know where you live and work . . . we even have your Hotmail email.' Quite rightly, he then blocked her again, but all to no avail. The emails from a man started arriving under the subject line 'BLACKMAIL – DO NOT IGNORE'. They contained death threats and he reported the matter to the police, who were not in the least bit interested. But, they did give David one bit of advice. 'Ignore it all and they'll soon get bored and move on.'

He did ignore them and he hasn't had a problem since.

So, where did David go so fundamentally wrong, like so many tens of thousands of people who are being scammed online every day of the week, with a few of them ending up being blackmailed or murdered?

David's first mistake was that although he had read a copy of my book *Murder.com*, he failed to take even a blind bit of notice of the advice this book offered, so here are a few simple precautions that can save anyone from losing their shirt.

Had David immediately used a very valuable and free internet tool called a 'Reverse Image Search', such as 'Labnol', he could have saved himself a lot of money and worry. Had he saved the girl's photos, then opened 'Labnol' and uploaded a photo or two there, within thirty seconds he would have seen that both women were high-end porn models with online sex forums, and obviously earning a mint.

Had David looked more closely at the selfies that had been taken only by the girls specifically for him, in a few cases he should have noticed down in the bottom right-hand-corner tiny logos. But his eyes were more fixed on what was above the waterline and not on the finer points that pointed directly to 'SCAM'.

But it is the use of gift cards that should have been the most obvious giveaway. Western Union and MoneyGram transactions *do* offer a high level of security. The sender has to have valid ID, as does the recipient, thus making these types of scams more difficult to pull off. Gift cards, however, are untraceable and easily converted into cash anywhere across the world with no ID required at all.

And he should never have given out his Hotmail address, or sent naked photos of himself for now he was a target for blackmail.

David should have demanded to see some form of valid US ID before he had parted with a dime, but he didn't. And, even if these were offered he should have checked online to see if it were fake or not.

In Miss Rose's case, had he checked out the zip code of her alleged home address, he would have readily twigged that it was not in California at all. It was pretty much a barn in the middle of a field in Montana.

And did these girls, who both claimed to have gone to university, possess a reasonable degree of competence in the English language? No, sir. When he read 'You are my King', and the use of 'dat', he should have smelt the slums of some shit-hole tin-pot city from thousands of miles distant.

In one exchange of texts between Miss Cherry and David, he received line after line of beautiful poetic love prose. This was, or should have been, an obvious red flag when taken in context with the rest of the garbage she was sending him. Had he cut and pasted even a few lines of it into his browser he would have learned that it had been actually penned by some well-known poet.

So, who were the scammers who hit David for his hard-earned cash? In this instance they were Nigerians working out of Lagos. They were part of a 'Scamming Factory' one of many set up with the specific intention of, in this case, 'Sex Scamming'.

The scammers are *always* men, who, after some tuition learn how to trawl the internet for modelling and porn sites, cut and paste the girls' photos, and pass them onto more techie colleagues who know the ins-and-outs of our internet world. In most instances, once a single scammer knows your email address, or WhatsApp address or other communications program, the rest of them do, and these details can, and are, being on the Dark Web.

So was David stupid? Perhaps he was, perhaps he was grossly naïve, but he now frankly admits that he should have educated himself right from the get-go. There are hundreds of websites giving good advice on how to avoid being scammed, many of them put up by law enforcement, too. Indeed, even Hangouts and the other internet chat forums give great advice and issue warnings, but most people think they know better and suffer the consequences.

The World Wide Web is exactly that – a web. Used properly it is a fantastic thing to have at one's fingertips; the downside is that crooks, conmen, thieves and killers exploit it, as I hope this book goes some way in proving.

This book shows us that stalking a victim employs many a different form; in David's case, a web had been spun using the specific bait – sex. To him, this was a tempting offer, one he could not refuse and, once hooked, he spent months of worry before he managed to wriggle off the hook. He fell for an internet-generated honey trap, one that he willingly walked into: it is as simple as that.

Can we entirely blame the Nigerian scammers for their criminal sexual exploitation of Western males? I think not for I see them in the context of living in a country where the majority of the population are starving and business and political corruption is rife. These people have to eat, after all is said and done, and one gets it when one reads the amazing book written by the *Financial Times* investigative correspondent, Tom Burgis. *The Looting Machine: Warlords, Tycoons, Smugglers and the Systematic Theft of Africa's Wealth*, exposes that what the West sows it shall reap, and for the scammers out of Nigeria we also can provide for easy pickings, too.

So, in the round, it is up to each and every one of us to be more vigilant – more diligent, and more aware of our surroundings. And also of one's own behaviour and condition.

But is this just a new phenomenon of recent times? Of course it isn't, for we can trace *exactly the same* techniques of trawling, hunting down, the stalking, the raping and the killings going back to the Victorian era of Jack the Ripper, and before.

And here is the constant: we find a thread, as strong as steel wire, the almost unbreakable thread of the spider's web, running through to the present day, where the same victimology, the crimes – be they of financial or sexual in motive – and the heartbreak, remain *precisely* the same.

Afterword

One final observation, and I make this somewhat reluctantly, yet on a high note: the chance of you being stalked by someone with evil intention in mind is *so* small it is almost not worth considering – with the chances of being stuck by lightning being odds-on more likely. However, if you are foolish enough, and against all good advice, to hold onto a steel pole during a heavy thunderstorm, your chances of *not* being hit might be somewhat reduced.

Here endeth the lesson and I wish you a happy, safe and successful life.